D0929418

Community
Journalism

THE ENLIGHTENED COMMUNITY NEWSPAPER is intimately involved with building its community through consistently positive coverage that also strives to be accurate, comprehensive, balanced and fair. No wonder community journalism is so challenging. The spirit of our work is embodied in this photo of a victorious Special Olympics athlete being held up by a real-life professional athlete while the happy boy's coaches respond with applause and support. (*All photos by the author unless otherwise noted*)

Community
Journalism

THE PERSONAL APPROACH

JOCK LAUTERER

IOWA STATE UNIVERSITY PRESS / AMES

Jock Lauterer is assistant professor of journalism in the College of Communications at Pennsylvania State University, where he teaches (among other subjects) community journalism. Lauterer is in charge of the College's photojournalism component, teaches graphic applications, is co-adviser to the *Penn State Journalist* and on the Board of the *Daily Collegian*. Between 1969 and 1983 he was the joint winner of 55 press awards from the North Carolina Press Association for excellence in papers he co-founded, edited and published. In an eventful career, Lauterer has taught photojournalism at his alma mater, the University of North Carolina-Chapel Hill, designed the journalism program at Brevard College (N.C.) and published four books. In addition, he writes commentary for the local public radio station and community newspaper.

Photos on pages 12, 81 and 121 reprinted from *Wouldn't Take Nothin' for My Journey Now,* by Jock Lauterer. Copyright 1980 by the University of North Carolina Press. Used by permission of the publisher.

© 1995 Iowa State University Press, Ames, Iowa 50014
All rights reserved

Authorization to photocopy items for internal or personal use, or the internal or personal use of specific clients, is granted by Iowa State University Press, provided that the base fee of $.10 per copy is paid directly to the Copyright Clearance Center, 27 Congress Street, Salem, MA 01970. For those organizations that have been granted a photocopy license by CCC, a separate system of payments has been arranged. The fee code for users of the Transactional Reporting Service is 0-8138-2309-9/95 $.10.

♾ Printed on acid-free paper in the United States of America

First edition, 1995

Library of Congress Cataloging-in-Publication Data

Lauterer, Jock
    Community journalism : the personal approach / Jock Lauterer.—1st ed.
      p.   cm.
    ISBN 0-8138-2309-9 (acid-free paper)
    1. Community newspapers. 2. Journalism. 3. Reporters and reporting. I. Title.
PN4784.C73L28   1995
070.4—dc20   95-19990

ALL ACROSS THIS LAND every Tuesday night (or Sunday, Wednesday or Thursday) the lights are burning late at the *News* of Creedmore (or the *Gold Leaf Farmer* of Wendell or the *Weekly* of Wake Forest or the *Rocket* of Blowing Rock), the so-called small newspapers of our country. This book, which is meant to honor those late-night candle-burners, the men and women of community journalism, is especially dedicated to the finest community journalist I've ever known, Jim Shumaker, my first editor and second father.

The author, summer of 1993, doing "basic research" for this book in the backshop of the *Tryon* (N.C.) *Daily Bulletin.* (*Photo by Charles Barnett*)

CONTENTS

FOREWORD

BE CAREFUL WHEN YOU PICK UP this copy of Jock Lauterer's book; it could land you in a world of trouble. It could land you in the community newspaper publisher's world of tumult and trepidation, tenacity and triumph. Lauterer's narrative will put you in the editor's place at the hometown *Gazette,* working late into the night, often well into the early morning, seemingly always hours past deadline. And he'll have you reading at the take-no-prisoners pace that he describes as the editor's lot in life.

Maybe this book isn't for everyone. Maybe it's not for the cynical reporter who writes for the city desk downtown and sneers at the thought that good news could ever be *news,* or that there *is* any good news in Bigville. Maybe it's not for the journalism professor whose aim is to prep the next generation of writers for the *New York Times.* And maybe it's not for the reader for whom the term "local paper" means a 12-pound, plastic-bagged edition that is hurled in the direction of the driveway at 5 A.M. each Sunday.

Lauterer's *Community Journalism: The Personal Approach* is for readers who have bumped into a different kind of journalism. It's for readers who have bumped into the person who writes the editorials—the same one who covers the Little League games, who sells the ads, answers the phone and carries the bags marked "Second Class Mail—Do Not Delay" to the post office.

It *is* for readers with a sense of humor. It's for those who harbor an empathy for small towns and aspiring journalistic enterprises. And it's for the dreamers among us who still romance the idea of owning a community newspaper.

Here's an additional reason to be careful when you pick up this book. It's tough to put it down.

The delightful anecdotes and illustrations ring true because they're right out of the author's experiences. Lauterer delivers insight that has been tested by fire as an owner/publisher/entrepreneur/community journalist. His writing style is casual, easy to read, and he provides readers a genuine and user-friendly look at grass-roots journalism.

What would-be owners of small publishing empires (the Walter Mittys of newspapers) will find within these pages are good-sense lessons from Lauterer's years in the business.

What those who are already in the business of putting out their own small newspaper will find is a story they recognize; a story they've lived. And while Lauterer's tales may have them reliving their greatest struggles, his stories will also reaffirm the worth of their enterprise. This book may even help restore the vision that enticed venturers into the newspaper business in the first place, even if the vision has dimmed under the harsh and frequent glare of the midnight oil.

There's something here for journalism educators, too. If you, like me, have been waiting for a good text on community journalism, you'll find that Lauterer has provided it. His work speaks the language of community journalists. It puts into print the perspective of the grass-roots journalist. It's a perspective that has disappeared from textbooks as journalism has become a professional sport and community newspaper ownership a corporate quest.

Still thinking you'll read on?

All right. Go ahead. You haven't heeded my earlier warnings, but I'll leave you with another:

Catch your breath now while you can. You won't have time to do it again until you finish this edition. Welcome to the world of community journalism.

JOHN NEIBERGALL
Executive Director
Huck Boyd National Center for Community Media
A. Q. Miller School of Journalism and Mass Communications
Kansas State University

You know it's a community newspaper when you can't tell the editors and publishers from the production team. Unloading newsprint at *THIS WEEK* (Forest City, N.C.) the author (in overalls), then co-publisher and co-editor, is surrounded by the work crew that includes, clockwise, assistant pressman Jackie Arrowood (in Elton John T-shirt), co-editor and co-publisher Ron Paris, business manager and co-publisher Bill Blair, and pressman and business partner Don Lovelace. (*Photo by Joy Franklin*)

PREFACE

WE ARE DIFFERENT.

Not better, and certainly not worse.

Just different.

If you're an old-timer, a veteran with community newspapers, you already know this.

If you're new or have been at a community paper for a little while and can't seem to find the handle, perhaps this will help.

If you're a student of community journalism or an intern at a community paper, then you need to know this.

There is a fundamental difference between us and the big-city dailies. (And we're so different from TV that we might as well come from different planets.) At first glance, a community paper may look like just a dinky, unsophisticated low-budget version of a big daily. After all, some of us are daily; we run ads, print broadsheet, cover some of the same stories, print those stories and photos and headlines with ink on paper—so we *appear* somewhat alike. But that is where the similarities end.

There is a profound philosophical difference in the way we look at our community, at our readers, at our advertisers, and how we write, handle and package the news.

In a nut shell, it's the personal approach.

At a community newspaper, news is not events happening to sources. News is people, your people, and how the changing world affects their everyday lives. News is people being caught up in events.

Writers, photographers, ad people, editors and publishers who don't have or don't want to develop the human touch should look elsewhere for employment. Otherwise they will be miserable and make all around them likewise.

Writers, photographers, ad people, editors and publishers who cherish people, who either know how, or want to learn how, to celebrate the ordinary and who want to have a lasting impact for good in a community can find an intellectually stimulating, financially rewarding and emotionally fulfilling lifetime of work in community journalism.

But in the words of Ringo Starr, "It Don't Come Easy."

To borrow from the Peace Corps: It's "the toughest job you'll ever love."

According to the 1993 *Editor and Publisher Yearbook* there are 1,586 daily newspapers in America. The vast majority, 1,336 or fully 85 percent, have circulations under 50,000 and are classified by the American Society of Newspaper Editors as "small newspapers." Of those 1,336, another 1,089 have circulations under 25,000. According to the National Newspaper Association, there are presently over 7,400 weeklies, with an average circulation of 7,487, reaching over 55 million people. Ours is a country dominated by small newspapers, most of which are community newspapers.

And yet, most graduates emerge from university journalism schools and schools of mass media and communication largely untrained and totally unprepared for what they encounter at papers of that size and nature. To compound the irony, most recent college graduates, cub reporters and photographers find their first jobs at these smaller papers (while they're waiting for that call from the *Washington Post* or the *National Geographic*). The common misconception is that the community paper is a small version of the big-city daily. Nothing could be further from the truth. Little wonder then that newcomers find the community newspaper to be a bewildering journalistic briar patch.

While this book is intended to be used as a text and workbook for university students studying community journalism, it is the author's aim for it to serve also as a survival manual/field guide/handbook — a support mechanism providing sustenance for those of you already out there in the trenches. I mean it also to be an affirmation and a validation for all the long hours and crazy times, when you're feeling very alone, trying to stay sane and creative out in the boonies, or up against a thorny ethical dilemma when there seem to be no mentors, role models, allies or anyone else who's been through anything like this before. When it's late at night and it's just you and the problem, you and your fingers on the keyboard at deadline, you in bed in a cold sweat wondering if you did the right thing — take heart; we're all in this together. There are legions of enlightened, caring and dedicated professional community journalists who have gone before you and succeeded against great odds. And so can you.

ACKNOWLEDGMENTS

This book, too, is a community venture. It reaches publication only through the inspiration, support and encouragement of a community of friends. I can take credit only for having been in the right place at the right time. My most heartfelt thanks go to three models, mentors and friends whose personalities run through this book like a clear note: editors and professors Jim Shumaker and Ken Byerly; and fellow Carolinian and inspiration, Charles Kuralt. To my former "partners in crime" at the Forest City paper, Ron Paris and Bill Blair— Long live the spirit of *THIS WEEK*! Thanks to UNC-Chapel Hill School of Journalism and Mass Communications Dean Richard Cole for suggesting the idea for the book back in the early '80s; and to former Brevard College President Billy Greer for providing me a nurturing work space when the idea took root years later. Thanks also to former fellow workers who contributed good photos and wise guidance: Ron Paris, Joy Franklin, Pat Jobe and Maggie Lauterer. Inspiration came along the way from great friends: Virginia Rucker, Lin Redmond, Bill Byers, Mike Thompson and Lynne Vernon Feagans. At Penn State I have been constantly uplifted and empowered by the best friend a man could ask for in the person of Steven Knowlton, whose insightful essay enriches this book. Special thanks to David Perry at UNC Press for encouraging me early on, to Sally Heffentreyer for a first read-through and editing, and to media observer Elaine Pearsons who read the fledgling work-in-progress and proclaimed it "fit for humans as well as reporters!" In addition, I celebrate that readers are treated to a taste of the community journalism initiative at Kansas State University; John Neibergall's Foreword and Carol Oukrop's Addendum bracket my efforts with an appropriately scholarly yet enthusiastic framework. I would be remiss if I didn't thank the inaugural class in community journalism at Penn State, who, during the spring of 1995, "road-tested" this book using little more than galley proofs. Without their forthright feedback, the final product would be the poorer. In the end, this book is the result of Iowa State University Press believing in the vitality and fundamental importance of community journalism. To Gretchen Van Houten, Jane Zaring, Bob Campbell and all the gang at Ames I extend my sincerest gratitude.

Community Journalism

After an all-nighter putting out *THIS WEEK,* the author takes a break from inserting. Undoubtedly, someone just told a joke; you can go a long way with very little sleep if it's a happy shop. (*Photo by Joy Franklin*)

The flag ripples in the July breeze. The maple leaves spread their shade. A gospel tune plays on the radio. Reading quietly, this couple enjoys each other's company in their favorite front-yard spot. An enlightened small-town newspaper is like a benevolent mirror held up to the community.

1

With Apologies to Nike, But Why Just Do It?

ONE JOURNALIST'S LOVE AFFAIR WITH SMALL NEWSPAPERS

Just as there are no small parts, only small actors, there is no such thing as a *small newspaper*. Especially if you're the editor of that paper, every issue is like giving birth.

Though we call it community journalism now, it still requires that you test the outer limits of your underarm deodorant. From an eight-page weekly on up, the so-called "small-town newspaper" requires all your guts, sheer grit, creativity and energy.

Big-city newspeople who harbor pipe dreams of buying that little weekly in rural Pennsyltucky and settling down to the leisurely pace of Rotary Club editorship with banker's hours had better wake up—because that's what a pipe dream is—pure fantasy. My workday averaged about 14 hours a day during my 15 years as co-publisher, co-editor. And whole weekends off were rare.

Even as faculty adviser to the lab newspaper of Penn State's College of Communications, the once-a-semester 24-page tabloid, I devote heaps of commitment and hefty amounts of overtime.

A newspaper is a living thing. Just ask any newspaper widow or widower.

AT HOME IN THE BACKSHOP

As I write this, I am hunched over the light table in the production room of a small-town newspaper where the *Penn State Journalist* is being prepared for press. All my senses come alive here: the sweet, acrid smell of the backshop, the whir of the LogE negative-developing machine, the crank and clank of the copy camera easel, the whoosh of vacuum on the copy camera back, country music in the background, faces of the strippers and opaquers lighted by ghostly illumination from the light tables, the prolonged zzzzzaaaap of plate burner and clunkaclunka of the plate developer.

The backshop is my home. I was raised in this briar patch. When I was a kid hanging out in the backshop doing odd jobs they called the likes of me a "printer's devil." The paper became my nursery room. As a burr-headed, whistling newsboy, I couldn't get enough of the dusty, fusty confines of the *Chapel Hill Weekly* with its friendly Dickensian counting house of a shop, all a-clank and a-clatter with the busyness of collecting, collating and printing the news.

The printer's devil liked the backshop so much he decided to own one, and so a college degree and a career as a community journalist ensued. Along with two partners, in 1969 I started a weekly, *THIS WEEK* (Forest City), in rural western North Carolina. Within five years we had moved to larger offices, purchased a press and bought out the competition semiweekly. By 1978 we had grown into a 60-page weekly, and that fall we went daily, renaming it the *Daily Courier.* Yearning for another weekly, in 1980 I sold my interest to my partners and started a second paper with two young optimists in another community. We published this paper as a free broadsheet weekly until 1982, when we converted to paid and semiweekly. But the major recession of that year crippled us. After selling in 1983, I found my way into university teaching. (See Chapter 19 for Two Case Studies of Community Newspaper Start-ups.)

Never far from the newsroom or the backshop, I continued to freelance columns, features and photographs to the local community paper. All the while I began paying particular attention to the state of community journalism as only someone who had sat in an editor's chair for 15 years could do.

I started noticing things.

First, that during the recession of the late '80s (when major dailies were hemorrhaging, laying off reporters and folding at an alarming rate), the community papers seemed to be surviving in far better shape. Fewer lay-offs, fewer papers folding, less decline in ad revenues and circulation relative to the big boys. Plus, community papers were hiring all through the recession.

Perhaps not at the boomtown rate of the '60s-'80s, but there weren't hiring freezes either.

Secondly, community papers seemed better insulated not only from the recession but also from TV's insidious influence. In this age of instant global communications, this satellite-enhanced Information Age in which we're all regularly "CNN-ated," how can a small-town newspaper survive? Hasn't TV rung the death knell for community papers? Has the global village abrogated the need for the village news?

A flourishing community journalism industry says a resounding "no!" Happily for us, people are hungry for and needful of information about their community, its concerns and their neighbors.

So until CNN can come up with an uplink from Crooked Creek, Possum Trot and Gobbler's Knob, papers like the *Bugle*, the *Argus* and the *Tattler* will continue to thrive.

WE AIN'T AFRAID OF WORK

The plates for the *Journalist* are ready now and are being loaded onto the big gray Goss Community Press, the flagship of community papers everywhere. I can't help but think back to my favorite pressman, Babe Yount of Waynesville, N.C., whose Goss was emblazoned with two big signs on the press's folder: "U.S.S. YOUNT" and, "We Ain't Afraid Of Work."

The press operator, who you'd better get along with because he or she can make you look like either a king or a goat, fires up the press, which takes off like a chained locomotive. To stand beside a running press is to be in the presence of the essence of our trade. After all, before it was "the Media," was it not "the Press?"

I still prefer the latter, for it evokes the power, energy and vitality of the printed word rifling through the giant machine ... the oily pungent smell of printer's ink, washer and solvent ... the dry tang of paper dust that tickles the inside of your nose ... the concrete floor vibrating slightly as the press thrums a staccato chunkachunkachunka ... the solid schuss of paper blurring through the units ... the steady whining whir of metal rollers ... and the sticky tacky hiss of rubber rollers meeting, meshing and parting.

Standing at the end of the press, watching the stream of neatly stacked *Journalists* shooting off the press, I can't help but be reminded again why I am, and always will be, a newspaperman. And above all, a small town newspaperman. A community journalist.

End of sermon. Can I have an amen?

YOUR TOWN; YOUR TURN

Whether you're a student of community journalism, or a reporter, editor or even owner, here's a little sensitizing exercise.

1. Go into your backshop. Close your eyes. Listen to the place. Catalog the sounds and smells. How does it make you feel? Write it down.

2. Go talk to the press operator. Find out about his (they used to be press*men)* family, his history, how he got started, how long he's been with the paper, what he thinks of it. Ask him his opinion of how you could be doing a better job. But be forewarned; press operators are characteristically long on honesty and short on tact. It is one of their greatest occupational virtues; a press is a no-bullshit machine. Consequently press operators come equipped with what Jim Shumaker calls "a 100 percent foolproof iron-clad bullshit detector."

3. Think back to how you got into this game. How has the business changed since then? How have your standards and your dreams changed? Where do you see yourself in five years? In 10 years?

2

Who Am I? And
What Am I Doing Here?

SPEAKING OF PROFESSIONAL IDENTITY CRISES

"Who am I and what am I doing here?" Those unforgettable words spoken by Admiral James Stockdale, Ross Perot's stunning choice for running mate, echo down as one of the great quotes from the debates of the '92 election, further immortalized by Dana Carvey and Phil Hartman formerly of *Saturday Night Live*.

To use that quote as a metaphor, it's puzzling how many people who work at community newspapers will remind you of the charming but confused admiral. They're clueless as to why they're there and what they're doing.

WHAT DO WE DO?

Comedian Howie Mandel likes to open his routine by asking audience members what they do.

"What do you DO?" he demands simply.

Systems analysts, middle managers, etc., have a hard time explaining exactly what it is they really DO.

"Oh, so you analyze systems," says Howie in mock fascination.

"Well, not exactly," comes the embarrassed response.

"Well, then, what?" asks Howie with childlike innocence while his subject wriggles under the bright lights.

And the audience goes nuts as the poor yup stumbles all over himself trying to put into simple terms what he spends eight hours a day DOING. He can't do it—because he'd never thought about it before.

What do WE do?

If we in community journalism can't say very quickly what it is we DO, then it's a safe bet our work reflects that lack of identity, purpose and vitality. So right away, before we talk about the nuts and bolts of writing, editing and producing a community newspaper, let's figure out what it is we do DO, so that if Howie Mandel were standing here today pointing his finger at us and saying, "Editors, publishers, reporters, photographers, advertising sales people of community newspapers ... WHAT DO YOU DO?" we would respond positively in a chorus of unity, in the words of CBS legend Charles Kuralt, that it's our job TO BE RELENTLESSLY LOCAL.

There it is. That's the key. Or to borrow from President Clinton's 1992 campaign, "Keep it Local, Stupid."

Or to adapt another old slogan, we ought to be Covering our part of Dixie Like The Dew.

Years ago out West, an editor of the *Denver Post* is reputed to have told a sub-editor demanding to know why the Boer War wasn't making P-1 above the fold: "SON, A DOGFIGHT IN DENVER IS MORE IMPORTANT TO OUR READERS THAN ANY MASSACRE IN ZULULAND."

We can forgive our editor of old for being perhaps jingoistic, xenophobic and even racist, but the quote and its context serves our needs. Or, to put it another way: A gentle swell in the ocean is a tidal wave in our frog pond.

When Brevard, N.C., passed a liquor-by-the-drink law recently, it was the banner P-1 head in the semiweekly *Transylvania Times*—and so it should have been. For the nearby big-city daily, the *Asheville Citizen,* which led with Bosnia, as *it* should have, the little Brevard story was on page 24 along with a smattering of other stories from the 17 other counties the *Citizen* tries to cover.

The *Citizen* may have scooped the Brevard community paper by two days or so, but to what end? The detailed story, in full length came out later, and it was the 30 inches the story deserved and the local readers wanted. In short, people in Brevard got their first news of the vote's outcome by word of mouth, by radio, by TV, then maybe from the Asheville paper. But for the full story, Brevard readers waited until the Monday *"T-Times."*

8

THE ROLE OF THE COMMUNITY NEWSPAPER

Nobody should be covering Pottsville, Pa., better than the *Republican*; nobody should be covering Dixon, Ill., like the *Telegraph*; nobody knows Rutherford County, N.C., like the *Daily Courier*; nobody should get better coverage of the local Little League playoffs in McCook, Neb., than the *Daily Gazette*. Nobody.

At their best, community newspapers satisfy a basic human craving that the big dailies can't do, no matter how large their budgets—And that is the affirmation of the sense of community, a positive and intimate reflection of the sense of place, a stroke for our us-ness, our extended family-ness and our profound and interlocking connectedness.

In these days especially, the role of the community newspaper is far more subtle, important and far reaching than one might suppose. The sheer accretion of relentlessly local coverage of city council, planning board, Boy Scout field days, church suppers and even Aunt Maude's 100th birthday all add up to a shouted YES for Our Town. An affirmation of the community's identity and its vision for itself, a way of saying over and over again in words and pictures a fundamental truth that keeps getting lost—that yes, people are all that matter.

Community newspaper editors, publishers, ad reps, business people, reporters, photographers ... students of community journalism: Put that on your wall. **People are what matter.** If you're not already doing so, live and work by that slogan and watch your work and your product take off, your staff morale soar, and your community relations improve.

LESS IS MORE

In further trying to define ourselves we might start by saying what we *don't* do. For instance, a lot of us aren't daily. In fact, up until recently even we ourselves called ourselves "NON-dailies."

What else? We don't run a lot of color. We don't cover the whole globe. A lot of us don't have AP Leafdesks.

We don't have ... and we aren't ...

Too many of us tend to define ourselves by what we perceive as our limitations. As in: Philadelphia, Charlotte, Pittsburgh, Raleigh are the Big Boys. And we, by extension—the Southports, the Danvilles, Smithfields, Elkins and Wake Forests—we're the Little Guys. As in: Little is Less.

Please, don't insult yourself. Such pigeonholing is demeaning and self-defeating.

9

Let's come at it from a different tack. As in: Less is More and Small is Beautiful.

To the enlightened community newspaper, small is beautiful and less is more because it operates within "the human scale," a term that recognizes that people flourish when given one-on-one attention. But that 1-to-1 ratio is difficult to maintain in all transactions. However, the alternative is untenable.

The antithesis of the human scale is being caught on LA's Ventura Freeway in eight lanes of mad commuters at rush hour, where human values deteriorate very quickly. Total strangers shooting at one another? Not my idea of community. By contrast, the small town has the human scale automatically working for it. You can make it work for you, too.

Here's how small is beautiful and less is more can be a boon for the enlightened community newspaper.

• A community newspaper can turn on a dime, make major decisions about coverage, editorial policy, news judgment, editing, cropping and advertising—without going through layers of needless bureaucracy and personnel.

• And because of the lack of layers, the access to the top is usually easier. Unless it's a poorly run slack chain operation, the editor or publisher is Norm or Nancy in the next room, empowered to make decisions quickly.

• Because it is small, it doesn't cost a fortune to start and equip a community paper—especially now with the emerging technology in desktop publishing. (See Chapter 10 and Chapter 19.)

• Everybody does more. Generalists are needed. So it's a great place for (1) beginners who need to learn the holistic art of newspapers; (2) older folks who want variety because it's never boring at a community paper since you're always doing something different; and (3) people who care about the final product and want to maintain journalistic and artistic control over an entire project—all the way from conception to pressroom.

• Small is beautiful because you can limit your coverage area. Instead of spreading yourself too thin (as the big papers are trying to do with so-called local "Neighbors" editions—thinly disguised attempts to copy us!) we can spread ourself THICK. In most cases the exclusively local weekly, semi- or triweekly is more valued by its readers and perceived by the community as being more caring and possessing more personality than the daily. That's why a great community newspaper can compete successfully against a large metropolitan daily. And that's why so many big-city dailies are scrambling to localize their coverage with zoned editions and Neighbors tabs. Doesn't that tell us something? One canny media observer even has a term for it; Professor Olin Briggs of Central Missouri State University calls it "the de-massification of the mass media."

Ron Dalby, general manager of the *Frontiersman* and *Valley Sun* of Alaska, says that pulling the plug on the wire service machine was "the best thing I ever did." Conversely, when an all-local non-daily converts to daily and is forced by sheer need to add wire service to fill the voracious news hole, a strange thing can happen. Because national and international news tends to overshadow and dilute the local coverage, the reading public is liable to assume the editors no longer think that the local news is important. Community newspaper editors and publishers considering such a conversion should beware.

ABOUT THE *COMMUNITY* IN COMMUNITY JOURNALISM

The word "community" in the term community journalism begs definition. In the strictest sense, this text addresses newspapers located in communities as defined traditionally: small, rural towns separated geographically from large urban cities. But the new demographics of the '90s demand an enlarged vision of the word. Broadly interpreted, *Community* now is used to refer to any group bound by shared values, be it philosophical, political, professional, recreational, or whatever.

Today we hear references made to the military community, the African American community, the arts community, the gay community, the Native American community, the university community, the sailing community, the internet community—you name it and they've got a community for it. Not surprisingly, these aggregates have their own publications too, which validate and authenticate the shared beliefs and practices of the larger group, while providing highly localized information tailored for the specific constituency. In the larger sense, are these not "community" publications as well?

Swinging the focus back to the more traditional mainstream American print journalism scene, media observers note another dominant growth area, that of the suburban community paper right in the backyard of the large metro daily. These papers face a formidable challenge in establishing a sense of place when a suburb is little more than a highly transient bedroom community for the nearby city. Publishers can't just draw a circle around a bunch of neighborhoods on a map and proclaim that area a community, Professor of Journalism Michael Stricklin of the University of Nebraska—Lincoln

Celebrating the ordinary: Small town and country rituals need never
look the same. Quintenna Boone Hampton breaks beans while her
grandson shows off his pocketknife.

told a recent National Newspaper Association seminar on community newspapers and community-building.

A publisher attending that seminar lamented his position. He publishes a paper just outside St. Louis where, "people just don't seem to care about our community. They move in, buy a house, work in the city and only sleep in the house. They couldn't care less about our town."

If people living side by side have no sense of community—that is, a separate and distinct identity—a newspaper has a long, uphill struggle to inculcate those values. It will take time, risk and financial commitment, along with consistent, solid local coverage. Such a publisher has to bank on the formula that the accretion of many good works over a period of time will pay off in the end.

But for a paper in this dilemma it's not enough to just put out the news week-in and week-out. The paper will have to be pro-active in nonconventional ways of promoting itself and the community. It must find new and nontraditional ways of selling itself, selling the community *to* the community and of educating the newcomers about the social context in which they've chosen to live. Perhaps this text will suggest some dynamic solutions. In any event, it's going to take some bold and synergistic thinking on the part of the paper's management.

THE COMMUNITY JOURNALISM SPIN

Regardless of differences in subject, specialization, setting or circulation, all community publications share a common denominator. Their perspective, focus, balance and news judgment is driven by local interests first. The Nigerians even have an expression for the concept, according to Assistant Professor Anthony Olorunnisola of Penn State. The Yoruba proverb, "T'iwa ni t'iwa; t'emi ni t'emi," (Ours is ours, [but] mine is mine), when applied to community journalism, could be extended like this:

"The national news is OK, but how does this story apply to *me*?"

Americans have an expression for it too. "All politics is local," said Tip O'Neill, the late congressman from Massachusetts.

If there's such a thing as a universal community journalism formula, that's it. Whether the reader is in Lagos, Nigeria, or Lost Creek, Mass., he or she needs to know how the international, national or state story is going to affect his or her life directly. In practically every big story, there's a local angle to be found.

WHO'S WHO IN THE ZOO

• Broadly speaking, there are two types of traditional "non-dailies"—the independently owned community paper and the chain-owned paper. In both cases, these papers are most likely to be exclusively local. The community newspaper can concentrate its coverage on the local area completely.

• **The independent or family-owned weekly, semiweekly, triweekly**—the owner has an investment in the community as well as the newspaper. The level of involvement between ownership, staff and community is profound. For the beginner, this is the best place to find a job. You'll learn more and they'll treat you like family. But fewer and fewer of these papers exist now, as the chains pressure them into selling. Some independent family-owned papers that are left are legendary in their areas and those owners are fiercely resolved to keep the paper from the chains. But the pressure of big bucks is too much for many owners.

• **The chain-owned weekly, semiweekly, triweekly**—unlike the preceding category, the publisher here is not the owner. While it's a good place for a young journalist to get a start, chain-owned papers, at worst, can be plagued by uninvolved management, low-grade talent, bottom-line focus, and draconian edicts handed down by a distant, remote owner who cares little about the community or paper except the P&L (profit and loss) statements. There are many exceptions to this; in the best cases, the chain has allowed the former owner-family to stay in place as editors and managers.

• **The urban alternative weekly**—'zines. This is the newest type of community paper to emerge recently, mainly centered in urban areas, catering to a tight target market of young Generation X arts crowd. Focus includes causes, lifestyles, the environment, guerrilla local politics, leisure, music, poetry, etc. The "look" is often specific in garbage fonts and Seattle or "grunge graphics," projecting a hip and with-it image. Ownership is usually independent and not overly concerned with profit and loss.

• **The community small daily. Five-to-six-days-a-week daily—the semi-daily.** The small daily often publishes in the afternoon, and is still local but now contains a mix of state, national and international wire service copy. Often, this is a former weekly grown to semi- and then triweekly and forced to go daily by circumstance and competition. Uses mostly local copy and local photos, no AP photos, and uses AP copy only to round it out.

• **The teen-ager**—the 15-20,000 circulation daily that doesn't know it's an adolescent. What am I? What am I going to be when I grow up? No one knows, and its pimples and gangly appearance reflect that lack of vision. Every front page is like an identity crisis: city council arguing over loose dogs beside Moslems getting blown away in Sarajevo. The reader pines for clarity and finds it not. This paper is demanding of the reader in much the same way an unruly teen drives teachers and parents to distraction. What's he going to do or wreck next? People working at the paper are likely to be just as confused.

    • **The little big paper**—20,000-50,000. Still classified by ASNE as "small newspapers" these are typically chain-owned and usually have the resources and savvy to put out good products, but they're now too big to fulfill their former community journalism role. They have to start Neighbors editions to fill that slot. At worst, Neighbors editions and bureaus can be staffed by two types: those on the way up and those on the way down. People at these places long to have their own paper, and that gets us back to square one, five paragraphs back.

WHAT THE COMMUNITY NEWSPAPER IS

You're familiar with the paradigm of the Cup Half Empty vs. the Cup Half Full. How you fare in life is generally a function of your perspective and attitude. It's all in how you look at things. Whether you're working at the paper or studying it, think about the community newspaper along those lines. First, make a list of what the paper *is*. Remember, keep it positive. As Emmett Gowan says, "Pessimism has no muscle." For instance, the weekly *Boogersburg Bugle* is:

LOCAL. The primary source for in-depth local coverage. Readers get the full story from the *Bugle*. They get the details of everything from Little League games to City Council to Girl Scout cookie sales winners exclusively in the *Bugle*.

SECOND READ. It therefore follows that most likely, the *Bugle* is the second newspaper in the house if the reader wants complete state, national and international news. That's not our job. And it's not our problem.

WEEKLY, SEMI-, TRIWEEKLY. The publishing schedule is your friend. More often than not, you have more time to spend on any given assignment than your counterparts at the daily. You have more time to do the interview, more time to write the story, more time to craft the package. And the less the frequency of your publication the longer the shelf life of your paper. A weekly is liable to sit around on the coffee table for a week, whereas with a daily, it's very likely to be daily-in, daily-out.

ACCESSIBLE. Most community papers don't employ armed guards with TV monitors at a security desk out front. Any reader or advertiser can walk in the front door of almost any community paper in the land and immediately find the editor, publisher, a reporter, photographer or ad salesperson. This accessibility is one of our greatest strengths. It reinforces the human scale, serves as a reality check for personal values, as well as responsible and fair news judgment, while encouraging professional accountability.

LEADING. Whether its editor or publisher realizes or acknowledges it, a community newspaper is involved intensely with its community, always leading, teaching, reflecting and telling the community about itself. The words of esteemed Brevard College Math Professor Rachel Daniels fit this model; she says, "You're never not teaching." The same is true for the community paper. We're never not *leading*. Whether the paper's cumulative impact is for good or not is a function of the editor/publisher's vision of the paper and the community. It's a lot like being a parent. Once you have a child, it's not a matter of choice. You are a mommy or a daddy, and that kid isn't going away. How you choose to parent makes all the difference—in your child's life and yours as well. Like a great mother or father, the enlightened community paper relishes its unique role in helping its community grow in healthy and appropriate directions.

SMALL. As in Small is Beautiful. It keeps it manageable, humane, personal and personally satisfying. We can drive around our primary coverage area by car easily in one day. The paper isn't so bulky that it breaks the bank to mail.

WHAT THE COMMUNITY NEWSPAPER ISN'T

FIRST READ. The community paper doesn't provide the first news on state, national and international news. Isn't that nice? The *Bugle* doesn't need to have uplinks and support a correspondent in Bangkok.

BIG. The larger the paper the more it costs to support, produce, print, deliver and mail. We are also not the nearby big-city daily, so quit trying to be like it. Ever see an older woman desperately trying to look like a teenager? Bleached hair, fake bake, tight pants, too much makeup. It's obvious to everyone that she's straining to be something she's not. How sad that she doesn't embrace the appropriate beauty of her age with grace and dignity.

TV. We are not TV. Go ahead and let the big-city dailies try to copy TV; it isn't working. They look like comic books when they try. The community newspaper has something that both TV and the big-city dailies don't and can't have: true personal community authenticity in your town. This is your turf. Exploit that strength.

WHAT THE COMMUNITY NEWSPAPER SHOULD BE

Bill Fuller, former community journalism editor and now a Tallahassee-based newspaper consultant, likes to say that community newspapers have to be vital. Vital to their community and vital to their advertisers (see Chapter 16), while striving to be better still. We should be taking advantage of our medium's innate, traditional strengths of in-depth storytelling in both words and pictures. Be true to your school; do your best at what you're best at, i.e., thoroughly local coverage. And finally, we should be watching the technological curve and staying educated for the future.

THE DOWNSIDE OF COMMUNITY JOURNALISM

Just as big-city dailies have distinct disadvantages, there can be a real downside to our profession. Community newspapers can represent the worst of our business. We are smaller, and undeniably we have less resources—fewer reporters per newsroom, fewer computers, fewer photographers, fewer state-of-the-art cameras and smaller darkrooms, less financial support—both for the papers' production and for salaries. Beginning reporters, photographers, ad salespeople make less (relative to big-city daily folk) until they rise to editorial, advertising and publishing positions. For a beginner with big dreams, this can be discouraging.

Further, many small-town papers seem to attract and harbor washed-up derelicts of our business; community papers at their worst become sort of a stale backwater for the flotsam and jetsam of journalism. This results in poor management, terrible writing, uninspired photography and a community paper that resembles the journalistic version of a zombie. It just keeps coming at you, dead or not.

The proliferation of chain ownership in the nation's community newspapers spawns a farm system not unlike minor league ball clubs. Sometimes this can be good, if managed well. But much of the time, this farm system means turnover is high, and consequently, journalists in training miss the entire point of community journalism. They never get involved with the community. Often, they privately assume a condescending attitude toward the community, a superior attitude toward the readers. They're at the paper only long enough to get some experience under their belts, then it's on to the next rung on the corporate ladder.

This sad system can be exacerbated by lazy editors who have bought into the fallacy that their publication is "just a little paper," and therefore less of everything is not just OK, it's the norm. Quality, precision, professionalism, the pursuit of excellence all suffer because sloppy editors have sold out.

This situation is often compounded by a publisher who is a "bottom-feeder" of community journalism, caring nothing about professionalism or the community but only the all-sacred bottom line. Little wonder that community journalism doesn't get the respect it deserves. When a recent outstanding graduate of a major journalism school announced her intentions of joining the staff of a fine weekly paper, one of her former professors reacted with, "Surely you don't intend to *stay* in community journalism … ?"

For the quality-conscious young professional working at an uninspired community newspaper, the going may be tough. If you're not getting creatively nurtured, constructively edited, or professionally encouraged—remember, you are paying your dues, and your experience will serve you well. When you do choose to move on, wherever you go, what you've gone through will help. Many a big-city daily managing editor will tell you, there's no better beginning than to work on a community newspaper. For further advice on how to stay sane and creative in a nonsupportive community newspaper environment, see Chapter 20.

OTHER VOICES; OTHER NEWSROOMS

Before Steven Knowlton became an author and an assistant professor of journalism at the Pennsylvania State University College of Communications, he says he got one of his lasting life lessons while serving as editor and part-owner of a Maine weekly newspaper. He calls this parable: "A romance of the columnist, the police chief and the diner: How a hotshot young cityside reporter got his comeuppance."

The Columnist, the Police Chief and the Diner

by Steven Knowlton

Reporters on metropolitan daily newspapers often harbor a fantasy—most prosaically, it is to go to law school, more fancifully, it is to write a great novel, or, most wonderfully of all, it is to own their own paper. The notion of someday eking out a noble living with a shirt-tail full of type, a mouthful of irreverent wisdom and a heart full of deep compassion has sustained many a journalist for periods unfathomable to anyone who has never made or missed deadline, successfully interviewed a grieving parent or gotten a handwritten thank-you from a third-grade kid you've made a front-page hero.

Someday, the reporters say to each other and to the back-bar mirror after work, someday I'll chuck the daily madness and Own My Own Paper, routing the rascals, comforting the afflicted, keeping a watchful eye on a grateful world. Dreaming gets no grander. Sometimes, people actually try for it, usually in middle years or later, winding up their careers where journalism began and where in many ways it is still its purest and its best, in smallish towns and communities, publishing newspapers with circulations of a few thousand.

So I was unusual in that before I was 30, I was living the dream on the rocky coast of

Maine—with a few bucks and a bit of credit, I bought half of a struggling weekly and with it the gloriously long hours, the romantic poverty, the pride to bursting-point of press day, when the best of me that I could commit to type came roaring off the press 20 or 24 pages at a time. At the time I bought my paper, I was a journeyman reporter, self-confident to the point of arrogance and altogether dead certain that my 10 years at big dailies and the wires would inevitably translate into more and better readers, nobler American journalism and greater glory for all.

Before I was 32, I was dead broke, out of business and deeply humbled by a small town in rural Maine, home to lobstermen and clam diggers, shopkeepers and shoemakers, cops and schoolteachers and civil servants—a tough, resilant people, impenetrable as a lead-gray winter sky, folks with deep roots and long memories.

There's a joke in Maine that a friend told me once over coffee in a well-meaning effort to keep me from tripping on my own big-city shoes. In it, a New Yorker who had moved to Maine decades before asks his Maine-native friend what it takes to be considered "from Maine." The native gently tells the ex-New Yorker that his 20 years in Maine doesn't qualify. "But how about my children?" asks the "newcomer." "They were all born here. They're Maine natives, aren't they?" The New Englander answers, "If your cat had her kittens in the oven, would you call them biscuits?"

I laughed at the dry, rustic humor, finished my coffee and went back upstairs to the four-room store clerk's apartment that we had converted into the newspaper office. We had jammed three typewriters and old wooden desks to hold them into the larger of the apartment's two bedrooms, and had put the leased typesetting equipment into the smaller one. We had made a darkroom out of the kitchen, sealing it off with towels and duct tape to keep the dark from getting out. And in the large front parlor, we had put the makeup tables, waxer and everything else it took to turn notes and quotes and too-few ads into a quarter's worth of weekly wisdom about Downeast Maine, the coastal strip from Machias on the Canadian border down past Mount Desert Isle and Bucksport to Belfast and on to the summer playground of Camden.

We had a full-time staff of four, including the ad salesman, but not counting the high school typing-class whiz who set most of the paper's type on Mondays and Tuesdays after school. Plus, like most weeklies, we had a dozen or so local correspondents, non-staff writers who were paid embarrassingly few dollars to produce a few hundred words a week on the comings and goings of their communities—who was in the hospital, whose offspring had enlisted in the service, who had houseguests from out of town, and so on. They were almost always dreadfully but colorfully written, frequently in longhand, and, in my case at least, generated great ambivalence as to whether they should appear in the paper at all. The columns took up valuable space and both the authors and their copy were a nuisance to work with. On the other hand, the columns contained dozens of names, which translated into dozens of badly needed newsstand sales, and were a convenient place to fob off hundredth birthdays and baby christenings I had neither staff nor stomach to give the full coverage the relatives wanted.

Most such columns were written by gossipy old ladies, but I took it as a matter of big-city sophisticated pride that if I had to be burdened by such, we could at least have a little variety. An English teacher in a local community college provided 500 words of plausible erudition, an expatriate from Washington wrote about national politics with remarkable insight, and a fellow named Ty Cooper, who ran a bait shop, wrote pieces of wildly uneven quality about the changing life of the Downeast fishing and lobstering families. It was one of Cooper's columns that taught me volumes about newspapering in a small town.

Late one summer, as the tourist season was winding down and folks were starting to hunker down for the long hard winter of much snow and little income, Cooper's weekly column was about an off-shore squabble in which one lobsterman's boat was shot full of holes and sunk by another lobsterman in a quarrel over the number and location of the two men's lobster traps. Nobody was named in the piece, which pleased me well enough, since while I found Cooper's wry account screamingly funny, I had been Downeast long enough to know that lobstering was serious business and that lobster pots represented far more than the source of a fine dinner on the one hand or the base for a L.L. Bean-kitsch coffee table on the other.

I called Cooper at the bait shop and questioned him closely about the incident and his sources, but he swore as to its absolute veracity and even explained why there was no police record of the aquatic showdown, since lobstermen rarely saw fit to avail themselves of the urban lawmakers' sense of justice. In truth, I had a residual nagging doubt, but figured what the hell, it was Tuesday, crunch day for us, the column was already in type, and the boats weren't even very well described—one red stripe above the waterline on the one, two narrow green ones on the other, barely enough to tell them apart in Cooper's tale of High Noon on the High Seas. We ran it.

The next afternoon, after another late night of getting the paper out, then sleeping until noon in celebration of another issue on the streets, I strolled up to the police station to see what malefactors had been apprehended since last we checked, and to chat with the chief. He was an amiable ex-state trooper with a raconteur's gift for timing and the telling detail. It had become a high point in the rhythmic cycle of weekly newspapering to sit for an hour or so with him in his small, dark-paneled office, listening to tales of the lighter, as well as more chilling, moments of a Downeast cop's 30 years on the road. So I breezed into his office and plopped down in my accustomed spot, a black leather arm chair with a small tear in the seat cushion and brass-headed upholstery tacks worn shiny and smooth. "What's up, chief?" I said by way of greeting. "Have you got the bad guys all rounded up?"

Now, during much of life, three or four seconds isn't a long time, and the chief's silence probably didn't last much more than that, but the dead quiet of the room seemed to take an eternity to break. Then the chief looked up from the latest issue of my pride and joy, opened to Cooper's copy, and froze me with a glare that I'd never seen but that other cops had told me was legendary. "You ... stupid ... bastard," he said finally, and I was amazed how clear his diction was since I could barely see his lips moving. "I ought to shut your goddamn paper down."

"Excuse me, chief, but what did I do?" was the best I could muster, hoping it didn't sound sarcastic, because I didn't mean to be flippant, but was way too spooked to try the line out in my head first, and way too rattled to trust my own conversational skills.

"You ... got ... the ... wrong ... damn ... boat."

The "wrong damn boat" of course, involved Cooper's story of the lobstermen's quarrel. After a few minutes of the most blistering verbal hiding I'd ever received, the chief explained, as one might explain to a naughty but slow-witted child, that Cooper's story was all backwards, that one of Cooper's friends was one of the figures in the story, and that the chief's own brother was the other. The men had quarreled for years, their respective families for generations. The chief had hoped it was finally over. Now, thanks to my ignorance, Cooper had let the evil genie of generational hate out of the bottle again.

I hazarded an interruption. "Maybe you already know the story, chief, or think you do, but nobody's named in that story. There's nothing to identify anybody. If Cooper screwed up, I apologize, but there can't be any real harm done."

"How many lobster boats around here have a red stripe just above the waterline?" the chief asked me, no longer livid because a decent man can stay angry with a fool only so long. He stuck his right forefinger—his trigger finger, I noted—into the air and counted. "One, my grandfather's."

I slunk out of his office and back down the hill toward the sanctuary of my office, stopping in the diner for a midday coffee and muffin that was the usual breakfast after the weekly exhaustion of giving newspaper birth the night before.

"Hi, Linda. Coffee and blueberry," I said with none too much cheer to the diner's waitress and half-owner, a pleasant woman in her early 30s who was also my newspaper's landlord.

She didn't glare as the chief had. She didn't look at me at all, in fact, so I didn't see how red her eyes were until much later. She just turned on her heel and went off to scrub down the other end of the counter, which had apparently suddenly become very, very dirty.

Her husband, Dennis, moved over opposite my place at the counter. "Don't talk to Linda," he said evenly but with obvious checked anger. "She's been crying all morning. Because of what you wrote about her brother-in-law."

In half-hearted self-defense, I asked, "What brother-in-law. I don't know Linda's brother-in-law. I didn't know she had a brother-in-law. What did he do? Get arrested or something? Dennis, you know I can't keep people's names out of the paper if they get busted." I rattled off several more sentences, which clattered to the formica counter top and lay there like so many pickup sticks.

"Ty's story about the boat-sinking," Dennis said. "She's terribly embarrassed, and mad, too, that you said her sister's brother sank that other guy's boat. You got it all wrong."

I could muster nothing more eloquent or profound than, "Oh, Jesus." and swept a hand through my hair so I could stare harder at the counter top. I had known that Linda's family, and Dennis's too, for that matter, had been in Downeast Maine for generations. I didn't know about the sister's husband, but it was no surprise that she had one or that he was a lobsterman.

What else I didn't know, of course, was that the brother-in-law had two Kelly green stripes painted on his boat, just above the waterline. To these and a fistful of other details, I told Dennis weakly, "I didn't know."

"You are probably the only one around here who didn't," he said. "You'd better leave now. Get your coffee down the street."

The paper didn't fold that week, though it could have, and the earth didn't crack open and swallow me up, though for a day I wished it would. I was glum enough for a day—self-pitying would be a fair enough way to describe it—then I righted myself and yelled at Cooper for screwing up his boat story. He stuck to his guns, joined the chorus in calling me a fool, and said he'd just as soon quit writing the column anyway unless I wanted to start paying him cash for it.

I was flummoxed again because I figured we'd been paying him ten bucks or twenty bucks or whatever for his column. Not so, Cooper said, adopting the increasingly familiar tone of the wise man trying with waning patience to explain the obvious to the town dunce. It turns out the guy who sold me half the paper had worked an off-the-books trade with Cooper—the column, plus half a cord of firewood now and then, in exchange for a $50 display ad for the bait shop.

I'd love to say this story was an epiphany, that the scales fell from my eyes and I suddenly agreed wholeheartedly with Rousseau and his conviction of the wisdom of the common folk. But that wouldn't be true, either. After a few weeks, we resumed getting decent cooperation from the cops, and after a few more weeks I returned to getting my coffee at Linda and Dennis's diner.

We limped along another year before the paper finally folded with a thud almost nobody else heard but which still hurts with a pain usually associated with the death of a pretty good friend or fairly close relative. But I still hadn't lost all my arrogance, so I blamed everybody but myself for the failure. The economy, the chief, Cooper, of course, Gerald Ford, who was president at the time, Richard Nixon, who wasn't but whom I still blamed him for almost everything. Epiphany is too strong, too sudden a term for the learning that the sunken boat story provided.

In the 20 years since then, I've been beaten up a lot, both at other small papers and at some more big ones, and greatly humbled in realizing how arrogant and brash are the young, even when they are, as I was, bright and clever and "fast copy"—perhaps the most highly regarded of all big-city reporters' virtues. And I don't know about Rousseau, but I do know that there's a great deal of difference between small-town papers and metro dailies in the way they fit into their communities. And while I love, truly love, the New York Times and the Washington Post and what they stand for in American journalism and American democracy, there's an intangible something, almost familial, about community journalism.

I think I am almost old enough to own my own paper again, a small weekly, perhaps somewhere on the New England coast.

YOUR TOWN; YOUR TURN

1. If Howie Mandel were to ask you, "What do you do?" what would you say?

2. If you're a professional, examine your paper. What kind of community paper is it? Does it have a vision? Of itself? Of the community? Can you put it into words? If you're a student, analyze your hometown paper.

3. If you're working at a community paper, ask yourself this: Why are you in this business? How'd you get started? What do you like, dislike about the community newspaper business so far? If you're a student, why are you taking this course? What attracts you to community journalism?

News Is Like a Hurricane: The Closer It Gets, the More Important It Becomes to You

THINK GLOBALLY; REPORT LOCALLY

When in early September 1989 a low-level tropical disturbance deep in the Caribbean made the first national weather news, Bill Collins of the Summerville, S.C., *Journal Scene* took little notice. But within 10 days, the storm assumed a force unparalleled in recent history. From the satellite photos Hugo looked like a giant's fist poised to deliver a roundhouse right to the Southeastern coast.

Summerville, just outside Charleston, was directly in harm's way.

In the next 48 hours, editor Collins would live through an unforgettable nightmare of monsoonal rains and high winds that all but destroyed his community. That little blip on the weather map had turned into the biggest headlines of the century, and many papers would be hard-pressed just to get to print at all that week.

Collins, camped out at the *Journal Scene*, says he vividly remembers roofs blowing off all around town within sight of the newspaper office, of how his own roof rattled and groaned, how his building shook as if with fright. And how they managed somehow to put out the *Journal Scene* that week in spite of trees down all over town. "Summerville looked like a bombed out war zone," Collins remembered. "But thank the Lord no one in our town was killed."

Repeat: Our town.

For community newspapers, that's the nature of news. News is like a hurricane; the closer it gets, the more important it becomes to you.

ENTER THE HUGONAUTS

In the aftermath of Hugo, national news organizations from the big TV networks to the major dailies sent teams into the Carolinas, and specifically into the Charleston area. Along with the influx of others taking commercial advantage of the area's plight, the media earned the local moniker of *Hugonauts*. And when they had "covered" the story, and national interest seemed to grow weary of angry lowland residents standing forlornly outside destroyed houses, the media went back home to the big cities.

Bill Collins stayed. He lives there. He cares. Summerville is his town.

That's the major difference between community journalism and the major media. They usually show up in your town only for a disaster, and then when it's over, they go home. But for the area's community newspapers, the Summerville *Journal Scene*, the Goose Creek *Gazette*, the *Coastal Times*, the Myrtle Beach *Sun-News,* the story continued. It continues today; there are still people in the Lowcountry trying to cope with the after-effects of Hugo.

Community newspapers collect, report, handle, write and package the news in a fundamentally different way from any other news medium. Remember Bill Collins, holding on that dark night in the *Journal Scene* office, praying for "his town."

For us, news is not some detached, impersonal set of occurrences happening to nameless, faceless news sources. What a terrible word: source. Join the human race, folks, we're talking about *people* here.

At a community paper, news is not events happening to inanimate objects. News is people, *your people*, and how the changing world affects their everyday lives. News is your people being caught up in events. Our job is to record that changing human condition in such a way that we provide not only an accurate and fair representation of what happened, but also understanding, compassion, context and hopefully, growth.

In addition, great community news coverage (take the Hugo example again) provides a place for community sharing, healing and growth. The Summerville *Journal Scene* became a platform for a communal rite of passage, a dependable scrapbook that said to its community: *Look, you stayed here and took it and you survived. We* (including the paper) *may be small, but we're still standing*. Once a community and its paper bonds through such an experience, you have the makings of true and lasting communication.

24

WHAT IS NEWS ANYWAY?

News can be broadly defined as an event that has one or all of the following characteristics. The following time-honored list has been called the *factors of news judgment*, and you can use this to help you assess the newsworthiness of a story or story idea.

Timeliness
Audience
Impact and Proximity
Significance/Importance
Magnitude
Prominence
Disaster/Tragedy
The Odd or Unusual
Conflict and Controversy
Human Interest
Humor

From Peter Jennings at "ABC Nightly News" to Bill Collins at the Summerville *Journal Scene*—we all use this list, albeit intuitively at times, to determine:

What is the lead?
What is this story really about?
Who cares?
What is the most important thing?
What is the head?
How do we play or place this story?

Remember, the community journalism response to news is profoundly different from that of the big-city daily. Again, not necessarily better, just different, and therefore more effective for our context. Here's how the above list takes on a community journalism spin:

NEWS AND THE COMMUNITY JOURNALISM PERSPECTIVE
Timeliness

It's been said the media is in the new/s business, not the olds business. News—as in new information. CNN is the apotheosis of this credo, in which the "data stream" is constant and unrelenting.

In community journalism form follows function. If your paper is weekly, then it's one thing. If it's semi- or triweekly, then it's something else again. If your paper is daily, then it can carry breaking news. The less frequent the publication, the more explanatory and in-depth it should be. The longer we have between the news event and the time we hit the streets, the more we should be putting things in local context and providing background for our audience.

That's how we compete with the big daily and TV. The nearby TV station might give the story in your town a minute; the big daily four inches. You can devote 20-40 inches—the whole front page if you're the editor and want to. With apologies to Miller: If you've got the time, we've got the paper.

Audience

When you buy a house, according to the old saying, you look for three things: location, location and location. It's the same in community journalism. Your location is your audience and your audience is in your face. It's very specific. It starts here, from your desk in the newsroom and ripples out to the edge of your prime coverage area. Perhaps that's the county line.

If it happens to anyone within the county, then it's news. And similarly, anyone in the county can become news and generate a news story (or a feature, or a sports story, or a sports feature, or an editorial or an editorial column or a … you get the picture).

Our audiences are what geologists call "site specific." Writing for the Lowcountry community of Summerville with its Gullah influences requires a different understanding of the local people, language and dialect, culture and historical background than writing for a newspaper in central Pennsylvania, where the influences are predominately Germanic with virtually no African-American influences at all.

Impact and Proximity

Think about your audience again. And about the old Denver editor with his "dogfight in Denver" edict to the young reporter. During the summer of 1993 the national story broke of the impending closings of military bases all across the United States. It didn't cause even the slightest ripple in Lewistown, Montana, where there isn't a base anywhere in the area. No local news peg; no story. But let's go back to Summerville, where much of the local economy is based on spill-over and from folks working at the Charleston

Naval Base and Supply Depot, which was on the list. Defense Secretary Les Aspin's list of proposed base closings hit the Charleston area like a second Hugo, editor Collins says. His follow-up stories reflected the impact—the significance and importance—of news like this on his community.

It's a given truth in our business that anything that impacts your community is going to impact your paper too. If the Charleston Naval Base closes, it will body-slam all of Summerville, including the *Journal Scene,* which will likely lose circulation and advertising. Talk about the trickle-down effect, if you're a cub reporter at the paper, the base closing could mean you don't get that raise you were hoping for. Worse yet, it might mean you get laid off.

Bottom line: The community paper possesses an inherent intensity of community involvement that simply can't be matched by any outside big-city daily or area TV, no matter how neighborly they try to be or how chummy they may appear on camera. Their survival is not inextricably woven into the fabric of your community; yours is. Professional intensity is a function of caring. Caring comes from an honest sense of our connectedness. Small communities are profoundly connected.

Magnitude

The larger the crowd at the Christmas parade, the more people at the conference football playoffs, the bigger the voter turnout, the more money raised for United Way, the faster the car was speeding down Main Street—the community journalism response to this factor of news judgment is similar to the other media, except that we try to place it in a local context.

Prominence

Important people always are news. But in the community journalism world, important means Big Frog Little Pond. So it's all relative. If the chairman of the county commissioners is pulled for suspected DUI, that's extra big news in your town. How your paper handles that story will have repercussions beyond just that edition. For instance, if you whitewash it or don't print it, you risk a complete loss of public credibility because everybody will have heard about it already by word of mouth. Consider the old saying: *I already know the news, I just wanted to see if the paper had the nerve to print it.* On the other hand, if you do print the DUI story and sensationalize and overblow it, you may have to live with the consequences.

Disaster and Tragedy

Just as the rest of the media, the community paper must report on disasters and tragedies—crimes, wrecks, fires and so-called "acts of God." But here again, the community journalism response to human suffering is notably different. For us, it's a matter of balance. How much gore to describe or show in pictures? Do we publish the name of the rape victim, of the accused? Do we publish pictures of dead bodies? People grieving over burned homes? For the big-city papers and TV this is standard fare. Why should we be any different? The answer is, the personal approach. Before you run any such story or photo which you think might contain content that would hurt people, use this rule of thumb: What if this were a member of my family? What if this were my daughter lying dead on the pavement? My grandmother's name in the paper as the rape victim, my father depicted crying hysterically in front of his burned-out home? Think twice. This is your town. And these are your people. What ends are served by publishing sensationalistic photos of human suffering or using lurid descriptions in hard news stories?

These are basic news judgment questions every community newspaper must grapple with and define, ahead of time if possible. The best of papers have policies on such subjects, and young reporters and photographers learn these matters of philosophical style in course. For instance, no, the *Express* doesn't run photos of dead bodies. That means if you go to a wreck where there's been a fatality, you take the shot from a discreet angle. Yes, we name the accused in a rape trial but not the victim. When it comes to grieving victims at tragedies or people hurt in auto accidents, allow them their dignity as best you can. At a disaster site, don't ask victims, "So, how does it feel to have lost your son (your home, your wife, etc.)?" We see enough of that reprehensible reporting on what cartoonist Jeff MacNelly calls "the Nitwitness News" on TV.

When taking photos, try to get permission either before or after shooting, or when your intrusion would be in poor taste, take such photos from a distance with telephoto—and then huddle with your editor before the photo is run. At the shoot, it's better to concentrate instead on the rescue efforts by firefighters, police and emergency personnel. We're not in this to sell papers by using prurient stories and gory photos.

Where do you draw the line? The line is always shifting. It's a judgment call. It's a gray area. And it requires a constant sense of balance. There are no right or wrong answers. On good taste and news judgment, the old *breakfast table rule* is still a good yardstick: If your reader can't read your

Putting the emphasis on the disaster and its effects is more tasteful than showing human suffering when it's not warranted. Many community papers used this style. (*Photos by Pat Jobe*)

paper and get through eggs-over-easy without losing it, then you've got a problem with good taste.

The public's right to know is not served by a bloody photo of someone's mama dead all over P-1. If you run such a photo, you have every right to expect "the solid waste matter to hit the climate control device." And remember, because it's a community paper, the kinfolk can walk right in the newsroom and knock you into next week. You probably deserved it. (More about questionable photos in Chapters 9 and 14.)

Conflict and Controversy

Because your backyard is so small, the community newspaper reporter, editor, even the publisher often finds himself/herself in the middle of that "Dogfight in Denver." Sorry kids, it goes with the territory. Local politics, public governmental affairs, law enforcement and the public schools all involve public tax funds and therefore need to be watched closely. The rule of thumb is to attempt to cover all as objectively and fairly as possible. When covering a controversial subject, make sure you get as many sides as possible represented in the story and that your report doesn't seem weighted one way or the other. This is especially important in community journalism, because the townspeople will make it their business to know as much about your private life as possible. Any possible *perceived* biases (whether or not they're true) or conflicts of interest will perjure your story's credibility. If you do have an ax to grind, admit it and bail out of the story quickly. If you're a young reporter and are working on a sensitive story, make sure your editor is closely involved in crafting the final product. If you're the editor and you're thinking about writing a scathing editorial, remember: don't write mad, and pick your fights with care. Are your arguments balanced and rational? Or shrill and strident? (More on this in Chapter 5.)

Unusual Occurrences and Odd Things

One of the town characters decides to take a coffee shop dare and dive head-first into the fountain on the square ... an old woman who's had a pet groundhog named Roscoe living in her spare washing machine for 16 years ... the community college president who's got to kiss a pig in public because he said he would if the soccer team went undefeated ... a truck overturns and spills its load of chocolate syrup across Main Street ... a woman who fakes a heart attack to scare off a burglar ... the first woman railroad engineer in your area—these and thousands of other little stories fall under the news heading of unusual or odd occurrences. People have an insatiable appetite

Concentrating on the scene and showing the rescue emergency—and in this case, firefighters at work—makes for dramatic shots.

for variety, things that are different and perhaps odd. We as a species seek relief from the boring humdrum of daily existence. Some papers, during especially slow news times, are famous for running photos of farmers with potatoes that look like dogs, tomatoes that look like they have faces. Is there anything wrong with this? Not really, unless that's all you're running.

Human Interest

Broadly interpreted, this term has come to encompass stories or photos that tug on the heartstrings a little. A mentally disabled boy was lost for a day and then found lodged in a drainpipe. He was found by local rescue crews because, though he couldn't speak, he wore a silver bell around his neck, and they heard him ringing the bell. When the rescue was successful it made a good news story, with an added dash of human interest. When one newspaper editor heard about the impending retirement of the local high school janitor, it didn't sound like much of a story until the principal told him that the old man loved to sit in the boiler room, playing his banjo while tending the furnace. Ah, now we've got a human interest story, and picture too.

Humor

Some maintain the media's job is to inform and entertain. Humor is the finest form of entertainment, but it's not so easy to come by. It takes a reporter, photographer and editor with a sense of humor, too. One of the real hallmarks of smaller towns is their innate sense of humor. A good community newspaper can reflect that sense of fun. The rule of thumb: Don't produce humor at the expense of somebody's feelings. Making fun of people is not good form. There's a fine difference between laughing at someone and laughing with them. In news and feature stories, avoid sarcasm, satire and parody until you've got some experience under your belt and your community knows you. Satire inevitably will be read straight by someone, who will not be amused. Reserve this form of humor for the editorial page, personal columns and commentary that is clearly marked as such. Examples? The eccentric old man who has stipulated in his will that he must be buried with his beloved '57 Cadillac Eldorado. The farmer who, when baling hay, playfully sticks a pair of boots in the center of the roll of hay, and then watches for passing motorists' reactions.

THE BIG THREE: NEWS, FEATURES, COMMENTARY

Everything written in your paper that is not advertising is one of three kinds of stories: news, features or commentary. How can you tell them apart? What are their distinct differences? Joy Franklin, editor of the Hendersonville (N.C.) *Times-News,* a thriving 21,000 daily, uses the following model to help young reporters and students get a grip on the forms and their characteristics.

NEWS
Lead: Lead is usually a summary lead (several of the 5W's and H).
Style: Story style is usually inverted pyramid.
Timeliness: The story is almost always timely.
Purpose: It is written to inform.
Perspective: The reporter remains objective.
Location: It is found on P-1 mostly, but elsewhere as well.

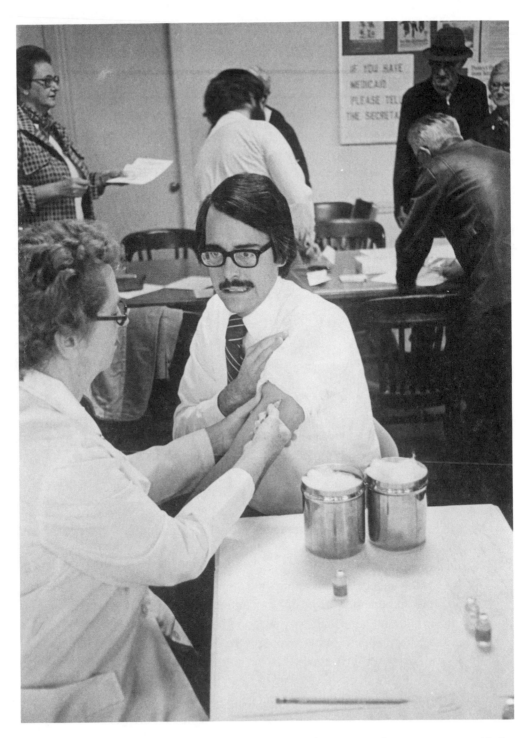

Helping to promote an inoculation program, the town mayor gets his flu shot, then for a brief second, clowns around for the photographer. A little humor in the news never hurts. But this does. Ouch.

FEATURES
Lead: Variety of leads can be used.
Style: Narrative, often anecdotal and other styles.
Timeliness: May or may not be timely. News peg not necessary.
Purpose: Written to entertain and inform.
Perspective: Can be either objective or subjective.
Location: Usually section fronts, occasionally as a "bright" on P-1.

COMMENTARY
Lead: Variety of leads can be used.
Style: Variety of forms and structure used.
Timeliness: May or may not have a time factor.
Purpose: Written to inform perhaps, but mostly to persuade.
Perspective: Opinion of editorial writer, or editorial board.
Location: Editorial page and in the case of personal commentary, in set locations in special
    sections: op-ed, lifestyle, sports.

ALL POLITICS IS LOCAL; ALL POLITICS IS STORIES

If the metaphor of news being like a hurricane is accurate, then local governmental affairs reporting could be called a veritable tempest. But it is not a tempest in a teapot. It is the very stuff of our calling as newspeople. Who else is going to provide in-depth, consistent and comprehensive coverage of city hall activities and meetings held by town council, school board, planning council, borough council, zoning board and the county commissioners?

Few beats covered by the community paper are more important.

The newspaper is there in proxy for the citizen who won't or can't attend the meeting. Such coverage is one of a community newspaper's main functions. Stories generated by action by such boards directly impact our readers.

If the county commissioners are considering raising the county tax rate, just look at how the factors of news judgment kick in. The story hits our audience right in the wallet; they need to know all about it right now; why has the rate been upped? What's going to be done with the funds? Joe Six-Pack (who may never have read a county commissioners story in his life) wants to know, "How much am I going to have to pay?" There's going to be a howl of disapproval, perhaps at a public hearing. "When is that meeting going to be held again? Where's that *Bugle*? I know I saw it here somewhere."

Local governmental stories are stories that matter to your reader. They may not know it right away, and they may not all know it at once, but it's vital that we be there at those meetings, providing coverage that goes beyond the mechanical reportage of agenda items one through five.

At one town council meeting that no newspaper deemed worthy of coverage, the board adopted a strict and sweeping sign ordinance. It wasn't until enforcement started kicking in, that town businesspeople began reacting angrily. "How come we didn't know about this?" they lamented.

If the area community newspapers aren't providing vital watchdog services, it's very likely no one will. Historically, American newspapers in general and community newspapers specifically have been that public watchdog. Some consider our surveillance role to be almost a sacred calling. It is certainly not to be taken lightly ... even though humorous, downright funny or odd things happen in council meetings—and they do.

In one town, the voters were preparing to vote on an ABC referendum, whether beer or wine could be sold in the city limits. The town council, all elderly conservative white males, held a public hearing. One noted liberal citizen stood up, called the council members all a bunch of puppets, maintaining that the council was completely controlled by the conservative church down on main street. And to dramatize that connection, he tied a piece of string from a large ball to the table leg used by the council, and marched out of the room, unrolling the string as he went.

Where was he going, trailing that string behind him? There was only one community reporter in the room, and he and several curious onlookers followed as the man stalked out of the county courthouse, down main street to the church in question. There he tied the other end of the string to the front door. "That's the connection," he said emphatically. "This church jerks the string and the council jumps. And you can quote me on that."

You're darn right we can. Great stuff. One can only hope our reporter had a camera with him.

Your reporting model for this area of the news might well be the late Tip O'Neill's famous motto, "All politics is local." When it comes to our business, we should add: And all politics is local stories.

State and national political stories impact our readers as well. If Bill Clinton is putting thousands of new police on the streets, how does that impact our town? It's going to get right down to names and faces. It's our job in community journalism to interpret these state and national stories by showing how such decisions affect our communities directly.

FROM THE TRENCHES

I awoke in the middle of the night, a strange smell in my nostrils. Smoke. Where could it be coming from? And what was that reddish glow outside my window? Suddenly awake, I could see from my second-story apartment over main street, Franklin Street, Chapel Hill, that something large was on fire in the middle of the block.

A cub reporter-photographer for Jim Shumaker's *Chapel Hill Weekly,* I scrambled into my clothes, grabbed my camera, and hurtled downstairs and up the street. It was the Varsity Theatre. If it went, half of main street could go with it. The firefighters let me pass and I shot some pictures of the fire-fighting efforts. But it was all smoke and darkness, and the actual fire was on the top and back of the roof. No way to get much of a decent shot, I realized with frustration.

Then as I was standing out on the sidewalk in front of the theater, I saw the Varsity Theatre's manager emerging from the theater. The look on his face was what held my attention. Without even focusing or thinking, I popped off a direct-flash grab shot, catching the soaked manager and his glazed look of shock. I shot it from about 20 feet out. One shot. One single flash. I didn't want to bug the owner. He already looked upset enough as it was. I was lucky. The shot turned out.

Shumaker grunted his approval when he saw the photo and ran it front and center P-1. He liked it because the photograph depicted not so much the extent of the physical damage as much as it showed the human reaction to a news event. The look on the manager's face was more telling than a shot of

The fire pictures of the Varsity Theatre fire were lackluster . . .

. . . but the shot of the soaked and shocked owner emerging from the ruined movie house told it all.

the burned-out building. That was an epiphanic experience for the young reporter-photographer.

YOUR TOWN; YOUR TURN

1. Think about your paper, or a target paper. Find an example of how the community journalism response to a local news event was different from that of the nearby big-city daily and area TV.

2. Find an example in your paper of how the publication schedule affected how the paper treated a major news story.

3. What is your newspaper's audience? Be as specific as possible.

4. How does your paper treat hard news? Human suffering and grief? The depiction of death and dying? Does your paper have a set of standards for good taste and a stylebook for handling hard news? If so, what are those guidelines? Do they seem to differ from the big-city daily and TV? If the paper doesn't have one, why not? And what are some of the *implied* standards it uses?

Features: Pay Attention to the Signs

ONE THAT DIDN'T GET AWAY

The young feature writer stood puzzled at the open front door. An old man was supposed to meet him here for a feature about cider-making. But Hoyle Greene wasn't in sight. Disappointed, the reporter turned to leave. But wait a minute—what's that sign by the mailbox? A jumbled bunch of nonsense. It said:

LOOK.ROWN.
THE.HOUSE.
I.WILL.B.W
ORKN.—>

Staring at the sign intently, the reporter began to understand. The old man couldn't spell very well, and thought periods at the end of each word added weight. The message was starting to get through, when Hoyle Greene, all a-grin and eyes dancing, appeared from around the house where he had been working.

"Lahk ma sahn, young feller?" he inquired.

The reporter "lahked" it so much he took a picture of it. The old man who couldn't spell proceeded to teach the young man a world about apples, cider, and making do with what you had.

Over the years, Hoyle Greene would become a vast sourcebook for the writer, and eventually provide him the photograph that would become a jacket cover on a book about the old people and the culture of the Southern Appalachians.

And to think the young reporter almost walked away from that sign.

THE COMMUNITY JOURNALIST AS CREATIVE WRITER

There's a memorable photograph from Edward Steichen's landmark photography exhibit, "The Family of Man," depicting a clutch of small African boys sitting by firelight listening in rapt attention to a village elder telling a scary story. Both of the old man's hands are raised to mimic open claws, his eyes are wide with excitement and his mouth is forming a toothy snarl. The children stare back open-mouthed, hanging on every word of the story.

The art of storytelling, as old as our species, provides the basis for all newspapers. At the most basic, it is our reason for being and survival. (Even advertising, if you think about it, is about storytelling.) It's easy to lose sight of this fact in this age of TV gloss, hyper-grunge graphics and garbage fonts in the magazines, and in glitz over substance in many newspapers that emulate TV.

In light of declining big-city daily readership and many publishers' terror over TV's increased dominance, Max King, executive editor of the *Philadelphia Inquirer*, calls for a return to thoughtful, explanatory, in-depth journalism. A notable noncommunity journalist, King thinks newspapers ought to be relying on their traditional strengths and "the lost art of storytelling."

TELL THE STORY, KID. TELL THE STORY . . .

You bring your story to life by using anecdotes, writing in the narrative style, delivering vivid direct quotes and hooking the reader with imagery.

If you're doing a story about poverty in Appalachia, don't cite statistics. That will make for a MEGO (My Eyes Glaze Over) story. Instead, find someone from the region who is poor. Tell his or her story. Put a face on a problem, a name to a statistic. Through that one life story, you will say much more about poverty in Appalachia than all the stats in the world.

Remember: Put a face on it.

Then you'll really be Showing, not Telling.

Hoyle Greene and his sign.

Learning to find features requires that you stay prepared and keep your eyes peeled. You never know where you'll find a human interest story. A window-washing service station attendant finds a way to overcome his height disadvantage.

The late journalism professor emeritus, Phillips Russell of UNC-Chapel Hill, used to tell his writing classes, "If you're going to write *about* a bear—bring on the bear!"

COMMUNITY JOURNALISM AND FEATURES

Community journalism provides a unique platform for creative and engaging storytelling, especially for the enlightened community journalist. And because of the intrinsic characteristics of our papers, we have certain advantages over our big cousins from the major metropolitan areas.

First of all, the people we're writing about are more likely to already know us, or about us, so there's a ready familiarity working for us right away. We've got that all-important *access*. We're likely to have more time to devote to the interview and to the writing of the story. (See Chapter 6.) In writing the story, we can be more personal. Many community papers encourage feature writers to refer to the source by his or her first name, instead of the impersonal-sounding AP Style "last name only" rule.

We're more likely to get to do the story one-on-one, do our own photography as well, and therefore have a better creative grasp on the story and package as a holistic entity. If we're lucky, we'll get to do the headlines and layout as well. Talk about total artistic control. Big-city feature writers would kill to get into the backshop to toy with the layout. Ever walked into a union backshop of a big-city paper and had the whole shop freeze in their tracks and just glare at you, daring you to touch anything?

And finally, we'll probably have the luxury of more space in which to run the story and/or photos. At the community newspaper level, feature writing is likely to be more personal, less harried, more holistically creative and far more enjoyable.

So, as sportscaster Red Barber used to say, we're "in the catbird seat."

Go. Fight. Write.

WHAT IS A FEATURE?

Fluff? Puff? Filler? Some editors and reporters dedicated to only hard news would have you believe the feature is only "soft" news and is a second-class story. Some people on the business side will be openly disdainful of features and maintain they're just taking up space better served with ads. In short, a waste of space.

But if that's so, how come *People* magazine is such a runaway success? What fills the pages of *Rolling Stone, Mirabella, Ebony, Esquire,* and the

New Yorker? Indeed, canny large newspapers and magazines are realizing that the increased use of features is one way to combat loss of readership to TV.

We'll never be able to beat TV to the street with the news. But we can sure feature them to death. A well-written feature story may not be the lead story in the paper, but if you've done your job well, you can bet more people will read your feature than what's under the banner head. That's because people can't help but read a story with human interest, a feature with human appeal. If you're a reporter-photographer who is a people-person, features may be your strong suit.

THE FORM

As you recall, features can use a variety of leads, can be written in anecdotal and narrative style, may or may not be timely, are written to entertain as well as to inform, may be either objective or subjective and are found all over the newspaper.

What usually separates news from features is that a feature contains information that is not vital to your need-to-know, as they say in the spy novel business. You can probably live just fine without the information that Chubettes, the third fattest cat in the United States, lives right down the road from you, and is on a diet. However, knowing about this fat feline makes life just a little more goofy and zany, and therefore bearable. It's been said that the highest form of bliss is living with a certain sense of the craziness of it all. Features may entertain, enhance our sense of livability, inspire us, underscore a sense of place and time and touch us deeply with the human condition.

Another factor of features: time. Many if not most features are what we call "evergreen." That is, the vital leaves of information won't fall off with time; they'll keep—depending on the story—indefinitely. There are usually limitations, but they are more forgiving than the time-demands on a news story, in which the facts turn brown and worthless with age almost immediately. For instance, the feature on Hoyle Greene's cider-making is a good example of a relatively evergreen piece; it could be run any time all the way through the late summer apple harvesting season.

ENTERPRISE? ISN'T THAT A FEDERATION STARSHIP?

Even Captain Kirk and Jean Luc Picard would tell you, the name *Enterprise* has its roots in self-reliance, pluck and what they used to call in football "broken-field running," or "razzle-dazzle." In other words, thinking quickly on your feet, employing all your senses and body parts to overcome adversity and to win.

Beginning reporters all too often expect the editor to provide all the answers, all the ideas, and all the guidance, plus loads of editing. However, at many community papers that is not the case. For a variety of reasons, you may be very much on your own—especially in the area of generating story ideas.

At many community newspapers you will be expected to conceive, background and write the feature. That means, find the story from scratch, figure out how to do your own research beforehand, set up and conduct a successful interview, possibly even take the photograph, organize and write the feature (and even critique your own work because maybe no one else will).

Enterprise—that skill or talent or learned ability for sniffing out features—will play a large part in your success as a journalist, be it at a community paper or a large paper.

WHERE DO FEATURES COME FROM?

If you're lucky, your editor will give you suggestions. But don't rely on that. In fact, it's really not mentally healthy to expect to be spoon-fed story ideas; it deadens your curiosity. And as journalists, curiosity is our main strength.

News Events

Read the paper, yours and others. Find a news peg. What's going on and how does it affect people in your community. How does it affect one specific person? Put a face on the news. What's it like to raise a kid with Down syndrome in your town? Find a family and a kid willing to talk and be photographed. Look for the positive. What social services does your county offer the mentally challenged? Who are the people involved? Who pays for it? How has this family coped with the challenges? Features can and should provide inspiration when it's appropriate to reality. Robert Kennedy used to like to say that a tidal wave of constructive, creative, social change can start from the ripples of one small pebble thrown into the edge of the ocean. Your features can be a real agent for positive growth in your community. Don't discount them. The accretion of many good works will make a difference. Don't you want to make a difference?

People in the News

Important people in your community are almost always generating news and features. A personality profile, an "inner-view" on almost anyone in a position of prominence is a worthwhile piece. How can anyone claim there's nothing to write about? You are surrounded.

Some community newspaper editors without higher professional inspiration tend to get brackish. That is, they fail to see the new things happening around them. If you're a new reporter, take advantage of your fresh perspective. Suggest personality profiles on leaders and outstanding citizens who perhaps have been featured already, but maybe it was years ago. Just because they've had one story done on them doesn't mean they're dead. What's new in their lives? If they're truly community leaders, they've probably grown and changed with the times, even if your editor hasn't.

Newsroom Suggestions

Once you get a reputation going around the paper for being a good feature writer, you'll find that your colleagues at the paper will start coming to you with story ideas. The ultimate compliment is when someone from the backshop, pressroom, circulation, mailing comes forward with a comment and an idea. The wise reporter learns not to scoff too quickly at these folk. Their comments will be like a vision through a glass-bottomed boat, affording you a view of how the community may be looking at you, the paper and your work. Listen to their ideas with respect and respond graciously. If one of their ideas is good, it's liable to mean there are lots more where that came from.

Readers

A good feature writer at a community paper will develop a following. Don't get the big head. We're not talking about thousands of screaming fans, but a loyal core of folk who like your work and look forward to it. This can be a tremendous asset to you, especially when they begin to contact you with story ideas. You may receive notes in the mail or a phone call, but more likely it will come when you're the least prepared. You may get hints at the grocery store, or while getting gas. And remember, you're never not a writer. Or to put it more grammatically, you're always on duty. A writer is always at work. So be polite; readers are more likely to feed you story ideas once they like your work and find you approachable, receptive and respectful.

And of course you don't have to use every single idea. Just thank them for the tip, and go on. But remember: What seems like a goofy story idea at the time may eventually lead you somewhere worthwhile.

Yourself

But of course, it finally comes down to you. If you're new to this game, it may take a while to learn how to sniff out feature story ideas, because many features don't leap out at you (remember, they may not be timely, new or vital). So they're not as obvious as news stories. Still, old-timers in our business seem to have no trouble finding features story ideas everywhere they turn. What do they know that you don't? Not to worry; it's an acquired skill. And you have to want to do it. Carry a pen and notepad everywhere you go. Keep your eyes peeled. Read community bulletin boards—at the laundromat while doing your clothes, at the grocery store while shopping, and at church notice the church bulletin. Around town, listen to people talking. Call it creative eavesdropping. They may be talking about a story you can use. In other words, get your radar out and always be looking and listening. Develop a features ideas list with contact names and phone numbers and rank them according to priority of time and need-to-do. And be aware: In a small community one feature story often leads to another.

DR. JOCKO'S HELPFUL HINTS

• Before the interview, you should do as much background as possible on your source—on the person you're featuring, or on the subject you're writing about. Find out why this person is important to your community.

• Find out when the story is due. This isn't as dumb as it sounds. Because many features are timeless, maybe the editor is thinking about using it next week instead of this week. This will help you in your time management.

• Find out approximately how long it needs to be so you can craft the story toward a skillful ending. Features aren't like inverted pyramid news stories which can have their bottoms snipped; news stories just stop. Features end. That makes a big difference to a writer.

• Find out where it's going to run. A front page feature will have a different impact from something planned for an inside slot, or from a feature to anchor a section front. If it's to hold down an entire page, then you've got your work cut out for you.

• Find out if photos plan to be included, and who is expected to take them. With photos, your story has an added dimension, and the added dynamics on the job. Without photos, you must use more descriptive imagery.

• Give yourself more time than you think you need to do the interview—and to write the story. Here's a basic truth of feature writing: Because there is no formula for writing feature stories (such as the inverted pyramid for news), both the interview and the writing will take—and deserve—more time.

Before You Start Writing, Ask Yourself:

• Who is my audience? A sports feature will attract a different set of readers than a personality portrait on a classical pianist or a story about an old mountain man who lives in the woods alone except for Clyde and Lulabelle, his two bears. Also, ask yourself, who is my audience in the larger sense?

• Why am I writing this? Because it was assigned to me and it's "Time to make dah doughnuts"? If you've got that attitude, no muse will get near you with a 10-foot pica stick. Your answer should be: Because I care. I'm curious, and this somehow affects my community or is a reflection of the community, and because people need to hear this story. It will help them, entertain them, make them laugh, or help them cope. You may want to write it because it will strengthen your clip file or add to your portfolio. That's not the best reason, but it may honestly be one of your motivators.

• What is the purpose of this piece? After our own agenda, the story itself may have a life of its own. One community newspaper writer did a story on a couple who were planning a home birth. The reasons were myriad: The reporter believed in home birthing, she knew the story and photos would be dramatic and unusual, and she realized how rare it was to have found a couple who gladly consented to the story and photo proposal. It was probably a once-in-a-lifetime opportunity for a writer. She was right. The baby turned out fine, the public's reaction to the piece was overwhelmingly positive, and the story won first place in state press competition that year.

• What can I safely assume the readers already know? This is a tough one for community feature writers. You must know your audience pretty well. How well you know your audience will show up here. In doing the piece on the retired classical pianist, can I safely assume all my readers will understand all the classical musical terms my person is using? Maybe I better ask some follow-up questions and gently provide background information. How do you define Baroque music? The same goes for an old-time fiddler. Many of your readers don't know the difference between old-time string band music and bluegrass. Yet the differences are vital to understanding a fiddler's story. In both cases, let the source, the subject of the story, do the explaining. And please, spare us the clunky amateur construction: "*When asked to* define Baroque music, Mr. Boznowski said … "

• How can I get the reader to stay with me to the end? Yes, it is hard for a beginner to realize yet again that his or her words aren't Holy Writ and that the reader isn't necessarily going to stay glued faithfully to every word all the way to the end. Remember, the comics page is calling. The crossword puzzle too. Worse yet, the reader might put down the *Bugle* and turn on the tube. You've lost your reader and hc/she has bolted. So before that happens, ask yourself how am I going to make the reader stay with me all the way? You have to seduce the reader word by word, line by line, until, *voilà!* It is finis. The story she is all done.

• And finally, how do I want the reader to feel when he/she is done? This question needs to be asked before you even put fingers to keyboard. It means, where am I going with this piece? Do I want my reader to feel sad, empathetic, and filled with a sense of the difficulty of this person's situation? Or poignant, bittersweet, nostalgic? Maybe mad, outraged, and indignant. Perhaps inspired, uplifted, empowered and filled with a sense of well-being. Words can do all those things. Is that not the magic of writing?

THE IMPORTANCE OF IMAGERY

If you want your writing to improve dramatically, write from the senses: sight, sound, smell, taste, feel, intuition and common sense. Write sense-ually. It's called imagery, and when you're writing your sensory impressions, you're Showing, not Telling.

People get hooked right away on writing that contains imagery because they can't help but relate when you start writing about this big golden South Carolina peach you've just bitten into—that's so bursting with juice you had to go stand over the kitchen sink to eat it. The peach is as fuzzy as your old teddy bear, and the juice runs down your chin and you have to laugh at the mess you're making. But you don't care because the peach tastes like summer …

People relate to sensual writing because they've got senses.

Stop reading. Look around. What are you seeing? Swing your eyes around the room, the deck, the woody clearing, the classroom, the canyon. Whatever. Look hard. How does what you see make you feel? Sheetrock smooth and uniform, log cabin rough and rustic, small windowless office sterile and trapped, a forest glade free and calm.

Now, what sounds do you hear? Close your eyes if you have to. Isolate the sounds of the radio playing light classical in the next room, the hum of an overhead fan, a bird song trilling outside.

The cup beside you; take a swig. Is the coffee dank and lukewarm or hot and sweet?

How does the old pottery mug you've had since 1970 feel in your hands? Smooth with age and chipped around the edges from years of rough wear and roadtrips. Best mug you ever had. Fits the palm of your hand like a custom-made pistol.

If you're inside, get up and walk into the next room, close your eyes and smell. Of the Vidalias you fried for supper last night, of last winter's cold wood ashes in the stove, of the cat box that needs changing. If you're outside, what is that sweet, musky fragrance coming up from the woods? Old-timers call it sweetbush.

Those are the five senses. There are two more: the sixth sense, or intuition. After you've polled your five senses for their specific reaction, what's it all add up to? The sum of the parts are indeed larger than the total. As a writer, that's where your sixth sense kicks in. What do you intuit about where you are right now? Is it "good space"? Is there creative energy where you are? What is the light doing? Has any consideration been given to hu-

A local elementary school principal phoned the paper to say that the entire school was out to set a world record for "group sitting." The resulting photo was sent to the *Guinness Book of World Records* and anchored a fun story about the event.

man scale and needs for peace and harmony? Or are you sitting in a class-room built in the '20s, no air conditioning, with walls painted institutional green? Or are you crammed in a tiny newsroom with depressing fluorescent and little window light? What sort of a Borg designed this place anyway? Pretty hard to be creative in such a space, isn't it?

The seventh sense is common sense. You'll need a lot of it in this business.

WHAT COMMUNITY JOURNALISM FEATURES ARE REALLY SAYING

Great feature writing can make the difference between an average and an outstanding community newspaper. The news, some maintain, is all pretty much the same. But features never need be repetitive. They are the garlic to the sauce, the flower on the table, clean sheets on the bed, an un-expected kiss, a phone call from a dear old friend. ... We could probably get along without these things, but their surprising presence uplifts and enriches us.

Features are a mirror held up to the community saying "We're OK," en-couraging people through examples of folks who have toughed it out. If our stories don't add up to doing good, and helping, then what good are we? We're no different and certainly no better than the smut rags and checkout-line tabs. Oh, by the way, Elvis IS finally dead. Saw it at Food Lion. Now there's a story we can all use.

TYPES OF FEATURES
The Bright

This is usually a short piece, 2-3 inches, with a cute twist and a punch line, seen mostly in larger papers and used as fill matter to enliven the front page. This type of feature's appeal usually lies in the story's oddity. If done poorly, this type of feature strains at humor and can be vapid or cutesy. At community papers, many topics used for brights could be better used as longer features.

EXAMPLE: The woman who fakes a heart attack to scare off a burglar.

Personality Profile

Remember, what we're working toward is getting the Inner View of someone in your community, be s/he a mover and a shaker, a local artist, an outstanding teacher, or a town personality. If there's a news peg, then the personality profile puts a face on the news, a real person behind the events.

Even in the small town, it's enlightening to gain insight on personalities behind the headlines. This story can be written in anecdotal form with a narrative style. It can be a single-source story or involve as many people as you like, reflecting on your subject. In either case, research and background your person. Beginner's Alert: Rule No. 1: Stay out of the way of your subject. Don't upstage them. The story is about them, not you.

EXAMPLE: A local elementary school principal retires after 30 years. He's famous for handing out dimes to kids who bring him papers with A's.

News Feature

At the community paper, the news feature is similar to the same style of story seen at larger papers except that for us, this story can be written more informally and have a more personal feel to it. Unlike the evergreen features, the news feature usually has news peg that is timely. The story may have to be written under the same time constraints as a breaking news story it accompanies. Other news features have a harder edge to them. Again, it allows you to put a face on the news. After the tornado ripped through part of town, you might tell one family's ordeal of survival. Narrative anecdotal style works great here. Such personalized news features serve to reinforce your readers' commonality and sense of community-ness. In one small town where a long-awaited bypass project was lagging, two editors decided to inspect the 10-mile stretch on a bicycle-built-for-two. The innovative approach yielded not only a hands-on story on the road's condition, but several humorous editorial columns as well. In addition, readers were impressed that the editors would undertake such a zany feat.

EXAMPLE: When your town's veteran mayor decides not to run for office again, people want to know why. It turns out she wants to spend more time with her husband, who for years has been an ungrudging "Mayor's Widower."

Lifestyle

At many community papers, these features are found on what used to be called the women's page (see Chapter 12). Stories on weddings, engagements, anniversaries, fashion, child raising, women's health, home, food and cooking used to be the staple in an age that seems quaint and sexist to us now. While that lineup may be still true at many newspapers, others have expanded the vision to include stories on societal trends, the changing role of the sexes in general and women in particular, and issues in family life such as child abuse, father absenteeism, and issues of aging and health care.

Features about the unusual always appeal. A bagpiper at the factory? Instead of taking smoking breaks, Joe Ryan preferred 10 minutes of piping "Scotland the Brave."

EXAMPLE: A series of stories and photos depicting how local elderly on fixed incomes in a modest retirement community had gone about making their homes reflect their individual tastes and values. The overall effect of the series showed readers convincingly that they could do quite a lot with minimal expenditure and lots of imagination and flair.

Speeches

Many inexperienced reporters tend to see speech stories as news stories only, but in fact, visiting speakers can generate entertaining features. The trick is to find the local angle, that local "peg." When a local author who had made it big came to town to talk to the library club, one enterprising reporter found out who the author's third grade teacher was, and asked her what the author was like as an 8-year-old. The old woman shook her head in wonder and said, "Where did he learn to write like that? In my class it was all chicken-scratch." Again, in community journalism, the key is to find the local difference and ride it for all its worth. Yes, it takes more work. But anybody can sit in an auditorium with a tape recorder and go back to the office and pound out a passable story. It's infinitely more fun and worthwhile to find the local undiscovered nugget that lifts a speech feature out of the ordinary. Say MTV's Martha Quinn comes to your town's high school to give a speech. When she walks out on stage, the kids leap to their feet in a standing ovation and one young man thrusts her a bouquet of roses. Don't you think you've got a local angle with a human interest twist? Who was that kid and why does he idolize Martha Quinn? What was her reaction? Buttonhole her after the speech and see if it made an impact. Does this happen all the time? The kid might be the lead, and that could provide you with not only a local angle but the vehicle as well.

Jimmy Jones had waited all his life to meet MTV video jock Martha Quinn. Friday he got his chance.

Speaking to East Rutherford High School seniors yesterday, Quinn was greeted by a wild standing ovation—and Jimmy Jones with a bouquet of roses. "It was a dream come true," Jimmy said with a shy blush afterward. "I love MTV and especially Martha Quinn. I guess you could say she's my idol."

Quinn, on an MTV 10th anniversary speaking tour across the country, said following the speech she was moved by the gift. "Believe it or not, it doesn't happen that often," she said backstage. "I was genuinely touched."

After the audience had settled down, Quinn took them on a retrospective tour of MTV's first 10 years, narrating a scrapbook style video tracing the creation, development and success of music videos ... etc.

Rules of thumb for speech stories: Always go in armed with as much background information on the speaker as possible. Get a program; it's loaded with info. Try to talk with the speaker after the speech for another local peg. Who invited the speaker? Get their reaction. And especially, watch the audience for reactions. Who's there and what do they think of the speech? Consider spin-off stories: The above piece might lead you into a story with local teachers, psychologists and counselors on their opinions of the effects of music videos on teen-agers.

Arts

This may sound like heresy, but arts coverage on the community level is every bit as important as—gasp—*sports*. And look at how much space most papers, regardless of size, devote to that.

There is a real possibility for synergy on the community level between an enlightened newspaper and the area's arts community. Theatergoers, concert listeners and exhibit-lookers are great readers. Support them and they will support you.

In addition, if a community newspaper provides space and encouragement for a growing arts council or arts agency, the relationship can only be mutually beneficial. It's a proven fact: There's a connection between a great town, a great newspaper and a thriving arts community. It's all about livability.

On the community level, most performing and visual artists are not professionals. They belong to the local Little Theater, the Photography Club, the Community College Singers or the Arts Council Players. They're not in it for the money. They're in it for their own personal joy of self-expression and to enhance the cultural life of the community. That's why most community newspapers don't and shouldn't attempt to write critical reviews of community arts. It's pointless. Better to be positive, provide coverage, publicity and support for the people and groups giving of their time and effort.

The paper should provide coverage before and after each event. Features prior to the event should include the 5W's with heavy emphasis on the who, plus a synopsis. The easiest and most effective way to provide coverage after a production is with photos from the performance (or dress rehearsal or photo-call).

Story topics can include personality profiles of the lead in the play, the director, the painter, the dancer usually *before* the production or exhibit. The intent should be to give the reader, the viewer and the theatergoer an inner-view behind the scenes. This insight before the performance, exhibit or concert enriches the audience members' total experience, as well as giving them

A flourishing community arts program can be a good sign of active community growth and health. Enlightened community newspaper editor-publishers know these barometers are important. Editorial support for facets of community life can only help your paper grow as well. A broad cross section of community people came together for this production of *Oklahoma!* (*Photo by Gerald Gerlach; courtesy of the Rutherford County Arts Council, © 1972*)

information that will help readers decide if they want to attend.

Arts features require that the writer know a great deal about the piece and the artist before starting the story. Read the book, see the exhibit, attend a concert, listen to earlier tapes, study rehearsals *before* the initial interview with the primary source. With the arts especially, avoid the cold interview. You should have to turn in your press credentials if you have to ask, "So, what's the name of the play you're going to do?" The informed lead-in question should be more like, "I understand *Cabaret* is set in Berlin just prior to World War II. … "

The paper can also provide a platform for community arts, with an arts calendar, and a regular arts page covering the activities of local artists and arts groups. The community newspaper also has a special role in encouraging emerging local artists by spotlighting unknowns as their talent and craft are developing. Also, some papers publish poems and or short essays suitable for the format.

Smaller community newspapers, notably weeklies, need not shy away from arts coverage because they fear they need to add an arts editor. You don't have to hire another staffer to effectively cover arts in your town. It should simply be included in someone's beat. Also, the real key is to get the various arts groups, county arts agency or arts council involved in generating their own copy and photos.

The local community college, private college or university in your area are probably already doing that. One idea might be to have the director of the local college news bureau lead a workshop (co-sponsored by your paper) for the publicity people of the various arts groups and agencies on how to write and shoot for the paper. That's a win-win scenario. It's good PR for the college; it helps the arts folk, and it makes your paper look good while improving your coverage.

Education

Newspaper editor and former community journalism professor Ken Byerly was so right when years ago he said: "Few things unite or tear a community apart as much as schools. The community revolves around its school. It is so vital that in many a small town, if the school closes, the town dies."

News of school closings, openings, hirings, firings, changes in curriculum, busing, lunchroom policies, new programs, choice of textbooks, expenditures, improvements, cutbacks—all provide grist for the mill. In addition to your regular news coverage of school board activities, the local educational scene provides an endless array of feature possibilities vital to your readers.

As with the arts, the community newspaper has a unique role and responsibility with its education coverage. In short, nobody should be doing so much in-depth work as the *Bugle*. Your level of involvement should be intense. Ideally, as with arts coverage, education should be a beat. That way the community journalist gets a sure grip on the turf, the players and how it all relates.

Because education is such a hot topic in the '90s it deserves more attention and space in our papers. The American primary education system is undergoing dramatic changes; community newspapers should be on the front lines. Story ideas abound:

Features can be constructive and have long-lasting impact. In one project, a dozen high school creative-writing students wrote pieces on their grandparents or favorite elderly neighbors. The essays were published in the community paper along with photos taken by one of the editors who helped coordinate the project.

✓ Which are most important to the development of our children, major league baseball players or teachers? So how come we aren't paying our teachers more? Great teachers don't do it for the money. So they need to be supported, encouraged and recognized. Features on master teachers, their philosophies of teaching and what works in the classroom can make a difference in how the teachers feel about the community. Each school's nominee for teacher of the year is a good place to start.

✓ The local high school newspaper that began paginating its award-winning paper years ahead of the curve at the urging of the veteran faculty adviser (personality profile as well?).

✓ Photos of the new teachers joining the local high school each August.

✓ In the spring, profiles of retiring teachers who have taught long and well. If they're to be honored at dinners and parties, tie in your coverage with those events.

✓ Trends in education. Service for college? Is anyone in your area already doing this? What are they doing and how do the kids feel about it?

✓ Amazing students. A personality profile and "a day in the life of" photo coverage of the most profoundly disabled student who is excelling against all odds.

✓ Innovative programs that work. The local private college that instituted a two-week program for county eighth graders at risk of not finishing high school. Talk to the college administrator who dreamed up this notion. Why do it? Who's paying for it? Attend the camp, take photos, interview the kids, counselors, teachers, parents. Do follow-up. Did it work? How did the camp change their lives?

✓ International students. Exchange students either in high school or college make for good features because they reflect so candidly in ways we can't see on the nature of American life. What do they like most? The least? What do they miss? What's the funniest thing that's happened to them here? How has coming to America changed them? What will they take back with them?

✓ Class reunions in the summer. Talk with old-timers about how things have changed, their fondest memories, pranks, favorite teachers, and what they got from their experience at the high school or college. The best stories come out of attending a 50th anniversary dinner, taking notes as people are telling those stories, and then buttonholing the folks afterward for permission.

One innovative newspaper provides coverage for each of the three area high schools by offering a page a month to each school's journalism class. The kids write the stories; a staff photographer comes out and takes the pictures the school editors have lined up. The entire highly successful program is coordinated by the community paper's editor and the respective high school teachers. Little wonder that the newspaper wins educational coverage awards every year. But the best reward of all, the community paper gets to say to TV and the big dailies, "Can't touch this."

Coping, How-To, and News You Can Use

If there's a trend in print journalism, this is certainly it. Newspapers are picking up the magazine trick of niche marketing, being user-friendly to the reader, of giving the reader something he or she needs to know. Women's magazines particularly have been doing this for years; if the headline's a grabber, you've got to read it. How to Renovate Your Man, Nine New Great Ways to Make Love, Dating in the '90s: What's Safe Anymore?, How to Turn On Your Creative Juices, How to Survive Your First Job When It's Not

You can't pose the great ones. Be prepared for novelty. The most boring-sounding school event may turn into a winner. Go ready for the unexpected. When the editor went to photograph the fifth graders watching a Native American dance, he caught one wide-eyed boy obviously impressed with the hatchet-wielding Cherokee brave.

the One You Really Wanted, How to Enjoy the Beach if You're Fair-Skinned.

On the community level, the trick is to get a good topic, then plug in all your local sources for authenticity and balance. For instance, say you decide to use the beach survival story idea suggested above, you could talk to a local dermatologist about the danger of too much sun, talk to local doctors about skin cancer incidence, a high school science teacher about the ozone hole, local people who are sun-worshipers and local people who are not— get their various perspectives on why they sunbathe or don't, and talk to a sociologist at the local community college about America's changing beauty standard. If "pale" is coming back in, why?

With "coping features" or advice and how-to stories, be sure to stay in the background as the writer. Let the source, the authority do the leading. No one likes to be given advice in a condescending way; and whatever you do, don't preach. Rather, you must be like a master puppeteer, always unseen, but in control of the flow.

Other related feature topics that adapt well to local-angle community newspaper treatment: include the environment, health, science and the sexes. Such coping stories provide grist for the community paper's "Lifestyle" section (see Chapter 12).

FROM THE TRENCHES

How do you get a story on someone who doesn't want to be interviewed—and how do you get a photo of someone if they don't want to be photographed? Sometimes the answer lies in saying just the right thing. And with different people, that right something may be different.

Everybody in the county knew Aunt Kate Burnette as the grand old woman of Mackie's Creek. The 88-year-old matriarch prided herself on cutting all her cookstove firewood by herself with a trusty red bow saw.

I had to have the story and picture.

She didn't have a phone, so the only way to reach her was to drive out to her little house in the shadow of Mackie Mountain. There, I found her at her sawhorse, working outside the woodshed.

STAY OUT OR ELSE THIS MEANS YOU a front yard sign warned.

I parked the car on the shoulder of the road, and got out. Before I got to her yard, Aunt Kate hollered, "I see you, you old bald-headed thing. You can just get right back in your car."

I was not to be so easily put off. "Aunt Kate," I shouted as politely as possible. "I'd like to talk to you for the paper."

"I get your ol' paper," she hollered, and then with a little grin, "Use it to start *fires* with every morning! Now go on back to town."

I almost left, but then decided, having nothing to lose, I'd try appealing to her vanity. "Aunt Kate, I'm doing a book." I hollered, and let that sink in. "I'd like to put you in my book!"

You could see the old woman thinking, and then, almost shyly, she shouted back, not quite so loud, "Well, where do you want me to sit ... ?"

I was in.

YOUR TOWN; YOUR TURN

1. Find a dry statistical news story in your paper that could have been enhanced and made stronger if the writer had "put a face on it."

2. Analyze your paper. Clip all the features and rank them according to timeliness and their "evergreen" quality.

3. Make a list of your last five features. Remember where the story ideas came from. Is there a pattern? Where do you get your best ideas from? When does it happen? On the golf course? In the shower? Just before you go to sleep? Better keep a pad and pen handy.

4. Take a walk around outside the building you are in. Go empty-handed but open-sensed. Come back to your desk and write down as many of your sensory impressions as you can of what you saw, heard, smelled, tasted, felt and *felt*.

5. Take a feature you wrote that you hate. Rewrite it with a new anecdotal lead.

6. Go buy a *Redbook*; how many stories can you adapt and find local angles for at your community newspaper?

5

Editorials: The Rapier, Not the Sledgehammer

THE HEAT IN THE KITCHEN

The brassy, outspoken high school biology teacher buttonholed the young editor as she was coming out of the local post office. Repeatedly thrusting one pointed finger at her, the teacher spoke as if to an errant first-year student who clearly needed to hear her superior wisdom: "About your editorial this week … why don't you just stick to what you're *good* at—which is writing *features*."

So … they didn't tell you it would be like this in J-school?

Welcome to the wonderful world of community newspaper editorial writing, where all your readers think they have the right to take a pot shot at you for anything you say; and indeed they do. And they will.

Editorial writing on the community level is an entirely different ball-game from the insulated, isolated, anonymous editorial board rooms of the big-city papers. There, editorial boards craft editorial policy, and editorial writers are likely to be faceless to their readers. They can go to Bi-Lo and not get ambushed over the broccoli.

Not so with us. People know us, and they know where to find us, and they know they can get to us. If you say something that rubs folks wrong, you're going to hear about it quickly—and face to face.

The singularly peculiar nature of our business affords us the ability to reach the entire community with a single keystroke or the push of a shutter release button. Such power is not without its price. The old adage comes to mind: The price of public access is public opinion.

This doesn't mean you should shrink away from bold editorial stands. It does mean, as with everything else about community journalism, that you are professionally accountable and personally accessible.

Be bold when the issue calls for boldness, but choose your battles wisely. A community is a glass house. A loose cannon breaks many windows.

THE COP-OUT: CANNED EDITORIAL PAGES

Because they're timid, burned out, lazy or simply don't care, many editors and publishers use nothing but canned stuff on their editorial pages. It's the editorial equivalent of the military field rations, MRE (Meals Ready to Eat) or the K rations of World War II. Clipped "guest" editorials from distant cities, etc. No local copy. Not one jot. There aren't any letters to the editor, either, because there's no reason to read the edit page.

These zombie editorial pages are more widespread than community journalism leaders would like to admit. And the really bad thing about a canned edit page is that it sends to the community the worst possible message in italics with bullets:

• *This paper really doesn't think you're worth the trouble it takes to create a lively, local editorial page.*
• *We're lazy, and proud of it.*
• *And what's more, we don't care.*

LAZARUS! RISE UP AND WALK

If you want to make your editorial zombie page rise up and walk like the biblical dead man Lazarus, it's going to take a holistic approach from the editor and the newsroom.

The editor(s) have to commit to writing live edits on a regular basis.

Solicit guest editorials on relevant subjects from community leaders, similar to a "my turn" series pioneered by *Newsweek*. Accompany this with a headshot.

Get local writers on board as columnists. (If they must be paid, give them a small honorarium.) But many times, community-minded writers will do this for the creative rush and the opportunity to get published as well as

And in the win column: One weekly community paper campaigned vigorously for a proposed state park with stories and photos as well as editorials. Now, the South Mountains State Park is a reality.
(*Photo by Joy Franklin*)

the possibility of doing something good for the town.

Assign weekly columns to each of your staffers in the newsroom, even your photographers. You'll be pleasantly surprised what this can turn in to. Accompany the columns with good headshots.

Encourage letters to the editor.

The only thing that should be canned should be the editorial cartoon. If, on the other hand, you can find and develop a good local political cartoonist, all the better. But this is a rarity. So, if you run nationally syndicated cartoonists, be prepared for much of your reading public to assume that you and your paper endorse the political stance of the cartoonist on any given issue.

WHEN IS AN EDITORIAL AN EDITORIAL?

Nothing in the newspaper makes people madder than something on the editorial page with which they disagree. However, shouting at the newspaper over the breakfast table is a grand old American tradition. Look at the history of American journalism; our early papers were all political and editorial opinion. Even so-called straight stories were larded with unashamed editorial opinion until well past the turn of the century.

It wasn't until early in this century that newspapers began embracing the concept of objectivity and then separating opinion from straight factual reporting.

Nowadays we revere this concept as if it came down with the tablets from Mt. Sinai. In current usage editorials have clear parameters.

To quickly review Edit Writing 101:

• Leads: A variety can be used.
• Form: A variety of forms and structures can be used.
• Timely: May or may not be timely.
• Purpose: Written to persuade as well as inform.
• Voice: Subjective, opinionated.
• Location: Editorial page in most cases.

EDITORIAL WRITING AND THE COMMUNITY JOURNALISM SPIN

While some editorials are written to inform, explain, educate—and even at times to entertain—most are written to persuade. This subjective writing with a clear point of view is what separates editorial matter from newswriting.

Not so many years ago they called newspapers "the poor man's college." Newspaper editorials were supposed to be "molders of public opinion." That all sounds rather quaint now in the face of MTV video-editorials that reach a vast, hip audience that doesn't read newspapers but digs rock. The baton has been passed irrevocably to TV and CNN. Clearly, most big-city daily editorial pages have lost the exclusive, pervasive clout they once had.

But on the community journalism level, there is still much work to be done. And this isn't likely to change with the coming of the millennium. Indeed, communities need strong opinions on local issues (which TV typically doesn't have time or stomach to address), unafraid champions of small, lost and worthy causes, and informed reflection on matters local and beyond.

Why are we writing editorials? What is our agenda? It should be that of the *Transylvania Times* of Brevard, N.C. On their masthead it says, "If it's good for Transylvania County, the *Times* will fight for it." Similarly, it is implied, if it's not good for the county, the *Times* will say so.

A good community newspaper editorial writer knows that there are five levels to editorial writing and reaction. From the outset, you ought to be shooting for level five.

Attention: The reader is "grabbed" and reads the edit. Maybe it's the headline; maybe it's your writing; most likely it's because the subject matter is something this person already cares about.

Comprehension: The edit is read in its entirety and stored in memory.

Synthesis: The reader then reflects on, or "processes," the information and data along with the opinion and argument.

Action: On that rare occasion, the reader realizes that the edit creates a desire to *do* something physically about the situation. An edit on homelessness in your community prompts the reader to join a Habitat for Humanity work crew.

Reciprocity: We've already talked about the negative; let's look on the bright side. This is the most wonderful of complete cycles—when you the editorial writer are told by the reader that your editorial made him get out of his chair and pick up his hammer. Give your typewriter or terminal an 'atta'-boy. They can keep their Pulitzers; you've done a day's work. Because of the relative size of the goldfish bowl, the community newspaper editorial writer is more likely than his city counterparts to hear such positive feedback.

THE KISS (KEEP IT SIMPLE, STUPID) RULE

Editorials are usually confined to the editorial page, and to a "standing" or preset and predictable position, most commonly, top left. Editorial pages

Sometimes images are stronger editorial comment than words. The county's deplorable dumpster situation was best addressed with photographs—run on the editorial page.

are also consistently positioned in the paper. People like predictability. If you start peppering your paper with edits all over the place, you risk alienating readers. Many media experts even frown on the so-called "front-page editorial" which is often used by editors when they want to trumpet an opinion. It's simply too confusing and risky to mix opinion with a page that purports to be objective.

There are other reasons to keep edits off P-1: It smacks of sensationalism, and says, in effect, that you don't have much confidence in your edit page to get and keep the readers' attention.

Who writes editorials? That depends on the size of the paper. From medium-sized dailies on up, an editorial board formulates what the paper's opinion is on a given issue. The publisher, editor and editorial page editor usually make up this editorial board. However, it's a sore spot if half the newsroom disagrees with the editorial. And furthermore, some media critics claim readers don't understand the distinction between a newspaper's opinion (i.e., the editorial board's opinion) and that of a single writer.

On many five-day-a-week daily, triweekly, semiweekly and weekly newspapers, editorials are written by a single editor. An editorial board is a luxury few can afford. In much of community journalism, the editorial is simply the opinion of the editor, and that's it, pure and simple. It's not the opinion of "the paper." Newspapers can't have opinions; people have opinions.

So, if a small paper has several people writing editorials containing diverse views, they meet this challenge by having the editorial writers sign their edits. The simplest way is an initial tag line at the end of the edit. This way, an editorial page can comfortably reflect and accommodate diverse editorial viewpoints. It not only lets the reader know specifically who wrote the edit, but also it underscores the bedrock community journalism precept of individual editorial accountability. In this context, a newspaper won't have an editorial policy per se.

"Editorial policy" is much like legal precedent, and can be defined as the body of opinions as written over a period of time by a paper's editorial writers. Sometimes, an editorial stance is agreed upon by the editorial board before anything is written on the subject. Whether it's the result of an editorial board, or a single writer, people in town generally are aware of the paper's position on a given issue. For instance, readers know the *Bugle* is pro-environment yet pro-balanced growth because the *Bugle*'s editorials consistently reflect that stance.

UNCLE WALT'S ADVICE

For over four decades beloved veteran journalism professor Walter Spearman, of the University of North Carolina at Chapel Hill, gave legions of future newspaper editors the benefit of his benevolent spirit and generous vision. In his much-sought-after editorial writing class, the late "Uncle Walt" had this advice, which is especially pertinent for community newspaper editorial writers:

• **The rapier, not the ax.** When making a point, be precise, subtle and clever. Don't bludgeon the subject. It makes you look like a Roboeditor, a Cyborg with a Mac. Impress them not with your firepower but with the deftness of your argument.

• **Issues, not personalities.** Always concentrate on the issues of the question you're dealing with. Never go after personalities. If you've got a county commissioner accused of embezzling, the issue is misfeasance of office, the betrayal of public trust—not what a jerk you think the commissioner is.

• **Don't write mad.** Most beginners find it easier to write editorials, (as well as songs and poetry) when they're upset, hurt or angry. If you're so bent

And in the lose column: An out-of-town chain burger company bought the historic Old Jail on the city's main corner; they wanted it for a parking lot. After editorials and visits from the newspaper and Historical Society members, the management promised not to tear it down, and yet within the week bulldozed the irreplaceable building under the cover of darkness. The burger place soon went out of business, but the parking lot remains. In the bottom picture, the town's oldest still-operating car passes the ruins the morning after.

out of shape you can't see straight, go ahead and write it, *but throw it away.* Then sit down, maybe later, and do it over again, this time without the shrillness. Remember John Belushi's classic "editorials" sketch on the old *Saturday Night Live* Weekend Update where he'd start out calmly and then get so worked up he'd go ballistic and have a heart attack … looked pretty stupid, didn't he?

• **Avoid sarcasm.** Sarcasm depends on vocal delivery for its effectiveness. In other words, it's a sound gag. Because readers can't hear your tone of voice, somebody will read it straight, and completely misunderstand your intent. Of all the literary tones than can be used, sarcasm is the most prone to be misread by some humorless clunk. Better to ditch the snide comments, parody and overly dry wit, and write it straight. Especially if you're a beginner.

THE ULTIMATE SHOW AND TELL: COLUMNS AND COMMENTARY

Having a regular column is not like looking in on the neighbor's cat for a week. It's there, waiting for you, week in and week out. You're either thinking about it, or it's thinking about you. You're either thinking what will I write about next week, or was the last one worth about as much as a bucket of warm spit.

It's been said that having a column is like undressing in public. At first, it's downright embarrassing. But eventually you get used to the scrutiny. After several awkward disrobings, you learn to do it with style, one button at a time. Reveal yourself with restraint. Make it last. To be good at it, you need to have a little bit of an exhibitionist in you, with a smattering of stagecraft thrown in.

No part of community journalism baffles and eludes the beginner so regularly and thoroughly as column writing. Few young writers are naturally good at commentary, especially humor. Indeed, it is an almost impossible skill to teach. That's because it's a matter of accretion. Unless they have a singular gift or vision, young writers simply haven't lived enough to have worthwhile, meaningful stories or the vision to tell them—or they don't have the maturity to synthesize their life lessons and be able to write about them with clarity, humor, pathos and wisdom.

In spite of all this, at the best community newspapers everybody in the newsroom is required to write a weekly column, regardless of training or background. In spite of the C+ quality of many of these columns, it's still the right thing to do. Here's why:

At big-city papers, they have great columnists who do nothing else.

Their columns are fantastic. At community newspapers, if you're going to have a live edit page, everybody in the newsroom may have to pitch in. There's a real value-added bonus to this. At the community papers, columns need not be about great literature or knock-'em-dead writing.

Because of their first-person voice and standing headshot, columns can, in the most personal way, give the newspaper a human face, a fallible real personality behind the P-1 bylines. This is the true subtext and value of columns in a community newspaper.

On the community journalism level, columns say: We are community. With every live editorial page, your paper will carry that reassuring message.

Below the flag of the McComb (Miss.) *Enterprise-Journal,* it reads, *"The one newspaper in the world most interested in this community."*

It doesn't matter if you're the hottest reporter on the paper; if you've got a column, you can't ignore the fact that you just did the laundry that included your kid's bright magenta crayon. You called Crayola and they told you the way to get the stain out was by using WD-40 on the splotches.

Columns say: Just because I'm a reporter or the editor doesn't mean I'm any better than you. I've just come back from vacation and the plants I left for the neighbor to water seem to have multiplied. The apartment looks like the set for *Wild Kingdom.* What's this? A note pinned to a six-foot-tall cactus says, "We've moved to Arizona and they won't let any plants into the state. I hope you can adopt or find good homes for these little buddies. Good luck."

Columns say: We're All in This Together. Columns give your paper the human touch. By the way, what other kind is there? If the touch isn't personal, then it's impersonal.

The congregation may be seated.

LETTERS TO THE EDITOR

The Orlando *Sentinel* receives an average of 400 letters to the editor each day; it has room to publish about four to six. The other 394 don't get run, nor do the writers receive a response. How do you think that makes all those folks feel?

The *Bugle* will receive about four to six letters a week and run each and every one. How do think that makes those writers feel?

The human scale, the appropriate matching of people to size of externals, is again at work in favor of community newspapers. At our level there is a satisfying cause and effect at work in the dynamics of production. People are acknowledged as people, not units. The editor's rule of thumb should be: Run every letter when possible, and respond to every letter that you can't use. If the *Bugle* receives a letter that is inappropriate, the editor usually has time to phone the writer and talk about it.

This ideal breaks down once a newspaper or its audience gets beyond a certain size. There are simply too many letters and not enough editors to respond.

It's the same as going to college at a small school, where on the way to class everybody looks at you and says hello, vs. attending a huge university where there's no way for the above scenario to happen, so no one even looks at you.

Is bigger better? In some cases, yes; in some cases, no.

Once this one-on-one reciprocity breaks down, the human scale is swept aside, and even though the paper may now be daily and carry flashy full same-day color, the paper has lost something precious.

A responsive community newspaper with a lively editorial page can provide a platform for vital dialogue. During the blizzard of 1993, the daily Hendersonville, N.C., *Times-News* provided the only constant stream of local information and inspiration, as well as news weather coverage to a community without power (no TV) for a week. The editorial page was chock-a-block full of letters. Says Editor Joy Franklin, "We are the voice through which the community talks to itself."

How a newspaper handles its letters to the editor can be viewed as a barometer of its community health. If you're not getting any letters, then either your edit page is a zombie, or readers have never been given a chance to write, or simply don't know how to go about it. A user-friendly explanatory box run regularly on the edit page should fix this.

Most problem letters come from unsigned pieces, vicious personal attacks and libelous submissions. Since the newspaper is responsible for anything libelous on its pages, even including letters written by someone not on staff, the editor must be careful about letters with potentially libelous content. Most papers won't run letters containing personal defamation or letters that aren't signed.

Unsigned letters are booby traps waiting to explode. If the writer isn't courageous enough to sign his or her name, why should s/he be afforded the luxury of hiding behind the paper? When the solid waste matter hits the climate control device, guess who it's going to coat first.

So do you throw out all unsigned letters? Not necessarily. If you receive a letter on a compelling subject from a writer who did sign their name but requested anonymity, follow it up with a phone call, and if it warrants, arrange for a news feature or investigative piece to be done on the subject of the letter.

AIR LETTERS

Photojournalists like to joke darkly about the terminal error of forgetting to load their cameras, and then going out and shooting an assignment, only to discover that they'd shot without film. Photographers call it "air shooting." Like the guy playing his broom while pretending to be the lead guitarist with the Red Hot Chili Peppers, it was all fantasy.

Part of what we attempt to do in the news business is divide fact from fiction. But sometimes editors lose track of the thread of reason, especially when they run columns of unsigned so-called "letters" that they receive in the mail, or they or their staff invent.

The most recent trend—papers encouraging readers to phone in these so-called letters, which may be published without the caller's name—strikes many media ethicists as reprehensible. Responsible community papers don't encourage such guerrilla letter-writing. Cowards, in the self-appointed mantle of public watchdog, assassinate by innuendo. As in: "What was the Sheriff's car doing in front of Ruby Freshwater's house on Saturday night until all hours?—unsigned"

This is sniping of the worst form. Little public good comes of such pot shots. The paper is perceived as harboring a mad gunner, and besides, the sniper is most likely to die by his own ricochet.

THE LAST WORD

If you receive a stinging letter attacking you or the paper's performance or editorial position, take great caution before you allow yourself to respond in print. In some rare cases it may be appropriate to write a small "editor's note" beneath a misleading or vicious letter. But use this practice sparingly. It can make you appear mean-spirited, as if you must have the last word. Use restraint. Otherwise you'll probably invite a letter-writing slugfest.

FROM THE TRENCHES

From whence cometh the editorial "we"?

I don't know, but I suspect it originated from some editorial writer who either represented his newspaper's opinion, or thought "I" didn't have enough clout.

For a small-town editor, "we" sounds pompous. Who do we think we are? The Pope?

The reality check came from one of my co-editors years back who heard me use that second-person possessive pronoun.

"We?" he said with a laugh. "Whaddaya mean *we*? You gotta rat in your pocket?"

Since there may not be a logical or historical explanation of the origin of the term, maybe its etymology lies in myth. Here's my favorite tale, unearthed from a 1967 edition of the *State* magazine of North Carolina carrying a reprint of J.W. Clay's carlier piece excerpted from the Winston-Salem *Journal*.

You may have noticed that editors in writing refer to themselves as "we." I do not know where this custom started but I well remember the first time I noticed it.

I was a printer's devil on the *Press and Carolinian* in Hickory back in the 1890s. Our editor was a fighting Kentucky colonel. One day he wrote something about a local politician that made the man furious. He came in to lick the editor. I was sweeping out. After a few hot words, they mixed. They overturned everything in the office, which made more work for me. The editor finally got the politician's thumb in his mouth and bit it off.

They were both out of breath by this time. The editor spit the thumb out on the floor and yelled to me, "Boy, go get Jim—the **fightin'** editor!"

Jim was a big double-jointed printer from Kentucky also. He always carried a six-shooter in his holster. I ran back into the shop and told Jim. When Jim got to the front, the politician was lickety-splittin' it down the street.

After that I noticed that the editor always referred to the editor as "we." Perhaps to inform the public that if anyone wanted to fight the editor, there would be several of them.

OTHER VOICES; OTHER NEWSROOMS

On the subject of community service, former Chapel Hill Weekly *Editor Jim Shumaker recalls this story from the early '60s. After leaving the* Weekly, *"Shu," became an associate professor of journalism at the University of North Carolina at Chapel Hill where for years he taught community journalism.*

"I Don't Want to Know How You Got This Stuff."

by Jim Shumaker

The finest community service ever performed by the old *Chapel Hill Weekly*, with which I was associated for many years, was one that I could not counsel others to try to emulate, since it involved intentionally breaking several North Carolina laws.

The story began, for the newspaper, when silver and black decals with the initials TWAK began appearing in store windows in the county seat, a dozen miles from Chapel Hill. The owner of a restaurant whose window prominently displayed a couple of the decals told a *Weekly* reporter the initials merely urged people to Trade With A Kinsman.

On further inquiry, in the finest tradition of investigative reporting, the *Weekly* reporter discovered that the TWAK urged people to Trade With A Klansman, meaning members of the Ku Klux Klan. The reporter also found that the county seat was becoming a hotbed of Klan activity, involving several county officials as well as merchants and civic leaders. The reporter also learned the location of the Klan headquarters in a rural area near the county seat.

The reporter and the *Weekly*'s photographer were told to nose around the area near the Klan headquarters to see what they could learn—who frequented the place, how often, what they looked like, whether they made a lot of noise, burned crosses, and so on.

The Klan headquarters turned out to be a shack covered with tarpaper, sitting in the middle of a broomstraw field. The field was encircled by a barb-wire fence. NO TRESPASSING signs were hung all along the fence and on all sides of the tarpaper shack.

I learned much later, in my role as editor of the paper, that the reporter and photographer had climbed the fence, across the NO TRESPASSING signs, and gotten into the headquarters by busting the padlock on the door. Inside, the photographer shot the Confederate flag on the wall and lighted cross and the Klan flag. The reporter found the membership roll and the photographer shot each page with the names clearly printed.

When they returned to the *Weekly* office and I saw what they had, I told them, in a fine demonstration of journalism ethics, "I don't want to know how you got this stuff."

We ran the story and closeups of the membership roll and shots of the interior of the Klan headquarters all over the front page, in effect confession that we were guilty of trespassing, breaking and entering, or at least being accomplices thereto. Then we waited a couple of days for the complains to roll in and maybe a visit from the sheriff to charge us.

Instead of complaints and a visit from the sheriff we got a series of phone calls to the effect, "This is Jim Bob Jones of Route 2 and I just wanted ya'll to know I am not the same Jim Bob Jones that was on that Klan membership roll."

The Klan activity in the county ceased practically overnight and those black and silver TWAK decals suddenly disappeared from store windows. So far as I know, the KKK and the decals, and for that matter the Klan mentality, have never returned.

YOUR TOWN; YOUR TURN

1. Remember the young editor zapped by the outspoken high school biology teacher? ("stick to features.") What would be your response to such a comment?

2. Determine your or your hometown newspaper's editorial policy on some given local issue. How was it crafted? By a group or individual?

3. Think back to the events of this week in your life. Write a personal column of not more than three double-spaced pages. If you've never written a column before, share it with a friend and ask for his/her honest reaction.

The Art of the Interview

TUTTLEMAUS'S TERRIBLE TECHNIQUES

A local pianist who just returned from her Carnegie Hall debut stops by the *Bugle* to renew her subscription, and is spied by her old friend, the exec ed. They begin talking about the performance, and the editor suggests a follow-up story. "Actually," he notes, "it's a slow news day … could you give us an interview now?" The musician, a little surprised but mindful of the need for publicity, consents. The editor assigns an available writer from the small newsroom, Bob Tuttlemaus, a new reporter fresh out of J-school.

Tuttlemaus shakes hands with the pianist and explains he'd rather do the interview in the newspaper's conference room, but since that room is locked, he settles for the empty office of the vacationing circulation manager. Tuttlemaus seats himself behind the big desk and motions for the musician to take the chair facing him across the table. She hands the reporter a Carnegie Hall program (containing musical and biographical notes). He glances at the cover and doesn't look inside; he's too busy fumbling with the tape recorder and flipping his legal pad open to a fresh page.

The musician, sensing the beginner's nervousness, opens the small talk, asking Tuttlemaus how he came to the *Bugle*. Glad to talk about himself, Tuttlemaus explains that for his first job out of college he had to "settle" for a small paper, but that he doesn't see much difference between working at a community paper and a big-city daily, where he clearly thought he deserved to be. He regards the town as "kinda' hick" and with a desultory shrug adds that the *Bugle* "is an OK place to start." Then he proclaims, "Besides, the way I figure it, a crime story is a crime story is a crime story, and a fire story is a fire story is a fire story." He tells the pianist he won't be staying at the *Bugle* very long; he has bigger fish to fry.

Tuttlemaus turns on the tape recorder, picks up his pen and asks his first question. "So, where were you born?"

Ninety minutes later, the interview (laced with questions such as, "So, what kind of music do you play anyway?") is over, and the musician is leaving.

"Hey, Bob, wait," says an older reporter. "Did you get her picture?"

"Oh, yeh," Tuttlemaus stops the departing musician. "Gotta' take your picture." Grabbing a camera, he directs her to stand against a blank wall. He adjusts the camera and flash, then looks up and shoots off five shots quickly. "That enough for you?" he says.

The pianist nods, and leaves with a growing sense of dread at how the story and picture will turn out in tomorrow's *Bugle*.

Is it any wonder that the 20-inch story turned out shallow and weak, and that the photograph looked like a glorified passport mugshot? What could Tuttlemaus have done differently at the front end to have strengthened his story and photo?

THE IMPORTANCE OF BEING EARNEST

Great newswriting can be divided into three functions: gathering, writing and editing.

Let's take it from the top, with the gathering. In our business, we're only as good as our raw material. That comes from the interview, a critical stage that many beginners tend to gloss over, thinking that the true art lies in the writing. However, we are only as good as we are curious. A great interview almost always results in a strong story, while a weak interview invariably produces a weak story. Almost never does a great story grow out of a weak interview.

So first things first. Give credit, importance and dignity to this vital initial step. It cannot be overemphasized. We are journalists. We are not novelists. We do not write fiction. We do not invent people and conjure up quotes. We are completely at the mercy of our people, and they are only going to reveal themselves to us in truth, giving us stunning quotes and shimmering insights into their lives if we conduct skilled interviews. This comes with work, dedication and time. With apologies to Neil Young, you should be "a miner for a quote of gold."

Especially in community journalism, it all boils down to this:
Access = Rapport = Success.

CLOSE ENCOUNTERS OF THE FOURTH ESTATE: TONE AND DIRECTION

Psychologists who study a discipline called Transactional Analysis (TA) tell us that every encounter between two people can be broken down for the relative positioning of each person. From the most simple to the most complex encounter, all our dealings with others are "transactions." Listen to two college buddies passing each other on the way to class:

A: Hi, how are you?
B: Fine, how 'bout you?
A: Great. See ya'.
B: Yeh, bye.

Seems simple, but look again. A opens with a friendly greeting and a non-ego inquiry about the health and happiness of B, who responds with a report of his condition, and then returns the question in kind. A reciprocates and gives an appropriate farewell, which B accepts and returns. In short, the transaction went A-B, A-B, in a complete circle. A nice tight little interview.

Now, consider for a second what might have happened if the first guy had said only "Hi." It's very likely B would have only responded in kind with only "Hello."

The point of all this: If A doesn't *initiate*, B isn't required to answer. *From the very first question*, A is the interviewer and sets the tone for the entire encounter.

Consider poor Bob Tuttlemaus's botched interview. When he asked "So, where were you born?", that sent a clear message to our musician. Privately, she was thinking, "Oh brother, Wunderkind here doesn't know the first thing about me and is asking for my life story. He doesn't even have the common sense to flip open the program I gave him and find out simple facts for himself. … At this rate I'm going to be here all afternoon with this puppy."

CONTROL: CARPE DE INTERVIEW

From the very start, Bob Tuttlemaus had lost control of the interview.

Like it or not, recognize it or not, an interview is a control situation. Either you the reporter will control it, or your subject will control the encounter—or possibly if neither takes charge, the situation and events driving the interview will dictate where it goes, usually resulting in a story that wanders in a muddle or spirals aimlessly outward to la-la land.

The skillful community journalist knows how to steer an interview subtly yet surely. It's a lot like riding a horse. You impose your will over your steed with your attitude and your gentle yet firm touch on the reins. Relinquish control of the reins and your horse or your interview will run away from you.

Bottom line: It's yours to control. So don't just carpe diem. Carpe de interview!

THE INTERVIEW AS AN INNER-VIEW

Remember the old newspaper axiom that says the purpose of an interview is to provide an inner-view. And you'll get the clearest, quickest and most accurate picture of someone when they're surrounded by their *stuff*.

Therefore, the penultimate rule of interviewing is: Go to your subject's home or workplace. You want to meet the person on his/her turf, lair, habitat or environment—the author in his study, the dancer in his studio, the mayor in her office, the cop on the street, the musician at her piano.

In community journalism, where distances are shorter between office and interview site, and you've more time generally to do your interview, there are fewer excuses for doing interviews in the office or—heaven forbid—over the phone. (The exception here is if your person knows you well and is a continuing source, a public official, etc.) What is there to learn about someone by talking to them in the newsroom or a vacant office?—except how flexible and well they handle themselves in a strange situation.

Not only will the home turf reveal your person to you, but it will also make the subject more comfortable, allowing you to go deeper and get more details. Again, if you can get Access, and establish Rapport, then Success likely will follow.

Is it any wonder that Tuttlemaus, who sought access only to a spare office, and who never established rapport, ended up with a story that just sort of lay there flopping weakly?

> Establishing rapport usually makes all the difference in the quality of the story you get. While listening to an elderly woman tell a heartfelt story, reporter Maggie Lauterer knew she was doing something right when the old woman reached out and took her hand as the tale reached its climax. No longer is it a reporter interviewing a source; it's two humans communicating and sharing.

80

Perhaps Tuttlemaus forgot Lauterer's Law of Interviewing. "Warning: Shallow In, Shallow Out." If you go in weak and just wade around in the kiddie pool area, you'll never get to the deep end where the fun is.

By placing the interview in a neutral, no-person's land of a vacant office, Tuttlemaus lost even more control over the transaction. People kept walking in and out, and the phone kept ringing. To make matters worse, the intercom constantly interrupted them and Tuttlemaus couldn't figure out how to turn it off, further embarrassing the musician who felt sorry for the cub reporter. Tuttlemaus's ineptness and attitude inadvertently signaled the pianist loud and clear: "I don't have a clue how to run an interview, so don't expect much out of this story. After all, a musician story is a musician story is a ... "

HELPFUL HINTS FOR THE METEORS: THIS IS NOT LARRY KING LIVE

A great interview is not so much a science or technique as it is an acquired and subtle art. And as such there are few models or formulas we can use. However, there are some time-honored guidelines for interviewing in the community journalism context, where the last thing you want to do is the I-sit-here-you-sit-there-and-I-ask-these-10-questions technique. Leave the formalities to Larry King.

Be Sensitive

As you will quickly discover, if you already haven't, many if not most of the people you interview in community journalism aren't media savvy. Your story subjects, both in news, sports and features, have preconceived ideas about us newspaper types—most of which they got from TV! They are likely to be intimidated by the encounter, and for many, this will be their first and perhaps only face-to-face experience with what one old mountain man in all seriousness called "the meteors." What seems normal for you as a reporter is to them like a visit from an alien. The more you appreciate the novelty of your interview, the better your success in community journalism will be. (Also see Notetaking, below.)

Background

Avoid the "cold interview" at all costs. For anyone you interview, you should do background research—especially in a smaller community where so many people know each other. If nothing previously has been written about your subject, ask people about your subject. Nothing will establish your reputation as a lightweight quicker than a vapid, shallow story on someone who is well-known around town. Also, if you do your research, you won't have to waste time covering the basic biographical and professional info that any vita, bio, resume, book jacket, or program notes would contain. It will save you from truly stupid questions such as, "So, what kind of music do you play, anyway?" which only signals your amateur standing. And ultimately, truly stupid questions further distance you from the very person to whom you're trying to get close. If circumstances force you into the cold interview, apologize and acknowledge it up front—and then do research after the interview, and follow up with a phone call or two.

Visit

Be a person first. A reporter second. Visit first. Chat. Strike up a conversation. Leave your pen and your pad, your tape recorder and camera on the floor in the camera bag. Talk about what's in front of you. The pictures on the wall, the family, the decor, the garden. Comment favorably about what you see. Be politely inquisitive. The first question should flow out of that conversation, not leap off your notepad like a barb thrown by Mike Wallace from *60 Minutes* (unless, of course, it is a confrontational interview). Give it time. Then, when your subject is comfortable with you, ease into the reporter role.

Don't Upstage

While the conversation should be the vehicle, beware of what former radio commentator Earl Nightingale used to call the "dynamic monologue." In other words, don't talk about yourself too much, and never lose sight that this is an interview.

Spaces

Study body language. Putting some thing between you and your person, such as a desk, represents a philosophical, emotional barrier. It's a power statement. Bosses use it when they want you to feel small. If you're in an interview where you're going for that inner-view, try to keep the space free between you two so the information can flow freely and informally. Tuttlemaus should have come out from behind that desk, or invited the pianist to sit in a less discounting position. Of course, the canny reporter would have insisted they drive over to the pianist's studio, where Tuttlemaus would have seen her collection of 43 Beethoven busts of all sizes arranged like a menagerie on top of the pianist's polished black enamel Steinway grand. There's your lead. And what an image. Where's that Nikon?

Be Prompt

Be on time. "Well begun is half done," says the proverb quoted by Aristotle. Being prompt shows a measure of your respect and gets things off on the right footing. This is especially true if your subject has never been interviewed before. On the other hand, the quickest way to discount your person is to be late. That's inconsiderate and sends the message, "I don't care about you; my time is more important than yours." Being late will poison the friendly atmosphere you're attempting to establish, and you'll spend the bulk of the interview trying to play catch-up.

Be Good to Yourself

Speaking of time, give yourself the luxury of time. A good single-source interview takes one to two hours, depending on the subject, the situation, the novelty of that situation, how it unfolds and flows. And you may want to go back and visit again after your first draft. You may want to call on other people to expand the piece. That can be done over the phone if you're well known, but nothing beats face-to-face—the personal approach style of community journalism.

Easy Does It

Give your person the dignity of time. Don't rush it, no matter how rushed *you* are. You want to kill an interview? Just tell your subject something like, "OK, I'm in a hurry. I've only got 20 minutes. Now—where were you born?" On the other hand, respect your subject's time. Find out how much time they can devote to the interview and stick to it. Important people usually have tight schedules.

Quotes, Quotes, Quotes

An interview should be loaded with quotes. Nothing beats complete direct quotes used in context for bringing veracity, legitimacy and life to a story. A balanced use of paraphrasing and partial quotes is pleasing, so long as you let the direct quotes (accurate, word-for-word, of course) carry the load. Of course it's hard work. That's why beginners cop out and paraphrase too much. It comes down to knowing when to use which type of attribution. John Neibergall of Kansas State University offers these guidelines: "Quote the quoteworthy. Paraphrase when the subject's words do not reveal something of the subject's personality or address the subject in an especially clear or bright manner."

Dress Appropriately

Dress to suit the occasion. Use common sense. An interview with the mayor requires shirt and tie or dress or a nice business suit, while an interview with a country family making their fall run of molasses calls for jeans, T-shirt and boots. The rule of thumb here is to blend. Dressing inappropriately will make your subject feel uncomfortable and call attention to yourself. You'll have a more difficult time establishing all-important rapport. Wearing heels or wingtips to a corn-shucking will have your people wondering about you. The same goes for ratty jeans at city council meeting.

NOTETAKING

Since it's likely your subject is a first-timer in an interview situation, he/she brings preconceived notions about what newspeople are really like. Think about how reporters are portrayed or seen by popular American culture on TV. We are mostly gruff, aggressive, loud, insensitive, messy, self-serving, puffed-out, egotistical, impossible to live with (read: divorced) irascible curmudgeons who care nothing about people but only the story and our professional advancement—and that's just for starters. You've got your work cut out for you just earning your subject's trust.

When you sit down to do a community journalism interview, the first step in notetaking is to not take any. You read right. That means, you must show your person that the image they have of the stereotyped reporter just isn't true in your case. You must earn their trust. You can gain access by showing them you care, that you're a person first. Don't interview. Visit. How long you "visit" before you start taking notes is up to you and how quickly you establish rapport. But generally, with a first-timer, the rule of thumb is: Don't rush it. Then, when you can't stand it a minute longer, slip out the notepad while you or they are talking, but don't make a production number out of it.

Alecia Swasy, a fine *Wall Street Journal* reporter doing a story on poverty in the Kentucky hill country, found a poor woman who consented to be interviewed. But instead of sitting down with her, flipping open the notepad and firing pointed questions, our wise reporter spent one whole morning *doing the wash and folding the laundry* with the woman. Didn't take a single note. The reporter was being a person first. She spent one whole day just establishing trust. And because she had gained access and established rapport, the following day she got an interview that sizzled.

So it's a given that most folks have never had a camera lens or a mike thrust in their face before, and they're likely to never have the experience again. Knowing this should affect your style, whether you use notepad or tape or both, and how and when you go about taking photographs.

Even the simplest act of taking notes is likely to unnerve the first-timer. Your subject will likely lose their train of thought as you start taking notes. "Are you writin' down ever'thang I'm sayin'?" one old woman asked incredulously of a young reporter. "Why law, child," she said with an embarrassed laugh, "I'm jus' an old-timey country woman a-rattlin' on. Jus' as old-timey as I can be. Why would you wanna' write down what *I* say?"

Why, indeed?

While you will develop your own style with time, it will be obvious to most that the above situation negated the use of a tape recorder. Why? Because the notepad itself was intrusive enough as it was. The rule of thumb, the more primitive the setting, the most basic your technology should be. Remember, we were *writers* first. Even with all our technological wizardry back at the office, we're still writers, and we'll always *be* writers. We don't *need* electronic brouhaha. That means we can write anywhere on anything. Take notes on cafe receipts, match covers, old envelopes, napkins, brown paper bags, your own hand if need be. But never, and this means never, be caught without a pen.

That's rule number one: Find a pen you love and carry it (or them) everywhere you go. It should be a fast, dependable, long-lasting rolling-ball ink pen. Avoid pencils and fountain pens and ballpoints. They fade or run or won't write on some surfaces (such as the palm of your hand). Pilot Precise Rolling Ball V5 and Uni-Ball Micro by Faber-Castell are favorites of many.

Next, equally simple and just as important: Find a type of notebook that fits in your hand and with which you feel comfortable. It doesn't matter if they're the traditional reporters' notebooks, or steno-sized flip-top pads or little notebooks, just so long as you're consistent and keep your notes in order over the years, when such a system of sourcebooks will prove their worth to you. Not unlike the oak and the acorn, big books grow from little

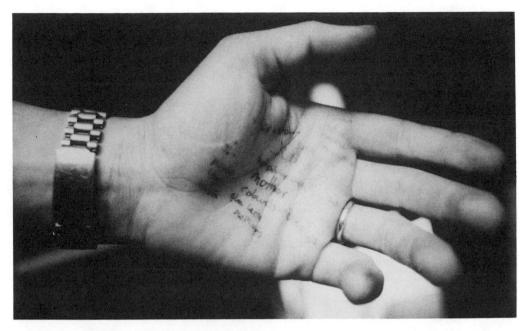

If you've got the right kind of pen you can take notes on practically anything. Be sure to copy your notes before washing for dinner.

(note)books. And you never know, you may someday have a book in you.

In high school journalism classes they taught us to write down 10 questions before the interview. That's not a bad idea, but if you take such a list to an interview, keep them out of sight. Who wants to feel like their life is a fill-in-the-blank quiz? Better to memorize them, and ask yourself before the interview: What's this story really about and who cares?

Before we go another second we've got to address the issue of tape recorders.

TESTING ONE TWO THREE . . . ARE THERE BATTERIES IN THIS THING?

You can safely assume in community journalism that you won't be doing many Inside-the-Beltway–style interviews. That's the running, hand-held tape recorder thrust in a politician's face and shouting-questions-style interview popularized by the "pack journalism" of the Washington press corps.

However, under certain circumstances, the tape recorder can be an invaluable tool for the community journalist: When the subject is media savvy, doesn't mind being taped or even *wants* to be taped for accuracy's sake, when it's someone who talks a blue streak, or someone with a dialect or colorful speech pattern you want to get down to perfection, and *if your subject doesn't mind*—then it's appropriate.

But there are no two ways about it, a tape recorder is not usually present in the course of a normal conversation. So to place a tape recorder on the table beside you and someone else and to try to have a conversation is unnatural. Normal conversation becomes theater. Face it, a tape recorder is an intrusion. (So too is taking notes, but at least notetaking is less threatening and doesn't take electricity.) Many people will simply go cold on you if you stick a recorder in their face. It says in effect: "Everything you say can and probably will be used to embarrass you in front of your family, friends and neighbors." To the uninitiated, the very act of recording every single "uh" and "er" will petrify them into yes and no answers.

Be wary of becoming too dependent on gadgetry. A tape recorder can be your pal, but it can (and will) turn on you. Anyone who's ever relied completely on a recorder during an interview knows about Murphy's First Law of Journalism: A tape recorder getting vital information will have dead batteries. Or, put another way: Tape recorders tend to fail in direct proportion to the extent you depend on them.

Lauterer's Law of Tape Recorders: If you have to use one, pretend it isn't there. Take notes like a wild thing. Not only does that intimidate the tape recorder, thereby negating Murphy, but it also guarantees you will get the data, possibly twice.

The wonderful thing about notes is they provide you with a visual picture, a map almost, of the interview. You can see repeating themes in your notes. If it's only on a tape, then you can't ever look at the interview and *see* what the person was saying. A tape recorder, used in conjunction with good notes, can be useful. However, be forewarned, this is time-consuming. If you use this technique, use your notes to organize and outline; use your tape to get precise quotes and nuances. Other pros and cons of tapes:

✓ Some reporters maintain that the presence of a tape recorder puts people on notice of the reporter's dedication to accuracy. It may even help guard against people being tempted to go "off the record" because the tape recorder is still running.

✓ Another plus for the tape recorder, it can provide you with an iron-clad defense against people who later claim they were misquoted (as long as you did get it right).

✓ One busy editor likes tape recorders because he simply can't get around to writing most stories right after he does the interview. However, he says the tape recorder keeps the story fresh for him. If he had used notes alone, he would have forgotten much of the interview.

✓ Tape recorders take batteries; pens don't. Notetaking exclusively satisfies the KISS rule and means you have less to lug around and less to worry about. Do I have fresh batteries? A fresh tape? Do I have enough tape? There's nothing worse than a tape running out before the interview is over, *clunk*, right in the middle of a sentence—and the reporter shutting down the interview apologetically.

NOTETAKING HINTS—PART DEUX

In the course of a normal conversation, people look at each other a lot. Granted, it's hard to take notes and maintain constant eye contact, but that should be your goal. Especially early in the interview, you should look at your subject as much as possible. The more you hunch over your notepad, eyes locked on your notes, the more you're expecting your subject to do all the work.

So how to do? Forget about Mrs. Fudnucker, your second grade teacher. Take big loopy notes. Ignore those lines. Notebooks are cheap. A lost quote is priceless. So let 'er rip. By the way, when you learn to do this, it will enable you to take notes in the dark, a most helpful skill for any reporter, for instance covering a speech in a darkened auditorium. Other stuff:

✓ Write in code. Come up with your own reporter's shorthand. Abbreviate as much as you can. If you're doing a story about sexual harassment, write SH every time your person says it in a quote. Come up with specific abbreviations for each story to speed you along.

✓ Learn the fine art of creative listening. Go for exact words and colorful, vital quotes. Write down key phrases, leaving out the articles, pronouns and prepositions if you have to. Fill in later.

✓ Avoid yes/no questions. ("Did you learn to play the piano here?") unless you intend to follow up. ("Oh really? Who was your piano teacher? Have you been in contact with her? What'd she say when she heard you were going to debut at Carnegie Hall?")

✓ Don't cheat your reader. Remember, this is not TV. When you can sneak it into your notes, or when your subject is off on a tangent you don't think you need, get down the descriptions and imagery of the person and setting. His bow tie, the beach shorts and shiny penny loafers, her hair parted in the middle, faded Pointer overalls, Gucci shirt—the details make the picture.

✓ Learn to end an interview, not stop it. When the interview is over, and when you've got enough material, go out gently, as you came in. Be friendly and supportive. If you're taking your own photo, this is the time to do it, unless you did it already during the interview. (See Chapter 9.) Tell your subject when and where the story will appear. Make sure your subject is amenable to any needed follow-up phone calls you might have to make. And finally, thank your subject for the interview and for the time given you. An interview can be exhausting.

If your subject asks to see the story (or photo) before it goes to press, politely explain that it's against your newspaper's policy, and that it's a matter of trust. The exception will be the technical story in which you or your editor may opt to let the subject review the story for content errors only—but never style or substantive editing.

✓ Right after the interview, go back over your notes and fill in blanks and abbreviations. The longer you wait to do this, the harder it will be.

If you've got something that looks like Russian in your notes, read all around it, and read the sentence aloud and see if the mystery word comes clear. Remember, it was your code. You knew what it meant when you wrote it. Go run. Take a shower. Come back and look at it again. Hold it up to a mirror. Really, sometimes that unlikely trick will shake it loose. Ask somebody else in the newsroom, or a friend, to attempt to read the whole sentence (without telling them that part of it is "Russian").

✓ Organize your notes with color-coded highlighters, circling repetitive themes so you can find them quickly when you start writing. This is also the way an outline will appear.

✓ Write the story as soon after the interview as possible. A story is perishable. The longer you wait, the weaker the story will be. Notes are meant to jog your memory, not serve as a substitute.

WOODY'S WONDERFUL WAYS

Watching Woody Marshall work an interview is a privilege. A veteran newspaperman, Woody is far more than just chief photographer and picture editor—he is also a consummate, committed and total community journalist. He understands his people, what they need, and how to treat real people. Long before a camera ever comes out of his bag, Woody is talking, being neighborly, asking questions, telling the curious who he is and why he is here—but mostly asking questions and making new friends at every turn.

Today the assignment is to capture the mood and color of a fall tobacco auction in the small North Carolina Piedmont town of Reidsville, just up the highway from Woody's Burlington *Times-News*. Woody has found out who's in charge of the morning auction at the Smothers Auction Warehouse and is establishing himself on a human level with the management, the buyers and the farmers alike.

"How long you been growing tobacco?" "Where's your farm?" "How's the crop?" "What do you expect to get this year?" "Really? That much?" "That's pretty good, isn't it?"

Woody scribbles notes quickly on a traditional, narrow reporter's notepad, while maintaining eye contact much of the time. Then, 20 minutes into the event, he sees something he can't *not* shoot, and out comes the Nikon 8008. Yet with this, Woody doesn't abandon his role as reporter, as human—just to take pictures.

Covering a tobacco auction in rural North Carolina, photographer Woody Marshall sits close and listens carefully and with respect as an old tobacco farmer talks about his life.

It's difficult to say what he's doing at any given time, for Woody is shooting, talking and writing so fluidly that the three activities appear to be the same physical act. In a word, his work is seamless.

Woody possesses, or has refined, the rare gift of being everywhere at once, while being virtually invisible. He is clearly a man in his element—now here, throwing himself on a tobacco bale for a low-angle shot—now there, dashing up a pile of tobacco bales for a high-angle shot.

Not surprisingly, he has worked himself into a towering sweat. His wet shirt flops open in front and clings to his back. Even the svelte, imperturbable auctioneer appears awed by Woody's efforts.

"Man's workin' his ass off," he comments with genuine admiration.

Woody, whose sweat-soaked hair is standing as stubble-straight as a new-mown hayfield, confides with a rueful grin, "I'm having too good a time."

Two hours later, Woody has a notepad full of notes and a Domke bag full of film. Is it any wonder that the final result was rich and fulfilling, for journalist and subjects alike? His photos accompany a story that starts like this:

> It might be the last days of a dying weed, but you'd never know it at Smothers Warehouse on auction day.
> Tobacco, which has taken its lumps, is still king at this family run operation in Reidsville. Each fall the old steel-sided warehouse resounds with the musical chant of the auctioneer as the season's tobacco is graded, sold, baled and shipped.
> Everybody at Smothers seems to be either chewing, smoking, breathing, buying or selling tobacco, the golden weed which today seems anything but deadly. Indeed, here, it feels life-sustaining. Across the brick front of the warehouse, the nickname speaks volumes, "The Money Box."
> Inside the cavernous building, illuminated only by open doors, dusty skylights and a lone, frail incandescent bulb far in the back, a ritual as old as the Old North State is played out. It is a feast for the senses ... "

HEY KID, THIS IS OFF THE RECORD

It's happened to every reporter. You're in an interview with someone, and you've worked so hard to get access, establish rapport, and now you're really rolling. Suddenly, your interview subject says the dreaded "this is off the record," and proceeds to tell you the greatest story before you can think of something creative to say to stop him. And if you did stop him, wouldn't that anger him and derail the interview? And by just sitting there listening, haven't you implicitly agreed to the conditions of nonuse?

In a community journalism setting you have.

At many large papers, the reporter would use the off-the-record material without a second thought. So what if the subject feels betrayed? He said it, didn't he? Besides, in a city of half a million, you'll never see him again. And just let him try to get past security downstairs.

But the whole issue of "off the record" in the community journalism context is made more complex by the inherent just-us-folks-good-ole-boy nature of small-town life, where word is bond.

Be forewarned. Just because you may be buddies with your subject doesn't give him the right to jerk you around journalistically. The great danger is that you will let yourself be used because of your ongoing friendship with many of the people you interview.

If you sit there and let Bubba tell his great story, which he thinks is off the record, and then you print it, you'll risk destroying not only a friendship, but also that source, that link to the community. And remember, in the community setting, there are just so many people you can alienate before you've got the whole place angry at you. You can bet he'll tell everybody you broke a confidence and that the *Bugle* can't be trusted. Worse yet, he'll claim he never said any of that and that you made it all up.

The recommended time-honored practice in community journalism is this: Respectfully stop your subject the moment he utters the expression, "off the record," and tell him politely you respect his right to ask for that status, however, if it's controversial, you'd just as soon he didn't tell you anything at all, because if it's a big deal, you're bound to find out about it from some other source soon enough anyway. In many cases, that independent stance will prompt the source to go on the record after all. Because here's the bottom line: Your subject really *wants* to tell the story.

Next, if the off-the-record segment is simply going to be something the source perceives as being slightly embarrassing if printed, you can try for the *conditional* off-the-record approach. You can say this—again, before the story's been told—"Now, I'll listen to this story, but if it's so great and colorful and contributes to the overall picture of what I think this whole story is about, I may try to convince you to let me use it. OK?" And then let him tell the story. If he still insists on nonuse afterward, you should comply.

For example, a reporter was interviewing an old man from the class of '37 celebrating the 50th anniversary at the local college. The gentleman wanted to go off the record when telling about the wild night he and his college buddies set squealing pigs loose in the hall of the women's dorm and later hauled a Model T Ford up on the library steps. Using the above technique, the reporter was able to convince the old grad to let him use the story. "You're right," the old man replied, laughing, "That was 50 years ago. I reckon we're not going to get in trouble now!"

Another way to handle the dilemma is the cop-out technique. In this approach, you stop the person before they go off the record and say you're sorry, but it's against your newspaper's policy to do that, or that you'll have to ask your editor. Sometimes, people want to tell the story so badly, at this point they'll tell it on the record.

And finally, there's "not for attribution," or "deep background" off the record. We usually encounter this situation when dealing with volatile data typical to investigative journalism. "Deep background" means you get your subject to agree that you can use the information so long as you don't reveal the source. However, you must substantiate the information from other sources. Needless to say, this is a dangerous game and should be approached with care and full knowledge and consent of your editor.

FROM THE TRENCHES

In 1965 I was a green cub reporter, working on my first internship at the *Transylvania Times* in Brevard, N.C. The editor, Johnny Anderson, was using me that summer to do mostly features, which had been my strength on the college newspaper. Fact is, I was the features editor/photo editor at the *Daily Tar Heel* and thought myself a Big Man on Campus.

My editor assigned me to go interview some famous out-of-town newspaperman vacationing at a nearby mountain resort. Guy with the odd name of Vermont Connecticut Royster. My editor told me Royster was the editor of the *Wall Street Journal*. Oh yeh, I thought to myself, that's the one with no pictures.

I drove up to the Sapphire Inn, found a chair in the lobby where we were to meet, and presently a short, white-haired, no-nonsense man in a gray tweed suit strode in, shook my hand, and sat down. I started asking questions, but he stopped me quickly.

"Son," he asked, "have you ever *read* my paper."

"Well—no," I admitted weakly.

"Interview terminated," he said, looking me right in the eye, and then he got up and strode back out of the room. I returned to the newspaper office in shame.

Twenty years later, teaching journalism at UNC-Chapel Hill, I found myself in the cap-and-gown line at Commencement beside a short, white-haired, no-nonsense man who fate had put there also as a visiting lecturer.

"You don't remember me, do you, Mr. Royster," I said.

"Ohhh, yes I do," he said, winking up at me.

You see, no matter how vaunted my career had been since that time, to him I would always be the boy who didn't do his homework before the interview.

YOUR TOWN; YOUR TURN

1. Reconstruct the scene of your last interview. Where did you stage it? How did location affect the outcome?

2. Arrange to do a feature story interview "on location." After determining the source has ample time available, make a point to just visit at first; don't take any notes or photos for at least 30 minutes. See how it feels.

3. Remember your worst interview experience, the Interview from Hell. How could you have strengthened the interview or saved the situation?

What do you do when the old peach-grower you're interviewing insists that you eat one of his juicy wares? This man's entire life has revolved around peaches. How could you hope to write effectively about him without immersing yourself in the fruits of his life? Forget your notes, camera and decorum; get gooey.

On Writing:
The Lesson of
Boone's Corner

THE COMMON TOUCH

Have you ever noticed how many people read their favorite news magazine backward? After glancing at the front page or cover, they automatically flip right to the back page—thus negating all that neat, well-thought-out graphic design packaging.

Are people being just plain perverse, or might not such a skewed reading practice reveal something deeper about the reading public?

What's going on here if it's not the readers trying to find a trace of something human and personal before they're ready to take on the burden of hard news in the front? Designers at *Time* and *Newsweek* got the message, and the current graphic redesign features lighter, more accessible, human interest packaging at the front of the magazine. Perhaps the publishers have even hired consultants and pollsters to ascertain whether this reformatting has converted the backward-reading subscribers.

You can count on it, people thirst for the human touch. That touch has made people their careers. If the great American humorist and humanist Will Rogers had published a newspaper, you can bet it would have been a community newspaper, one with the common touch.

Former CBS newsman Charles Kuralt who raised the newsfeature-gathering-by-wandering technique to a fine art with his celebrated *On the Road* series in the '60s, was one of the few people in the national media who

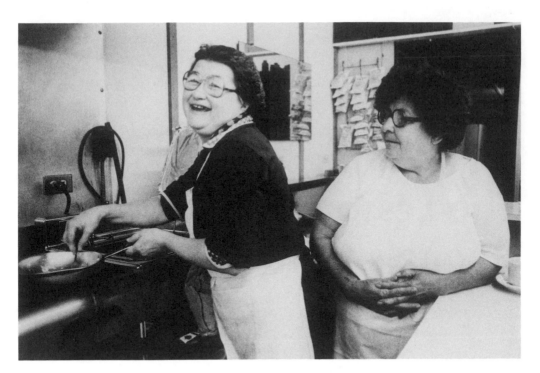

With apologies to Rod Stewart: "Every Face Tells a Story." Human interest stories are as close as your favorite lunch counter. Willie Mae Houk of Sutton's Drug Store in Chapel Hill was honored by the state's governor. Here, co-worker Margaret Durham watches as Willie Mae whips up another fried egg in her battered skillet.

was a community journalist at heart. What he called "innocent little features," vignettes of real people we'd never heard of but who were out there living decent, honest, productive and authentic lives along the backroads of America, ultimately said positive things about a nation and a people in need of an encouraging word.

What Kuralt called simply "neighborliness" centered around his journalist's knowledge that there were no taxpayers, no consumers, no homeowners, no homeless, no voters—but only people. Kuralt's secret for success, his sheer love of people, is central to what makes community journalism viable.

The enlightened community journalist embraces Kuralt's philosophy, and takes it a step further: That there are no readers but only people, that *people* are what matter.

And people love a rattling good yarn.

THE POWER OF THE ANECDOTE

The weekly editor had been asked to give an after-dinner speech to a year-end awards banquet honoring the high school yearbook, newspaper and literary magazine staffs and their parents.

The enlightened community newspaper is intimately involved with building its community through consistently positive coverage that also strives to be accurate, comprehensive, balanced and fair. No wonder community journalism is so challenging. That spirit is embodied in this photo of stump-clearing high school boys participating in a volunteer work day to build a nature trail for their community.

Driving to the high school, he sighed, thinking about the cafeteria rubber chicken and dutiful but probably bored parents and what he'd say about his assigned topic: What Journalism Has Meant To Me. It was like having to pick your own form of execution; no way to cram all that in 20 minutes. What could he say that would make any difference to these budding writers?

Stopping at the Boone's Convenience Corner, the editor went in for a cold soft drink—what old-timers in that region still called "a sodey-dope." Standing there wondering if he should get a pack of nabs as well, he could not help but overhear a local fisherman telling the patient clerk "how to cook a carp."

"You go out in th' spring-uh-th'-year and you catch you a carp," the old gentleman delivered the formula with a straight face. "Then you go home, roll him in cornmeal and butter and you fry him up good till he's nice and brown," the fisherman looked up from his story to see if the clerk and the journalist were paying proper attention to the fine details of his recipe.

"Then you throw away the carp—and eat the cornbread!" he finished with a flourish, while his audience groaned with appreciation.

That's when it hit the editor: What's the basic unit of exchange for the human race? Is it dollars, rubles, yen or marks? No, it's *words*. And writing is the word made *fast*. That is to say, fixed, photographically speaking, and permanent. People who know how to skillfully mold and string words together effectively—they are the wordwrights, the wordsmiths, the real power brokers in our society.

And what had he just witnessed at the little country store? A basic transaction as old as humankind itself, a form of interaction that TV can only mime: the simple yet pervasive act of storytelling.

Everybody who writes at all for newspapers, magazines, the electronic media—be they obituary writers, beat reporters, advertising copy writers, creative feature writers or artistic poets—their basic unit of measure is the story. How well they choose their words and paint their picture determines how effectively they communicate.

SHOW, DON'T TELL

Gene Roberts, now the widely respected managing editor of the *New York Times*, likes to tell how Henry Belk, his mentor and the former editor of the Goldsboro, N.C., *News-Argus*, used to edit copy. Because Belk was blind, Gene would have to read his stories out loud to the old editor.

Blind Henry Belk would sit there in his big oak armchair, head titled

Cartier-Bresson's "decisive moments" are all around us. Sometimes they can be as subtle and poignant as this vignette found in an elementary school trash can. Don't discount the possibility for novelty at even the most routine of assignments. The author found this shot after taking a school play cast picture.

back, the warm humid air blowing in off the city square, and Gene would read his pieces aloud. And if a story didn't work or didn't suit old Henry Belk, he'd cry out loud, "MAKE ME *SEE* IT, GENE. MAKE ME *SEE* IT."

Too often, beginning writers assume the reader knows all about the story and can see the people in the story just as clearly as does the writer. But this is not the case. Pretend you're writing for old blind Henry Belk, our visiting speaker told those kids. He said if you want your writing to come alive, assume your readers are blind and you have describe the whole scene from scratch—foreground, background, atmosphere, mood, lighting as well as the characters with all their details and differences.

What other writing tips had the editor gleaned from over two decades in the trenches of community journalism?

The bride worked at McDonald's and that seemed like the logical place to get married. Human interest? You betcha. But don't have fun at the expense of other people's feelings. The way to do this story is straight.

DON'T FORGET WHOM YOU'RE WRITING FOR

In journalism the term "human interest" has become so overworked that it's all but lost its meaning. To some, the term has a definite pejorative ring to it—connoting a soft filler story or a feature denigrated as "fluff." These same folks would never suppose that human interest had any place in a news story. But in community journalism, if a news story, a feature, even a commentary or an editorial doesn't have some element of human interest, then it's missing the key to connecting with the reader.

High-paid consultants who help business, industry and education leaders with the "strategic long-range planning sessions" take executives into brainstorming think tanks where they engage in hours of corporate soul-searching. The consultants challenge the leaders to identify deceptively simple elements of their businesses such as, "Who are our customers?"

That's a useful question for community newspapers writers to ponder. Who are we writing *for* and *about*—if not people and human interest?

Perhaps next to cats and chimpanzees, humans are the most curious species out there. We have an insatiable curiosity about each other. Dennis Gildea, a journalism professor at Marist College in upstate New York, says that the *Weekly World News* has a lot to teach mainstream American journalists about human interest.

Gildea says, just watch the eyes and face of any supermarket shopper waiting in the checkout line. Confronted with racks of baby-making aliens, reappearing dead Elvises and gay Wild Bill Hickocks, the shoppers who might never dream of buying a *National Inquirer*, *Star* or *Weekly World*

An emerging a cappella do-wop ensemble makes for an engaging human interest story and photo. The Lovemasters of Chapel Hill and Carrboro break into "My Girl."

News, still stare transfixed at the silly covers. Gildea wonders, why is that, if not sheer curiosity about our own humankind?

OTHER WRITING TIPS

The KISS rule: Write to inform, not to impress. Remember Fozz E. Bear. Get on the stage, do your bit, and get off. There's nothing worse than being held captive by a meandering after-dinner speaker enamored by the sound of his own voice. The old curmudgeons in the balcony are likely to start yammering insults at you. Get off the stage, Fozz E. Bear.

And since readers aren't held captive at all, you have nothing with which to hold them except the power of your words. You can't assume they're going to stay with you from line to line; they're free to bolt at the first hint of boredom. After all, there's always "Peanuts" and "Calvin and Hobbes."

Use imagery; appeal to the five senses. Show, don't tell. An apple that is bright red, taut-skinned and juicy is an apple that fairly leaps off the page.

Quest for brevity. Eschew obfuscation. Don't be very very redundant. Get a copy of Strunk and White's *The Elements of Style*. That's the writer's bible.

Use it or lose it. A good writer is like an athlete. A runner who runs regularly, a tennis player who practices three times a week, or a basketball player who is constantly shooting hoops steadily improves. The same with a writer. Work out. Write often. Do windsprints on paper. Work on your serve and delivery. No one ever said writing was easy. Folks who pump iron say, "no pain, no gain." Folks who pump keys agree.

So you don't know where to begin? You think you've got a case of writer's block?

Years ago, Mark West worked as a summer intern at the Asheville, N.C., *Citizen*. Mark remembers having trouble on a story with the deadline close at hand. He was just sitting there gazing at his computer when veteran City Editor Jay Hensley approached and asked what was the problem. Mark explained that he had writer's block—to which Hensley announced to the entire newsroom with a mocking, piteous wail: "OH MY GOODNESS

Look at the details in this photograph of Shorty Boyle, "the Running Boy of Sunshine, N.C." The grin, the hair, the teeth, the eyes, the hand-me-down clothes. If you were writing about Shorty, how would you describe him? Show, don't tell.

GRACIOUS! MR. WEST HAS WRITER'S BLOCK!"

"Mr. West," now a respected journalism professor in his own right, says that experience cured him instantly and forever. Since then, mysteriously, he has never had a reoccurrence of the fashionable writers' ailment.

Which is to say, if the beginning has you stumped, just start where it seems logical and forge ahead. The point is to get started. What will almost always happen is that once you get going, without even knowing it, you will write the beginning somewhere else in the story. This is something you can count on; the beginning will reveal itself to you. It's called the Eureka Factor. Cut and paste the lead at the top. Et voilà!

Get tight with your dictionary (*not* Spellcheck). Learn to spell. Expand your vocabulary. Read voraciously. Learn to listen well and pay attention. Very little happens in the course of the day that is not somehow significant to or fodder for a writer.

It's just like the old J-school admonitions said: Your Copy Ain't Holy and Good Writing Is Rewriting. Read your stuff out loud. If your writing sounds stilted or pontifical, then it's awk. And that's not a nearly extinct species of New Zealand bird. An awk is that little red squiggle English teachers and editors scrawl in the margin when your writing goes clunk. The fact that awkward sentences are almost always the result of a passive verb formation is something about which you can do. See? Wasn't that terrible? Try this: Passive verb formations create awkward sentences.

The fix: write in active voice. Avoid the "to be" verb in its many forms. Instead, use action verbs.

Give yourself permission—permission to be bold, to be creative, to have fun with words, and to make mistakes. You can always go back later and clean it up. Write fearlessly. Writing that sings won't come if you're filled with anxiety and fear of rejection and failure. Forgive yourself in advance. Get jacked up. Football teams aren't the only ones who need cheering. Instead of *Go! Fight! Win!,* how about *Go! Fight! Write!* Say to yourself, "Hey, I may be only human, and I'm gonna goof up occasionally. But not right now. Right now I'm gonna knock their socks off. I'm gonna make old Henry Belk see it."

And that's exactly what the editor told the young writers. He told them to go out there and knock the socks off their readers. As he finished and looked out at his audience of a hundred or so people, he saw in some of those fresh young faces that they had listened, and amid the sea of dull faces wanting to get home to Gameboy or *Bevis and Butthead,* some eyes were shining.

YOUR TOWN; YOUR TURN

1. Go to the local greasy spoon, the town's favorite cafe or coffee shop. Find a story with human interest there. You have 90 minutes.

2. Pick a person at random right now. Be like Yogi Berra who said: "You can observe a lot just by watching." Study their eyes, hands, mouth, hair, walk, clothes, how they "look out of their faces." Take notes and write about it.

3. Pick an impersonal prune of a story from the last front page of your newspaper, or your hometown paper and find a new human interest angle.

TRENDS
RECYCLING HITS THE
FASHION INDUSTRY
See Page 1D

OFF CENTRE
AREA STUDENTS PREPARE
FOR THE PROM
See Page 10D

LOCAL
SCHOOLS TO RENEGOTIATE
VO-TECH CONTRACT
See Page 3A

SPORTS
BRAIN SURGERY CAN'T
STOP KELLEY SAX
See Sports, 1B

SINCE 1898

CENTRE DAILY TIMES

Serving the Communities of Central Pennsylvania

Thursday, May 4, 1995

35 cents a copy

KENT STATE 25 YEARS LATER

Mourners march: *A parade of 4,000 people carried four coffin-like boxes around campus on May 6, 1970 — two days after the Kent State shootings. On that day two Kent State professors spoke to students and faculty, urging faculty members to work to keep the peace.*

'FOUR DEAD IN OHIO'

Kent State killings heightened tension at Penn State

By BILL SYKEN
Centre Daily Times

Twenty-five years ago this month, Penn State students decided they couldn't go on.

With three weeks remaining in the semester, students voted by an overwhelming majority to replace classes with workshops and discussions on current events. Professors were required to teach the standard curriculum to those who were interested, but few were. Many students went home, satisfied to be graded on their first seven weeks' work.

Such was the state of the university after a semester of local protest and the tragedy of national scale that happened in Ohio 25 years ago today. On May 4, 1970, National Guard troopers at Kent State University killed four students who were protesting the Vietnam war.

The killings raised the stakes of university protest higher than people ever

thought they would go.

"(Students) felt the government would never turn their guns on them," said Phillip Stebbins, who as a young Penn State faculty member in 1970 participated in many protests. "Kent State made it clear that was a miscalculation."

The Kent State students had been protesting the April 30 expansion of the Vietnam war into Cambodia. America at the time was supposed to be pulling back its involvement there.

A few weeks before the shootings, several observers said Penn State almost seized Kent State's ignominious place in history.

The most violent confrontation at Penn State took place on April 15, 1970, during an occupation of Old Main. While Stebbins said Penn State wasn't the kind of place where something as radical as Kent State would happen, others said that if tempers had become a little more out of

See PSU page 10A

Kent State 25 years ago

What happened: On May 4, 1970 at 12:27 p.m., four student protesters were killed and nine injured at Kent State.

Cause of protest: The expansion of the Vietnam war into Cambodia at a time when America was supposed to be reducing involvement there.

Thirteen seconds: 28 Ohio National Guardsmen in 13 seconds fired up to 67 rounds. Some protesters had thrown rocks at the troops.

Findings: A presidential commission ruled the governor should not have sent troops in with their weapons loaded. After three trials, no one was able to definitely determine how the shooting started.

Grief's cry: *Mary Ann Vecchio, 14, screams as she kneels by the body of student Jeffrey Miller on the campus of Kent State University in Kent, Ohio, on May 4, 1970. National Guardsmen had fired into a crowd of demonstrators, killing four and wounding nine others.*

AP PHOTO

Ohio university marks anniversary

By RICH HARRIS
Associated Press Writer

KENT, Ohio — The Kent State University campus looked back at tragedy Wednesday, 25 years after National Guardsmen opened fire and killed four students, and Mary Ann Vecchio's moment of agony was frozen in a Pulitzer Prize-winning photograph.

Vecchio, then a 14-year-old runaway, was pictured kneeling with arms upraised in horror over the body of Jeffrey Miller. She returned to campus for a cameo appearance as herself in a play

about the May 4, 1970, shootings.

She had one line to speak to actors portraying the slain students: "You don't have to be dead to be in purgatory."

At the Wednesday afternoon close of a two-day symposium, veterans of campus protest tried to put the Kent State shootings into larger context.

Charlayne Hunter-Gault, a "MacNeil-Lehrer News Hour" correspondent who was one of the first two black students admitted to the University of Georgia, said

SEE KENT, *page 10A*

Execution may open floodgates

By HEIDI RUSSELL
The Associated Press

PHILADELPHIA — Time seems to be running out for many of the nation's 2,984 death row inmates.

This year could set the record-setter for the number of people put to death in the country since 1976, when the U.S. Supreme Court made the death penalty constitutional.

And states that have not carried out many executions in recent decades could see more, said Richard Dieter, executive director of the Death Penalty Information Center in Washington, D.C.

Dieter said most death row inmates have been awaiting execution since the early 1980s, when the murder rate matched that of the 1930s gangster era at 10 victims per 100,000 people.

Many of the condemned have received execution stays during the last 15 years. But now they are at the end of their appeals processes, Dieter said.

"It's not necessarily a resurgence for the death penalty in America. This was all put in motion a long time ago," he said.

Although Southern states lead the nation in the number of people put to death during the past two decades, other states — particularly Pennsylvania, California and Illinois — could catch up, Dieter said. The three states rank in the top five with a total of 743 condemned inmates.

"It appears that there's a movement spreading out of the South. But with the large numbers on death row in Pennsylvania and California, the numbers will be shifting," he

SEE INMATES, *back page*

Zettlemoyer's death a first for coroner

By BARBARA BRUEGGEBORS
Centre Daily Times

BENNER TOWNSHIP — His business is dealing with non-natural death ... determining causes, pinning down times.

Then came Tuesday night, when Centre County Coroner Kerry Benninghoff was summoned to the death house at the State Correctional Institution at Rockview . . . to certify the distinctly non-natural demise of one Keith Zettlemoyer.

There never was a more open and shut case.

At 10:14 p.m., Zettlemoyer, 39, received a lethal injection of barbiturates and paralytics.

Ten minutes later, the attending physician went over the body strapped to the gurney and pronounced the man dead.

Benninghoff was there moments later and removed the IVs. He conducted a quick, external postmortem and filled out Zettlemoyer's death certificate.

Cause known. Time known.

For a coroner, dealing with death doesn't get any easier — or any harder.

"Something like this makes you sit back and re-examine your values," Benninghoff said. "I've done a lot of soul-searching the last couple of days."

SEE CORONER, *back page*

THIRD IN A SERIES

TALE OF A CITY?

S.C. council opposes referendum

This is the third part of a series looking at the issues surrounding the May 16 municipal consolidation referendum in State College Borough and College and Patton townships.

By JIM MACKINNON
Centre Daily Times

Elected officials from the three Centre Region municipalities involved in the consolidation referendum have been largely on the sidelines.

Informed, opinionated and vocal, but mostly on the outside looking in.

That is, until Monday night.

That's when the State College Borough Council voted unanimously to formally oppose the May 16 ballot proposal that asks residents whether they want to combine the borough and College and Patton townships into a new city in January

1998. The council voted 6-1 to mail its reasons for opposing the measure to borough residents.

The heads of the two township governments, on the other hand, say it's likely their boards will stay formally neutral with individual members expressing personal opinions.

State College Council member R. Thomas Berner voted in favor of opposing the consolidation referendum, though he cast the sole dissenting vote on sending out the mailing at taxpayer expense. Berner said he supports consolidation, but not the ballot proposal.

"Consolidation without home rule is regression," Berner said. "We're talking about uncharted waters."

The sad part of the public discourse over the issue is the forums that have been set up about consolidation have been in a pro-con format instead of general discussions,

SEE CITY, *page 10A*

SENIOR EXPO '95

From 10 a.m. to 9 p.m. today and Friday, the Nittany Mall will host the annual Senior Expo, designed to inform and educate senior citizens about businesses and services of interest to them. This year's event will feature nearly 70 exhibitors and 12 free health screenings.

NEWS OF NOTE

FORECAST

Cloudy today with showers starting by mid-day, high 58. A mix of rain and sun on Friday. For details, see page 2A.

COINING THE DOLLAR

Republican budget-cutters are eyeing billions of dollars in savings that may result from replacing $1 bills that wear out in 17 months with a $1 coin lasting 30 years.

Though opponents have over the years succeeded in blocking the coin, the proponents' cause has been given new life this year by Congress' struggle to balance the budget.

Graphics, Design and the Community Paper

DESIGN SHOULD ENHANCE COMMUNICATION, NOT DEFEAT IT

Someone once said the ultimate function of design is to make us feel good. When we look at a well-designed page, we are drawn into the page, and find ourselves reading everything, almost effortlessly. If we look at an ugly newspaper page, our reaction will be to bolt, and head off for the predictable. That usually means the comics or TV.

Only three elements comprise newspaper design: words, pictures and space. How we integrate those three elements conspires to form a content of its own greater than the mere parts.

A wonderfully written story on a page without photos looks drab. A gorgeous photo illustrating a poorly written story is as sad as a rose on a streetwalker. A fabulous and inventive design that is forced to use weak photos and a poorly written story is as transparent as a flashy used-car salesman trying to hawk junkers with nothing but hype and shouting.

Since the advent of *USA Today* in 1982, larger newspapers across the country have been jumping on the color bandwagon—converting to the use of more color photographs, "spot color" for headlines and color bars, and colorful informational graphics such as explanatory maps, charts and graphs.

This is expensive stuff. Community newspapers, with small budgets, may think that what has been called "the new graphics" is out of their

109

league. But it ain't necessarily so. There are plenty of things a paper can do to look better without breaking the bank. Smaller community papers, many of which are competing with area metro dailies, can have a sharp and savvy presentation too, without hiring an expensive outside design firm. But it takes someone who cares and/or a flexible management courageous enough to take risks.

NOT JUST UGLY, BUT REALLY UGLY

Matt was bummed; there was no other word for it.

After a tough first year as managing editor of the *Bugle*, what had he got to show for it? Oh sure, a whole raft of second-place awards from the state press association. But he couldn't get one judge's comments out of his mind.

"If only the *Bugle* looked as good as it reads," the judge had written on the runner-up award for General Excellence. And in the Typography/Design division Matt's paper hadn't even placed.

Stung by the realization that appearances are important, Matt resolved to redesign the *Bugle*. But where to start? At college it had never occurred to him that a course in newspaper graphic design might someday be vital.

The young editor decided to do a little informal market research on his own. For his "focus group" on graphics and design, he decided to approach the most opinionated bunch of old coots in town, the 9 o'clock coffee club down at the Village Cafe, where caffeine was in and tact was out. This crew may not be experts in newspaper graphic design but—as with everything from high school football to national foreign policy—they knew what they liked and didn't like; moreover, they weren't afraid to say it.

"Why sure, son," said the retired mayor, "the *Bugle* is ugly. But then it's *always* been like that." And with a laugh: "We wouldn't recognize the *Bugle* if it wasn't ugly."

When Matt approached the paper's publisher about the subject, Mrs. Hinson told him he could do as he wanted—within reason. She said she would be especially pleased if the proposed design changes resulted in more readership and increased ad revenues. Matt replied that he had no idea if there was any such correlation, but that he'd look into it. They ended the meeting agreeing that a better-looking paper should attract more readers, and hence, more advertisers. At least the idea was worth a shot.

But Mrs. Hinson cautioned Matt to phase in his changes slowly. "Remember, people don't like change," she said, adding with a chuckle, "people think of the *Bugle* as *their* paper, not our paper, and certainly not my paper."

Additionally, the publisher told Matt the *Bugle* couldn't afford an outside design consultant, but that she would be supportive of sending him to state and regional press workshops on newspaper design. She further counseled him to simply look at the better community papers in the region and try to absorb what the winners were doing. And finally, did Matt have any informal contacts whose expertise he could draw upon?

That's when Matt remembered Gloria.

Matt's next move was to contact his old college buddy who had become a graphic design editor for an out-of-state newspaper. After hearing Matt's situation, Gloria agreed to critique the paper's existing design and offer simple alternatives. Two weeks after sending her a packet of papers, Matt received them back, covered with Post-it Notes and accompanied by a long letter that started like this:

> Dear Matt,
> You were right. The *Bugle* isn't just ugly, it's really ugly …

The graphic designer's comments were divided into three areas: type, photos and space. Gloria's recommendations follow.

TYPE

The Flag—Let's take it from the top. Your nameplate is so archaic it's almost comical. That *Bugle* you've got there looks like the Old English Gothic typeface came off the front of some hymnal.

But I also realize that changing a newspaper's nameplate can be tricky business. So consider this: Many people in town will be very upset if you summarily trash your old flag and go with a new, more modern typeface.

When my paper was considering a redesign last year, we ran a reader poll, and actually put the choice for a new flag design up for a reader vote. We published our top five choices, and the readers wrote and called in their responses. When we finally incorporated those changes into our final new nameplate, the readers felt they'd been a part of the process. Oh sure, some people were still miffed, but many more said they appreciated being included in the decision-making process.

Headlines—Honestly, Matt, what is that stuff you're using, Futura Bold Condensed? Anyway, it's too black and dense. I'd suggest lightening up by converting to a more friendly-looking and airy Roman-style font, perhaps a nice Bodoni, Times or Garamond. If you must use sans serif, find a lighter, less-condensed Helvetica or Avant Garde.

Body Type—Typeface choice is critical. Most newspapers including the *Bugle* use Times Roman for their body type. Nine point is average. Make sure your horizontal spacing (leading) between the lines is not so crammed. The *Bugle*'s body type looks like boiler plate. I suggest airing it out by increasing the leading at least one point.

Column Width—In addition, you need to convert from eight to six or fewer columns. An eight-column format causes too many strange hyphenations in justified copy. If you go to a six-column layout, your copy will become far more inviting, accessible and readable. Right now, frankly, it hurts my eyes even to look at your paper. Sorry, but you asked.

Just a thought, but try setting your commentary (on the edit, lifestyle and sports pages) ragged right instead of justified. That style signals the reader that this is a more informal piece, and it's a good way of airing out the pages, thus introducing pleasing white space.

PHOTOS

The quickest and easiest way to dress up your paper and boost readership is with good local photos displayed well.

Photos First—Did you know that readers look at photos first? Not only that, but the presence of a photo doubles the likelihood of readership. A lot of word people hate to acknowledge what's been proven in reader research, but it's true.

Photos Bigger—The *Bugle* needs to run its photos bigger. That means you've got to be bolder with your layouts. The photos I saw weren't that bad; you just ran them like postage stamps. In my experience, if photographers realize beforehand that their photos will be running large, they produce far better work. Try and see.

Color vs. B&W—I would advise using all the color you can afford; but this is not nearly as critical as the quality of the photos. A great black-and-white shot is extremely powerful. Other suggestions:

Dominant Image—Make sure every page is anchored by a Dominant Image Above the Fold.

Dominant Image First—Lay out your page around that dominant image. In other words, start with the photo as your main building block and then make the copy and heads work around the photo. Not only will this result in a more pleasingly designed page, but your readers will like it and your photographers will love you.

Crop Carefully—Don't crop photos without conferring with the photographer first. Slash-and-burn cropping is the surest way to discourage any future creativity from your shooters.

Use Photo Pages—What about a photo page? I didn't see any photo essays in the papers you sent me. You need to showcase your photographers more. Turn your people loose on the county fair, the Boy Scout field day, a barn-raising, a farm auction, the local fire department at a practice burn. You get the idea. Occasionally devote B-1 to some creative visual space. Your readers will like it, and your photographers will blossom.

Use Headshots—Is there some reason you're not using headshots for your editorial columns? I recommend good mugshots for *all* columns, including commentary on lifestyle and sports pages, and even your community correspondents and the lady who writes the community college news roundup. Good headshots personalize the paper by connecting faces with the commentary. It's also an easy way to dress up the page by breaking up the gray of copy.

Informational Graphics—The *Bugle* probably can't afford a full-time graphics editor now, but someday, I hope your publisher starts thinking along those lines. One of the things a great graphics person could do for the paper is to bring informational graphics to your pages. These infographics include charts, graphs, maps and simple computer-generated illustrations that enhance stories and make them not only more readily understandable but visually appealing as well. Matt, I'd suggest you might start by taking a computer course from the local community college. Also, I've noticed from time to time that the state press association offers hands-on computer graphics workshops.

SPACE

If you'll follow some of the above suggestions, I think you will be introducing "white space" into the paper in a pleasing way. White space refers to the creative use of what artists call "negative space," in other words, anywhere that there appears to be nothing. Think of the paper like an art gallery. For the pictures to have the desired impact at an exhibition, there's got to be enough wall space between each hanging, otherwise the effect is crammed and difficult to look at. The same goes for your newspaper. Give each story its due by providing enough white space between different stories, and between heads and copy, photos and story and so forth.

PACKAGING

Some thought needs to be given to packaging. That is, the consistent grouping of like stories. The *Bugle* appears to have a mysterious organization concept known only to its editors; I couldn't figure it out. For your size paper, I'd suggest devoting the front page to almost exclusively local coverage, then group state, national and international news on Page 2 under a clearly marked section header.

Use Section Headers—I'd recommend that formula throughout the paper: 48-72 pt. headers denoting each section or page following: sports, editorial, lifestyle.

Strive for Consistency—In addition, try to keep pages in consistent positions. For instance, Editorial should always be found in the same position. I like 2B.

Start a Page-One Briefs Box—Finally, I found little news announcements scattered all through the paper like filler stories. What about compiling all those bulletin board-type community announcement stories into a front-page, left-hand briefs column?

Gloria ended her recommendations with a wrap-up set of comments that addressed the overall feel she got from looking at the paper.

OVERALL FEEL

With just a little work, the overall feel of the *Bugle* could be so much more visually reader-friendly. Recommendations:

Sky Boxes—Create a space above the nameplate to highlight what's inside the paper. This is also a great opportunity for spot color.

Indexes—You need a clear table of contents on the front to help out the reader.

Captions—If the photo is the first thing the reader looks at, the caption is often the second thing. Call this a point of entry. Think of captions as little leads. They should be written as if the reader is not going to read the story the photo accompanies. Captions also offer opportunities for "refers," flagging an inside story that relates to the photo.

Phone Numbers—On the *Bugle*'s editorial-page masthead, you don't list any way of getting in touch with the editors. A listing of phone numbers would make the paper more reader-friendly and accessible.

Letters Policy—If the *Bugle* has a "Letters to the Editor" policy box, I couldn't find it. A regularly published and clearly stated policy box not only serves to encourage letters, but it also establishes your guidelines, prevents potential confusion about unsigned letters, etc., while graphically breaking up what tends to be a gray page.

***

Good luck, Matt. Let me know what you decide to do. I'll be especially interested in the community reaction to any changes in the paper's design.

CENTRE DAILY TIMES

Oklahoma stops to mourn, pray

Police sue over job status

Pregnant teens face risks

Student group wants Pepsico out of Burma

Pipeline explodes in Russia

Jostens plant mixes with rich, famous

CENTRE DAILY TIMES

KENT STATE 25 YEARS LATER

Execution may open floodgates

'FOUR DEAD IN OHIO'

Kent State killings heightened tension at Penn State

Ohio university marks anniversary

TALE OF A CITY?

DAYBREAK

Comics Page 7

Spock champions 'old-fashioned' parenting

The Slob Sisters

Crazy about clutter, business team is really in a mess

Hip-hop kids have the 'word up' on slang

---

thursday TRENDS

greenwear

Women find Internet unfriendly territory

You don't have to leave home to go shopping; it's all happening online

Some boomers never grew up

DESIGN WRAP-UP

Matt studied and then incorporated many of Gloria's suggestions for enhancing the graphic design of the *Bugle*. And as Mrs. Hinson advised, he introduced the changes gradually over a period of three months. In fact some readers didn't even realize the paper was changing before their very eyes. Circulation and advertising did increase that quarter, but it was difficult to determine if the new design changes were solely responsible. Most gratifying to Matt was the comment from the former mayor down at the coffee club, "Well son, I couldn't help but notice," he opined, "the ol' *Bugle* doesn't look *nearly* as ugly as it used to."

Matt was betting that the judges at the coming year's state press association contest would notice too.

YOUR TOWN; YOUR TURN

1. You have been put in charge of redesigning your paper. What changes would you put into effect? Remember, you need to be able to verbally justify each proposed change.

2. Does your newspaper have a reader-friendly design? Find some examples of design features that help readers through the paper. If you think your paper could do a better job in that area, make specific suggestions.

3. Evaluate the typography and graphics of the paper's flag, or nameplate. Find out something about its history. Who designed it and how has the flag evolved through time and use?

An example of a redesign: The *Centre Daily Times* of State College, Pa., spent many months on a comprehensive self-study before unveiling its dramatic redesign. The newspaper (a Knight-Ridder morning daily with a circulation of roughly 20,000) wanted a graphic presentation that enhanced their new local coverage emphasis and community-intensive initiative. Reactions from readers were mixed; people seemed to either love or hate the redesign. Regardless, the redesign process itself, while exhausting, energized the newspaper from within. Most staffers liked resulting fresh, airy look. (*Pages courtesy of the* Centre Daily Times)

Thigh-deep, the community newspaper editor covers a 'coon hound water race. Notice the notepad safely stowed in the jeans. (*Photo by Maggie Lauterer*)

Photojournalism:
Put That Camera Down
and Dance, Boy!

COMMUNITY NEWSPAPER PHOTOGRAPHERS: BE A PERSON FIRST

We can forgive the master photographer Henri Cartier-Bresson when he says photography "doesn't take much brains. It doesn't take any brains. It takes sensitivity, a finger and two legs."

Cartier-Bresson, the very personification of Gallic intuition, is best known to students of photography for having coined the expression "the decisive moment," that pie-slice in time when the action and intensity of any given event reach their peak. He elevated to high art the ability to record precisely that decisive moment on film.

Photography *is* a snap—as easy as a diminutive click. At least, that's what generations of Kodak advertisements would have us believe. Little wonder then, when the serious beginning photographer feels frustrated and betrayed when s/he finds, in the words of the lyricist Ira Gershwin, that "It Ain't Necessarily So."

For the student of photography, here's your challenge: You start out basically visually illiterate. Then over a period of time you commit yourself to learning a new visual language. You must learn to reconcile the three eyes: the mechanical eye you hold in your hands (be it a point-and-shoot or a Nikon F4, it's the same thing); our physical eye which "sees" exactly what we point it at; and our mind's eye, the latter an untrustworthy witness, because it's so full of visions and ideals.

117

Learning to train your physical eye to coordinate your visions with the mechanical eye can be a lifelong work.

Increasingly in community journalism our profession is crying out for well-rounded photojournalists. That is, writers who can shoot, and shooters who can write. It is no longer enough to be just a reporter or just a photographer.

The irony is that this new twist is being heard from the very highest places as well. Now retired *National Geographic* photo chief Robert Gilka told a national press photographers gathering back in the early '80s that his magazine wants photographers who can sit down at a terminal and intelligently and confidently write about what they saw. After all, who should better be able to explain the picture? To borrow from Eric Sevareid: "One good word is worth a thousand pictures."

The positive impact of images on the printed page has taken on a new significance in American newspapers in the last couple of years. With readership sliding, many large American newspapers have begun copying TV and *USA Today*. This has caused a trickle-down effect on many community newspapers which assume that gratuitous spot color and color-for-color's-sake photos will automatically make the paper more appealing. But make no mistake about it: The weak-content color photo, no matter how vivid the colors, will never be as good as a great content-rich black-and-white photo.

We no longer question whether a photo will make a story or a page more appealing. The evidence is in. Readership soars when a photo accompanies a story. Enlightened editors and publishers now demand visually exciting pages. For the community paper, photography is the simplest and most inexpensive way to make any story or page more appealing.

In spite of this increased emphasis on visual communications, many, if not most, journalism school graduates emerge into the real world with no working knowledge of cameras or graphics. See if this scenario doesn't ring true: The new hire from State U is told to interview the new police chief and bring back a headshot to dress up the story. When handed a 35mm camera, the new reporter is struck dumb with terror. The M.E. might has well have handed a snake to the new recruit.

But many if not most community papers have *always* expected and required reporters to be able to shoot. Community papers traditionally have not been able to afford the luxury of specialization. And because editors and publishers historically have been word people and put more emphasis on reporting than visuals, it is usually the photos that suffer—as a cursory glance at many community newspapers will reveal.

On the other end of the spectrum, at the better large dailies, more emphasis is being put on newspaper graphics and design. Therefore, photography is receiving nationwide attention from savvy publishers who regard pictures as a new marketing tool—a way to hustle papers.

Here is where community newspapers should be paying attention to their big cousins. Rich Clarkson, *National Geographic*'s former photo chief, told photographers at the Southern Shortcourse in News Photography, "One of the trends I see is the nationwide growing awareness in the importance of graphics and intelligence in packaging ... that means planning the shoots and tying the photos well to text. But of course, that requires committed editors committed to visual reporting." Clarkson said that "the thoughtful use of thoughtful pictures," is what wins Pulitzers these days.

However, many community newspaper publishers are less concerned with winning Pulitzers than they are with winning the local Food Lion account. Still, enlightened editors and publishers of community papers should be paying attention to the national curve. Much is in ferment. What goes around comes around.

Clarkson agrees with his old boss, Robert Gilka, that "photographers have to get out of the darkroom and into the newsroom," if we are to have any influence on how the photos are used. On the more progressive papers, the old line in the sand that separates word people from picture people is becoming less pronounced. Emerging technologies have had a lot to do with that.

But tradition dies hard at the big papers where change occurs glacially. *Washington Post* reporter Linda Wheeler is representative of the new breed of reporters who carry a camera as well. Community newspaper photo-reporters may smile inwardly to learn that the newsroom has branded Wheeler as a WASP (that is: Writer And Sometime Photographer). Wheeler, who, when she spoke to a recent workshop, was covering the D.C. drug beat with pad, pen and camera, said, "I get more satisfaction out of my work now, because I can better control the whole package of my work. I think of my stories accompanied by my photo as a visual bloc; I try to create a whole coordinated entity."

Welcome to most every community newspaper journalist's world. The big papers are beginning to discover what we've known for ages: It's infinitely more effective and satisfying to do it all yourself.

Another thing you'll hear at national photo conferences that reinforces the pluses of community journalism: the resurgence of minimalism. Often the best in our business are using the most basic of equipment—quality stuff to be sure—but devoid of superfluous gadgetry and mechanical brouhaha. Motor drives, once the auditory prerequisite for the macho photojournalist,

All around you in your community there are talented, emerging artists who will give you great copy and photos. Your coverage of their endeavors is important both to them and to the artistic life and intellectual growth of your community—whether it be a visiting artist in pottery . . .

. . . or a local unsung craftsman who has been laboring quietly for years in his backyard shop.

are increasingly viewed as photographic overkill, as in duck hunting with an Uzi, especially when used in quiet situations where sensitivity is called for. "Throw away your motor drives," says *U.S. News and World Report* staff photographer Darryl Heikes. "We don't need any more Machine Gun Kellys."

As anybody who's ever shot for a small paper knows, equipment isn't nearly as important as attitude and access. Pulitzer-prize-winner Bill Strode, whose credits include *Life* magazine covers, says, "Access is all important. Be a person first; then a journalist; then a photographer."

Strode speaks as if he comes from a community newspaper background. He says, "I am so tired of hearing national press photographers complaining and whining all the time. It's time for photographers to dig up good pictures within yourself. It's time for us to try to do good in a grander sense ... even in small ways. If you can help your local United Way by taking a better photograph ... then if we have this attitude ... that your photo just might help ... then that will change your entire attitude about your work."

Strode concluded with a quote from the late great combat photographer Robert Capa, which could be adapted as a motto for whatever kind of creature you are or want to be: photographer, community journalist or just plain person: "If your pictures aren't good enough, you're not close enough."

THE POWER OF THE IMAGE

Look at your paper's or your hometown newspaper's front page. Examine the covers of this week's *Newsweek* magazine, a copy of *Rolling Stone* or the *National Enquirer*. What is the common denominator that links all of these fronts?

That the cover is to the publication what the lead is to a story.

It should beckon; it should entice; it should seduce; it should grab; it should make you *stay*. It should make you *read*. It should make you turn the page.

The eye is a lusty hunter and also a fickle one.

Bored, our eyes leap for new game.

A drab front page tells our eyes, "Bummer. Gotta split. Go find something to entertain us. How 'bout the funnies?"

If it was your job to shoot the lead picture or to design the front page, you just failed. You lost a reader.

A reader?

Go loaded for bear. Carrying your camera with you at all times will result in some great shots. The old photojournalists who carried Big Berthas and Speed Graphics could define the formula for a great shot: "F/8 and Be There." There's no substitute for being in the right place at the right time with the right lens—as demonstrated with the telephoto shot of a tobacco-spitting contest.

What are readers?

Before we were readers, we were *lookers*. What do we look at?

Pictures.

From the dawn of time, from the cave drawings of early humankind through the span of civilization, man—and woman—have been lookers first. Lookers of pictures.

It is a particularly human trait that other animals lack. Our eyes quest for more than just functional information, as in: Where's that gazelle I'm going to have for dinner?

Our eyes quest for entertainment, relief from boredom. But deeper still is the quest for new information. The human mind is not content to remain static; it needs and wants fresh images to scan and process.

And finally, and most excitingly, our kind are gregarious. *People* magazine is not so different from a busy-body lead dog in the prairie dog village. Who's Hot and Who's Not. Arf Arf. Sexy Hunks of Daytime TV. Bowwow.

You may laugh, but why is *People* so terrifically popular? It's because we love ourselves. We love to find out about other prairie dogs—people with two-headed babies and too many wives and people who want to be buried with their Cadillac and people who want to go to the jungles of Zaire to work with AIDS patients. Homo sapiens is the only species so intensely curious about and utterly fascinated with itself.

Back to the cave drawings. Recall the little stick figures running beside the huge prehistoric bison? People. People talking to people.

The earliest way we had to talk to each other—over time and over physical space, even before there was the word—was by pictures.

We don't know the language of the ancients, but we know their brush strokes. We have no written tablets from the caves, but we see their bravery and their fearless stature in their artists' hands. Pictures were the earliest form of impersonal communications, an exchange of information that didn't have to rely on Thag's grunts and hand-waving to Grog.

Pictures were our earliest basic language and have endured as an international form of communication because it is a language we all know. Take your photographs seriously. Run the good ones big. People love pictures; always have; always will.

COMMUNITY PHOTOJOURNALISM 101

Bill was a good reporter; he prided himself in that. But he was not prepared for what he ran into at his first job out of college. They wanted him to take pictures. "But I'm not a photojournalist!" he tried explaining to the ed-

So much of what we do involves wise use of time. The high school football story from Friday night has to be written, and yet there's this feature photo you've heard about: The late Gwen Cole's old dog sleeps faithfully on his grave. To get the shot of the skittish dog, the author took a typewriter and AP paper (no paper changes required) and set up shop beside the cemetery until the dog obliged.

itor. "You are now," came the reply.

It wasn't fair. The editor had started out as a photographer and grown into writing. Somehow that struck Bill as an easier progression.

Bill had to admit, he didn't know diddly about photography, and his early work showed it. Every time he'd turn a photo in, it was so bad that it invariably resulted in the editor hollering something like "This isn't just bad—it's *really* bad!" or "You call *this* a photograph?" Such outbursts were usually followed with an admonition of how Bill should have shot the picture.

Gradually the editor noticed that Bill seemed to be improving. One day, while talking to the young reporter in his office, the editor caught a glimpse of something strange taped to the back of Bill's door. At the top, the large lettering caught his eye: *How Any Idiot Can Take Good Pichers.* And scrawled on a four-foot long sheaf of AP paper were the preachments. Every time the editor had hollered, Bill had gone back to his office and written it down.

They may not have been the community photojournalism version of Strunk and White's *Elements of Style*, but all of the editor's hollerings had been therein recorded almost verbatim:

1. Is there film in the camera? Are you sure it's loaded correctly, dummy?

2. You can tell if there's film in the camera like this: Shoot a picture, wind the film, and see if the rewind knob turns. That's the knob at top left. If it's not moving, you're taking fantasy pictures. Pay no attention to the frame counter on the top right. It turns even if film *isn't* going through the camera.

3. Don't shoot into the light. Instead, get the light behind you, for the most part, so the subject is illuminated.

4. Don't bring me any Dead Snake Pictures. That's a photo taken of a dead snake made by a photographer who wants to put as much distance between him and the snake as possible. See 'em every summer in the *Bugle* on slow news days. What—Are you terrified of your subject? You gonna catch something from him?

5. The most valuable and inexpensive attachments you have for your camera are your two feet. Step closer to the subject. Also, you have knees? They do bend, don't they?

6. Fill the frame with significant matter. Look what's really in the viewfinder. I don't want tennis players with power poles growing out of their heads.

7. Remember Peter Pan? Watch your shadow. Keep it out of the photo. The photographer's shadow in a photo is a sure sign of a rank beginner—which you are, but you don't have to broadcast it.

8. Speaking of shadows, avoid direct flash. It makes people look either guilty or nuked. For softer, more humane lighting, bounce your flash off the ceiling. Open up two stops to compensate for the light falling off. Oh, for God's sake Bill, that means 1/60th at F/5.6 instead of F/11.

9. People look at pictures to see people. Put people in your pictures. This campus scene you just brought me looks like somebody dropped a neutron bomb on the place. All the buildings are intact, but not a living soul in sight. How'd you do that?

10. No butts. Give me people's faces. Not their behinds or their backs or their butts. Their faces. And I want to see their eyes.

11. Whoever said Ansel Adams got the shot with a single try? Take lots of pictures each time you shoot a single subject. Three frames per assignment is the bare minimum. Film is cheap compared to the lost shot or your having to drive back to do a reshoot, because the guy blinked and you'd only shot one frame.

12. Be paranoid about focus. A fuzzy picture is acceptable only in combat photography or pictures taken during an earthquake.

13. Don't trust your light meter. What do they know? You've got eyes, don't you? Bracket. That means, after shooting the picture like your light meter tells you, open up one stop above that setting, shoot some and then reset one stop below the advised setting, and shoot some more. It's called life insurance, cause I'm gonna kill you if you screw up again.

14. Take lots of pictures. If you want to get better, do it like a sport. Practice. And Bill, let me tell you, when it comes to photography, you need to practice bad.

15. Bill, you screwed up again. But lemme tell you something, son, that's all right. Because infinitely more can be learned through defeat than from victory. Take advantage of the lessons afforded by a really good screwup like this one. Figure out what went wrong. The picture is blurry; it's gotta be one of only four things: You shot it out of focus, you shook the camera, your shutter speed was set too slow for the action, or your enlarger slipped out of focus in the darkroom.

16. Bill! These pictures look like they were taken by the Doughnut Man. You remember that little fat bald guy that used to be on the TV doughnut commercials. You'd see him stumbling around blearily before dawn, repeating to himself automatically, "Time to make da' doughnuts … " Don't take pictures like a half-awake robot. Nothing is automatic. Every situation

is different. Novelty is everywhere. Any picture could be your best.

17. Hey Bill! This photo actually isn't too bad. Keep clickin' and windin', son, and we'll see what develops.

CAPTION WRITING 101

Here's a short course in what the AP's Mike Putzel (a former small-town newspaper guy) calls "the fine art of effective caption writing." Some guidelines:

✓ Don't assume that just because captions or cutlines (the latter name derived from a block or "cut" of wood on which the metal photoengraving used to be mounted) are so short that they don't deserve our attention.

✓ Don't give short shrift to this highly compacted journalistic form. The cutline is a mighty mite, a vital byte of data, a veritable nugget of information. Consider the caption like the piccolo of the paper; it may be tiny, but yet it can be heard over the blaring trumpets of a 60 point headline. Done right, a caption can justify and enhance a good or even fair photo. Done poorly or sloppily, it can ruin a great one. When writing the caption, give it the full weight of your attention.

✓ Consider the caption a little lead. Provide the 5 W's in three to four accurate, cogent, concise, pithy lines.

✓ About names: Be paranoid about accuracy and spelling. Nothing kills a photo deader than a misspelled or wrong name.

✓ For starters, try the Subject-Verb-Direct Object sentence construction.

✓ Write in the present tense unless your paper dictates a different style.

✓ The caption must provide not only vital information on the photo's content, but it must also set the picture in the correct context—not only what is happening in the image, but also perhaps what happened to lead up to the event portrayed, and maybe what happened just following the making of the photo. Write as if the reader will *not* read any story accompanying the photo.

✓ The caption is a potential point of entry. Be aware of its power to draw the reader into such a story, and hence, into the entire paper in a way that even headlines sometimes can't do.

✓ If there's an inside story to which the photo refers, make the caption user-friendly by providing the reader with a refer (pronounced *reefer* by pros)—as in "see related story on A-12."

Photo credits are important too. They're not so much about ego-stroking as they are about assigning responsibility and accountability. Local

Here's what former professor and now community newspaper publisher Ken Byerly calls a "tree full of owls" photo. Don't laugh. For every one of these cast members in the local play, there are at least four family members who want copies of that edition of the paper so they can cut it out and tape it on the refrigerator door. Here's the arithmetic of community journalism: There are 71 people in this picture. Lessee, four times 71 is … Now you got the picture. (*Photo by Gerald Gerlach; courtesy of the Rutherford County Arts Council © 1972*)

photo credits serve a subtle but profound function in community journalism. Photos credited to local photographers signal the community that the paper is on the job; that they didn't rely on AP to do their work for them. Maybe it's only tiny agate type, but it's another way for a paper to tell the community that it cares.

Who writes the caption? At many large metro dailies, shooters only shoot, and turn in assignment sheets with caption information. Someone else—whom the photographer may never see or even meet—may write the caption. This strikes some photographers as an odd division of labor. Who else is more qualified to comment on the subtleties of the scene or event depicted than the person who was there in person? At the larger community paper, if captions aren't written by the photographer, then the caption writer should at least secure data from the photographer and ideally check out the final version of that cutline with the shooter. At the smaller community papers, the photographer, who might be a reporter or editor as well, enjoys the luxury of writing her or his own cutlines.

FROM THE TRENCHES

So you wanna be a photojournalist ... ?
Can you eat a taco and drive a car at the same time?
　—Woody Marshall
　　Chief photographer
　　The Burlington, N.C., *Times-News*

The great five-string banjo picker Snuffy Jenkins was coming home to Harris, N.C. I couldn't believe my luck. Snuffy, an old man and a famous figure in old-time and bluegrass history, had his roots in my county. I had been invited to interview him at his ancestral home in Harris, not more than seven miles from the paper's office.

Arriving at the Jenkins home, I was directed to a wicker chair on the front porch, where I began taking photos and conducting my interview without much preamble. I admit it; I was young and didn't understand the subtleties of interviewing country folk.

Snuffy, however, had his own agenda.

The music began with his daddy, Roy Jenkins, striking up a clawhammer tune on the banjo. Then one of the brothers got out of his chair and began buckdancing around in the red clay of the front yard. Snuffy joined in with his banjo. The front door opened and out came Ma Jenkins. Now there were several more dancers afoot. I was going nuts taking pictures.

But Snuffy would have none of it; maybe he knew I was missing the real essence of the moment. Or maybe spoiling it. Wagging his head at me as he flailed the banjo, the old man grinned at me and hollered with what almost sounded like a square dance call, *"Put that camera down and dance, boy!"*

And I did.

130

The Jenkins family takes to dancing in the yard. What's a photographer to do? Make a quick shot and then join in as Snuffy commanded: "Put that camera down and dance, boy!"

YOUR TOWN; YOUR TURN

1. Pick a newspaper at random, your hometown newspaper, or the paper, where you work. Identify the lead photo on the front page. Is it a "grabber"? Is it the dominant graphic image on the page? How could it have been strengthened? Would color have made any difference. Would black and white have made any difference?

2. Look at that same photo. Do the photo and page appear harmonious? Can you tell if the page was laid out around the photo or was the photo made to work within the confines of the page layout? Does the photo appear oddly cropped?

3. Again, the same photo. If it relates to an accompanying story, was it taken by the reporter? If it wasn't, does it relate well to the story? How could the photographer have done a better job coordinating with the reporter in tying the photo to the story?

10

Emerging Technology: That's the Way We've Always Done It Here

COMMUNITY NEWSPAPERS AND EMERGING TECHNOLOGY

On a chilly January day in 1960 Bub the pressman was standing beside the thrumming Goss flatbed letterpress, its sound filling the room, indeed, permeating the whole building with the authority of an approaching World War II Sherman battle tank. Alex, his assistant, wanted to know what he thought of this new-fangled thing called "offset."

"Shoot," said Bub, spitting tobacco juice on the already begrimed and colorless ink-stained floor. "I don't know what it is, but they'll never get me to change." Then waving at the lumbering steel behemoth dominating the basement pressroom, he said with finality, "Besides, that's the way we've always done it here."

When Bub's newspaper went offset later that year, he was as good as his word. Refusing to learn the bold new emerging technology of photographic-based printing, Bub was relegated to an old press in the commercial printing shop where he puttered on until his retirement.

His rationale for not changing: *That's the way we've always done it here*, has been called the Last Eight Words of a Business.

CUTTING EDGE OR STEALTH EDGE?

Twenty years later a Big Three automaker would be fond of saying,

The way it was: In 1957 founder-owner-publisher Roy T. Cloud (in hat and vest) sheet-feeds printed pages of his Pleasant Hill, Mo., *Times* into the folder on the back of the Babcock flatbed press. The Cloud family sold the 2,000 circulation hot-type weekly in 1961 because of the coming of offset printing. In addition, the *Times'* old printer died and couldn't be replaced easily. (*Photo courtesy of Bill Cloud*)

"You either lead, follow, or get out of the way."

Communications futurists would have us believe that if we don't get on board the technological bandwagon, we'll end up like Bub—roadkill on the information highway.

But how heavily should a community newspaper invest in emerging technology? Should your paper be trailing edge? Leading edge, cutting edge, or stealth edge? Should it be on the edge at all?

The answer is: It depends.

Here are some of the factors that determine a community paper's need to embrace emerging tech:

- size and frequency of publication,
- scope of coverage,
- the competition,
- corporate vision and matching budget
- and, in the case of very small papers, who prints you and how?

EMERGING TECH: NOT NECESSARILY THE MAGIC BULLET

Ultimately, the publisher must ask himself: Why invest in the latest CD-ROM Bigothing ×4000 in the first place? What does it do for my paper?

In the case of offset in the '60s, the change that swept the community publishing business was so pervasive because offset papers *looked great* compared to the smudgy images we had been getting from the old hot-type presses. The investment in new technology was tangible: The paper flat out looked better—better than it was and better than the competition. Again, the bottom line is the reader and what they want.

And here's the good news: Because community newspapers are small, they can invest in new technology incrementally and not break the bank. The *Bugle* doesn't need to spend millions for a whole newsroom full of Bigo-things; it may need only one Lilothing.

For this very reason, 30 years ago the community newspapers quietly led the offset revolution in the publishing industry, while the large metro dailies have embraced it wholesale only after decades of competing with ter-rific-looking outlying and suburban community papers. For years, big-city newspaper management had maintained that replacing those immense stereotype presses would be just too expensive. Some people say the advent of *USA Today* in the early '80s changed those publishers' minds. But many community newspaper folk think it was another thing.

Community newspapers, with more forgiving deadlines, smaller over-head, tighter territories, more dedicated and loyal readers, can afford to look at emerging technology quite differently from the major big-city dailies which are always competing with television. First of all, remember, we're *not* competing with TV. Until they can air the equivalent of a 24-page broad-sheet of local news, we've got them beat cold. However, the biggies have to stay out there on the cutting edge of emerging technology if they hope to win back readers lost to TV. Hence the color revolution. Hence redesigns at pa-pers coast to coast. Frankly, they can put all the bows and trinkets they want to in their sky boxes, but until they catch the community journalism spirit and sell that concept to the entire staff, no technology known will stop their slide.

DESKTOP PUBLISHING: FORM FOLLOWS FUNCTION

In the last decade our business embraced another emerging technology before their counterparts in the big cities. Within the publishing industry, community newspapers adopted and popularized the use of the free-standing PCs, mainly the Macintosh desktop publishing systems.

When it came to computerization, community newspapers, with their intrinsically smaller economic base, turned to the free-standing PC out of need. Here was an affordable technology that didn't require a huge, complex and expensive mother computer and sophisticated network system. If you had one Mac, the right software and one printer, you could put out a paper. Pagination? No problem. You think that drove the big boys nuts? You bet. Little publications have sprung up like dandelions all over the country—right in the front yard of the big-city dailies—spunky alternative weeklies, gonzo little 'zines, arts and leisure tabs, newsletters of every ilk and walk.

It only stands to reason that community newspapers would latch on so quickly to this relatively inexpensive, simple and fun way to turn out type on paper. Both the technology (the Mac) and the product (community journalism) are user-friendly. It was a marriage made in heaven. Or at least Silicon Valley.

STAR WARS PHOTO EDITING, READY OR NOT

If you're a student of journalism and haven't been in the newsroom of even a middle-sized community daily lately, you're likely to be startled by what you find there today. In the last two years there has been a quiet but profound technological revolution that has thrust itself on all community newspapers subscribing to Associated Press's photo service.

Whether you call it the electronic picture desk, the electronic darkroom, digital image manipulation or digital photo editing, it's "Star Wars" photo editing, and it's here now—at a paper near you.

AP's conversion of their old analog land-line transmission system to digital satellite transmission in the early '90s has catapulted photographers, graphic designers, photo editors, systems managers, editors and publishers alike into the computer age, ready or not.

This new technology offers a myriad of time- and cost-saving advantages: It cuts the transmission time for a photo from eight minutes to 30 seconds; and it allows the photographs to be encoded, broken down, and reconstituted as images on a very special computer known as the Leafdesk Digital Darkroom.

Another very tangible advantage: The Leafdesk requires no new camera technology. You can use your old Nikons, Canons and Pentaxes just like always. So publishers don't have to go out and spring $16,500 for the new digital Kodak and AP NewsCamera 2000 (though if the publisher wishes to, the Leaf system can incorporate those images for even greater speed in delivering images).

Nor does the publisher have to buy a new wirephoto receiver. The photos coming in from AP still arrive on the old faithful laserphoto receiver (LPR), circa 1973 technology. Of course, optional, newer, faster receivers are on the market.

The Leafdesk, a keyboard and monitor which looks and behaves pleasingly like a Mac, is rented from AP and is fast becoming the only way to receive AP wirephotos. Indeed, they don't even call it that anymore. Now it's AP Photostream.

Publishers claim it is cost-effective because photographers no longer have to print color photos in the traditional "wet" darkroom. The Leafscan 35 negative scanner (Kodak, Nikon and Polaroid make them too) reads the color negative film directly into the Leafdesk.

Newspapers using this system either develop their own color negative film (Ektapress 400 and 1600 being the most popular, along with Fuji 400 and a new tight-grained 800) using small, automatic tank Jobo developers (about $1,500) or the larger, more versatile and expensive model by Wing-Lynch. Or, believe it or not, some papers take their film to WAL-MART's one-hour photo-processing.

The savings in photo paper quickly pays for the scanner, which the newspaper must buy. When the system was introduced in 1990, scanners were pricey. But with competition and time, the prices have plummeted. Now even the smallest daily can afford the Nikon Cool-Scan at under $2,000.

Here's how the system works. First, consider the source: AP Photostream, in-house photos, or photos coming in over modem or disk, the latter being still the most distant technology and as yet impractical for most community papers.

Photostream

The picture editor accesses the day's AP photos available by clicking on the day's menu, using a Mac-style mouse. She sees a screen of 12 images arranged in a grid, selects the ones she wants, and one by one, isolates them and edits each for density, contrast, brightness, tone, color, burning/dodging, cropping and size. In other words, everything the photographer used to do to make the print using an enlarger in the darkroom, the Leafdesk operator now does on computer.

Saving the final alteration, the Leafdesk operator sends the commands to the Laserphoto receiver or some other in-house printer, which prints the photo to be sent to the backshop for screening. Or, in more sophisticated set-ups, the Leafdesk operator hits the "print" command and the photo is automatically screened on an Autokon automated photocopy camera.

The Leafdesk shows its prowess in the case of color, breaking the photo down into prints for color separations and quickly producing cyan, magenta, yellow and black (CMYK) screenings. With Leafdesk technology, papers can have same-day color, where previously they had to go out-of-shop, pay roughly $100 per photo and wait two days for color separations. Hence, a savings of time and money with the Leafdesk.

In-House Photos

Staff photographers produce color negatives which are scanned by the negative scanner into the Leafdesk, where they can be called up on the monitor and edited as above. The scanner will also read color slides if needed, but photojournalists are finding color negative film to be more forgiving, and thus Kodak Ektapress has become the film of choice for the industry. The scanner also accepts black-and-white negatives, again saving time and darkroom printing costs. However, since the Leafdesk can scan color negs and convert them into B&W prints if needed, many papers are shooting only color film for the sake of uniformity in the field and simplicity in the darkroom.

Modem and Disk Sources

The photos come in either by disk or over the modem and are fed directly into the Leafdesk, where they are edited as above, representing a further savings in time and darkroom costs.

BOB GILKA WOULD BE PROUD

Twenty years ago *National Geographic's* venerable photo chief, Robert Gilka, was preaching the doctrine that "photographers should get out of the darkrooms and into the newsrooms." Ironically, it is the Leafdesk of the technologically roaring '90s that has forced that change.

In what's being called "the new newsroom," or "open newsroom," photographers are out there in the newsroom because that's where they have to be. The placement of the Leafdesk has forever altered the dynamics of the journalist's workplace. No longer are the so-called word people segregated by work areas from the picture people. The result is that the two have to talk to each other. Not surprisingly, this results in a better product and a happier staff.

And, because there is usually only one Leafdesk workstation per newsroom, someone has to be in charge. Just as a single new Mac in a previously non-Mac environment can cause a jealous uproar, a single Leafdesk can have an unsettling impact if there's not a strong editorial hand. So we now have a new job description in our lexicon: the Leafdesk Manager. At many papers this person is the former picture or photo editor, while at smaller papers the responsibility rests with the chief photographer.

It is his or her responsibility to manage the time and the photos for the various editors (lifestyle, sports, city, news, etc.) so they don't clash over the use of the facility. No longer can various editors wander over and finger through the dozens of AP photos methodically printed out by the old Laserphoto receiver. At many papers it's been a daunting task to convince older editors of the advantages of the Leaf system. At larger papers, where they have multiple Leaf workstations, this is not a problem.

NEW TECH, NEW PROBLEMS

The real demon in the box here is the computerized abuse of authentic news photos. Using the sophisticated Leaf technology and digital imaging manipulation (DIM, or computer-altered imaging) the computer operator can fundamentally alter the contents of any given picture, thus compromising the photo's veracity. Because present imaging technology has the capacity of altering images drastically (moving people around, interchanging body parts, excluding objects from the image entirely) this alarming trend raises questions of fundamental photojournalistic authenticity and credibility.

Community newspaper folk need to realize the depth and inherent dangers of the digital technology. At smaller papers, where visual decisions may rest with a single person who may not have to answer to anyone until the paper hits the streets, there's a real potential for someone abusing the new technology of digital imaging. While the Leaf technology is a fabulous deadline tool, it is also a Pandora's box. And the box has already been opened.

Across the top of every Leafdesk in the land, from the weekly *Bugle* to

the mighty *TIME* magazine, editors should tape a copy of the NPPA Statement on Manipulation of Photographs from the Code of Ethics. It reads in
part:

> As journalists we believe the guiding principle of our profession is accuracy; therefore,
> we believe it is wrong to alter the content of a photograph in any way that deceives the pub-
> lic ... altering the content of a photograph, in any degree, is a breach of the ethical standards
> recognized by the NPPA.

You could hardly have been an American during the summer of 1994
and not known about the *TIME* magazine cover with the computer-darkened
face of O.J. Simpson.

Whether they tried to justify it by calling it a "photo illustration" or a
"computer-altered photo-montage," to you and me as readers, it was a fake.

How'd they do that? Moreover, why'd they do that?

Both questions deserve in-depth answers. Practically since the inven-
tion of photography 150 years ago, dishonest operators have been abusing
the power of the camera. And sadly, from the outset the public has been de-
ceived.

Look at Roger Fenton's photographs from the Crimean War in the
1850s and you'd think it was a Sunday picnic in the park. He was commis-
sioned by Queen Victoria to make the war seem heroic and attractive so as
to spur enlistment back home.

How about one of Matthew Brady's photographers, Alexander Gard-
ner, who at Gettysburg made a photograph of a corpse and titled the photo
"Union Sharpshooter." Then for his own reasons, he dragged the poor fellow to another spot, took another photo, retitled this one "Rebel Sharpshooter" and sold it to the paper of the day, *Leslie's Illustrated.*

Later, in the tabloid era of the '20s, editors began cutting and pasting
photos together and passing them off as the real thing. One of the most
nauseating abuses was the cut-and-paste nonsense performed by the New
York *Evening Graphic* at the Rhinelander divorce trial. The paper's editors,
angry that their cameras were denied court access, concocted a fake trial
scene, and called it grandly a "composograph."

Now we're into the latter-day roaring '90s, and what those unscrupu-
lous cut-and-pasters of the yellow journalism days could do with scissors,
we can now do with a Mac and a mouse.

The technology was upon us in the '80s before we knew its ethical implications. Consider the seemingly benign example of *National Geographic*
magazine moving Egyptian pyramids around in a 1982 cover shot to make
a vertical out of a horizontal picture. What's wrong with that? It's art, the editors reasoned.

Consider the cover of the 1980s photo book "Day in the Life of America" in which the horizontal shot of a silhouetted cowboy, lone tree and crescent moon was condensed to fit the vertical cover layout. Anything wrong there?—other than the fact that the photographer who made the photo said he didn't recognize it when he saw the book?

In 1989 when *TV Guide* published a cover that depicted a newly svelte Oprah, nobody thought much about it—until it was later revealed that *TV Guide* had put Oprah's head on an older photo of Ann-Margret. *TV Guide* hoped nobody would notice. By then many of us realized we had a tiger by the tail.

Digital imaging technology allows a Leafdesk operator to not only print and crop in the traditional "wet" darkroom style, but also to fundamentally change and transmogrify anything about any photograph. It's so easy it's scary.

And it's also so technologically advanced that even the most sophisticated reader can't tell when a photo has been altered. We must rely on either the caption or the publication's integrity.

And sometimes all that fails. Covering the winter Olympics of 1994, the respected Long Island daily, *Newsday*, published a full-cover photograph that depicted Nancy Kerrigan and Tonya Harding skating together at Lillehammer the day *before* the event actually happened. The caption, which was dwarfed by the big color photo, shamelessly explained "Nancy ... and Tonya ... appear to skate together" and called the image a "*Newsday* composite illustration."

Understandably, everybody who cared anything about photojournalism integrity and ethics went ballistic.

And that gets us to *TIME* magazine's altering of O.J. Simpson's photo. The police mug shot was "computer enhanced," they call it—as if that makes everything OK—eyes and face darkened, stubble emphasized; the image out of focus and a dark, sinister pall thrown over the brooding face. Though the cover "photo illustration" was derived from the same police mug shot, it looked completely different from the version published by *Newsweek*. It boggles the mind that it never occurred to *TIME*'s computer artist or the managing editor that darkening the photo would be construed as racist.

The next week, even after a firestorm of protest from readers, the editors were unrepentant. In a letter almost as insensitive and infuriating as the doctored photo, they said they considered the cover an illustration, or "art," and as such that justified the darkening and altering.

No, they were wrong. AP and the National Press Photographers Association are clear on the guidelines. No tampering with news images. Nothing beyond what we've always been able to do in the wet darkroom: cropping, and minor adjustment of tones and contrast. No moving trees, no moving the moon, no moving a Diet Coke can. If you shot it like that, you run it like that. Period.

In the words of NPPA President Joe Traver of Buffalo:

> If the cover is an "illustration," it had better look like one. Great documentary photos derive their power ... from their content. Their power is in their truth. No one has the right to distort this truth. ... If a photo looks real and is used in a context where the viewer expects to see actual photos, then the photo had better be real.

That's it then. If a news photo isn't real then it's a lie. When photographers, artists or editors distort photos for the sake of a scoop, art, sales, layout—whatever reason—they are striking a death blow at the very heart of what makes authentic photojournalism so valuable.

If the media keep creating fantasy images where readers expect to see unfettered objectivity, our public will begin suspecting the integrity of every photograph they see. Once we've lost our credibility, we've put ourselves out of business.

Since the digital cat's already out of the bag, here are some suggested guidelines for community newspaper treatment of images:

If you're the publisher or editor, see that your key people get updated on the latest ethical considerations regarding the digital revolution. Your state press association, the NPPA and the Poynter Institute for Media Studies have excellent programs and workshops which are designed for professionals to be accessible and comprehensive. In short, get your people current. It may cost something, but the savings in grief will be immeasurable in the long run.

First, every community paper should craft, adopt and then publish its own statement on photojournalism ethics. Tell your readers your aim is accuracy, in both content and context. Tell them your paper stands for that accuracy and against visual deception.

Explain, explain, explain: Never knowingly deceive the reader. Don't assume the reader knows how a picture was made. If a long lens was used and the resulting image is highly compacted with distances condensed, explain how the picture was made. The same goes for extremely wide-angle shots with distorted distances as well. In both cases, when an image is not as it appeared in real life, it is the paper's duty now to put the photo in accurate context.

If you print a digitally altered or computer-enhanced image, tell your reader in plain English right there in the cutline. Geographically connect the photo with the explanation. Don't bury the explanation on another page. To do so is to deceive, because many readers have no idea how *we* think they should read a paper.

If you publish an "illustration," say it plainly and place that explanation right beside the art. And, it had better *look* like an illustration and not a news photo. If the image purports to be a truthful, documentary image, and it is not, then you have nowhere to hide when the truth comes out.

WHY FIX IT IF IT AIN'T BROKE?

What drives emerging tech in our business? And what is the catalyst for change? Sometimes it's the competition. You want to stay a jump ahead of them in how to you look, how effectively you serve your advertisers, and how smoothly the delivery system works. Anything that can help you keep that edge is worth looking at. Sometimes it's a corporate vision for the publication, as in the case of chain papers getting an upgrade. Clearly, if your paper is a daily subscribing to Associated Press's Photostream, the future has been thrust upon you. Your paper has no choice but to embrace the modern computerized digital photo editing system. In 1992 Pottsville (Pa.) *Republican* Editor Jim Kevlin observed, "The Leafdesk has become the industry standard in just nine months."

APPROPRIATE TECHNOLOGY

Hendersonville, N.C., *Times-News* Editor Joy Franklin says, "Unless you stay up with the technology, it's going to walk off and leave you." A *New York Times* paper, her publication tries to stay up with emerging technology but must wait in rotation for New York to approve other than system-wide modifications.

But at what point can a community paper afford to be less than trailing edge? Both Kevlin and Franklin's papers are 20,000 circ. dailies with lots of color and national-international news.

Here's the answer. There's sort of a hierarchy of high tech. If your paper is a small daily that generates all its own photos, and subscribes to AP but not Photostream, then you've probably got a satellite dish on your roof to get the stories, but there's no need to get Leaf technology. Instead, your paper might consider a Mac with Adobe Photoshop to do in-house color separations.

If your paper is a totally community-oriented newspaper and you carry no wire service copy, then investing in that technology wouldn't be worth it. Use your common sense. There's no point adding bells and whistles if they're not somehow improving the paper or making life better in the newsroom or backshop. High tech for high tech's sake is fine if you've got the money to throw around. But wise community publishers say the smart thing to do is to add *appropriate* technology. For some, that will be a Mac in the ad department, for others a full-blown Leaf system. For others, it might be the purchase of their first press.

If in doubt about where your paper should be headed in regard to emerging technology, call on the expertise of a community newspaper consultant. The knowledgeable outside opinion could save you thousands, as in the case of Jeff Byrd at the *Tryon Daily Bulletin* (see Chapter 18).

WHO PRINTS YA', BABY?

It's also a fact of this business that many smaller newspapers don't own their own press, requiring them to be printed at a nearby town. Usually, that press is located at a larger, more technologically sophisticated community daily newspaper. Many of these smaller nonpress papers have been forced to adopt new technology to suit their printers' needs. This was especially true in the offset revolution, and now we see nonpress newspapers being told by their printers to get ready to come to press with everything on disk or relayed by modem.

COMMUNITY JOURNALISM AND THE FUTURE OF PRINT

Whither the ink-on-paper newspaper industry? At this writing, large metro newspapers are scrambling to get "on-line," but it remains unclear if America is going to start taking its newspapers and magazines this way. For one thing, the service is expensive and impractical.

"So let me get this straight," said one observer. "For nine bucks a month you no longer have any phone service?" On-line computer services (America On-Line, CompuServe) tie up your phone line, and the only feasible alternative is to have two phone lines. Now ask yourself, how many of your readers can afford two separate phone lines? Just by dint of the economics alone, digitized newspapers and magazines on-line would seem to be the plaything of an upper middle class. Not exactly the demographics of our readership.

Going in another direction, futurists predict that the newspaper of tomorrow might be some sort of a free-standing, thin, silicon-based computer pad displaying stories and photos. They claim the days of the ink-on-paper newspaper are numbered.

Interactive community newspapers may be coming someday, just as fission energy may be practical someday. But for the foreseeable future, the smaller newspapers of this land can rest assured, in the words of *N'West Iowa REVIEW* publisher Peter W. Wagner, "I have seen the future—and it is print."

It's hard to imagine your average middle-class reader of your average small daily, weekly, semi- or triweekly calling up his *Bugle* on a computer. It may yet happen, but at least for some years to come, it's a safe bet that people closer to the earth will want to have something physical to *hold* in their hands, to look at in their leisure, to roll up, fold up, take anywhere, cut out, and finally, to keep.

How is Mom going to make a clipping of Jimmy's winning basket at the Mighty Mites game when all she's got is something flickering on a screen? What about birth announcements and obituaries clipped and placed lovingly in the family Bible?

It is that sort of solid, tactile connection with reality that will keep print alive in community journalism longer. When newspapers start converting from print to something like hand-held personal digital assistants in earnest, we'll see it happening at the big metro papers first, where they'll be using the changes to their advantage, enabling them to compete directly with TV.

Community newspapers with their own presses will have the luxury of waiting and then choosing which printing technologies they want to adopt, while letting the big guys take the risks and get the bugs out of the emerging technology.

A REPORTER'S NOTES FROM THE STEALTH EDGE

> Newspapers—remember them? They're where people used to get their infotainment before CNN, Hard Copy and the Letterman Top 10 list. Kids don't read them much anymore; newspapers are nostalgia items for the geriatric Gutenberg generation.
> —Richard Corliss
> *TIME* magazine, March 21, 1994

The writer can be forgiven for that curmudgeonly swipe; anyway, coming from *TIME,* one supposes there is a certain amount of irreverent, intrafamilial humor in that sassy pronouncement.

Nevertheless, it is too early to read the eulogy for the newspaper business. After attending the 1994 America East Newspaper Operations and Technology Conference in Hershey, Pa., I'd say print is alive and well.

And furthermore, that the much heralded demise of the American newspaper reminds me of Mark Twain's premature obituary. Like Twain, I hear newspaper folk saying with a wry grin, in Twain's words: "The reports of my death are greatly exaggerated."

Send back the flowers, boys. There's life in that old codger yet.

Here's what I observed during the two days of workshops, networking with publishers, editors, reporters, photographers and vendors: that American newspapers know they're in trouble, that readership is down, ad lineage is down, that TV is siphoning off young readers, the recession hurt us deeply—but that's old news.

The *new* news is that emerging technology has re-energized the American newspaper, that emerging technology has and is making "us" competitive with the T-word—and in so doing, we've got a new lease on life.

Multimedia, high tech, Star Wars—call it what you will—in a word, the way to the future is fully integrated computer systems in production, meaning digital everything: reporters with powerbooks, fax modems and cellular phones; shooters with digital cameras that can turn a photo around in seven minutes; laptop-carrying ad reps with computerized marketing plans based on databases and site-specific demographics. And finally, newspapers will survive as we know them because we're going to learn to "zone down to the doorstep," says media futures expert David Cole, providing "targeted, tailored newspapers that will beat the direct mail bogeyman."

The "New Newspapers," ones with fully integrated systems, will be the papers which survive and flourish, according to Cole. His admonition: "You have to be pro-active. Go out and look for this stuff ... " Or else, he warns, "We will cede our business to Bell Atlantic, TCI or the broadcasters."

Television, a word spoken little at this conference, hovered like a malevolent cloud in the collective subconscious at America East. Chuck Blevins, the man who successfully masterminded Gannett through the production nightmare of setting up *USA Today* in 1982, said that one way to beat television is to do something they can't. Newspapers have to become more customer driven, he said, doing "bigger things in smaller areas, pinpointing subscriber interests and becoming highly segmented."

And finally, getting the product out quicker will make newspapers more competitive. New production technology will help drive that speed. Said Cole, "Time is the enemy of newspapers."

Speaking of speed ...

EMERGING TECHNOLOGY AND PHOTOJOURNALISM

Nowhere in print journalism has change come so swiftly and profoundly than in the area of photography. Digital photography, which requires no film, no paper, no chemicals, is here in a big way.

Photographers who try to ignore this sweeping change soon will be looked upon as the photo-troglodytes of the '60s who wouldn't give up their 4×5 Speed Graphics when 35 mm cameras blitzed the scene.

Leading the workshop on digital photojournalism, Jim MacMillan of the *Philadelphia Daily News* said electronic photography will be one of the things that helps stop the so-called "impending extinction of the American newspaper." He pointed to the Oscars-night coverage in which AP was able to transmit a photo of Spielberg accepting his Oscar. The photo was shot about 1 a.m. on the new AP/Kodak NewsCamera 2000 and transmitted in only minutes, allowing papers everywhere to make deadline with a front-page, high-quality color shot.

The NewsCamera 2000, unveiled by Kodak and AP on Feb. 8, 1994, has implications as far-reaching as the stunning introduction of the Leafdesk four years ago. There are only 10 to 12 NC 2000s out there right now being used by AP photographers, but orders are being taken from other subscribing papers (for $16,500) and in the space of nine months, the NC 2000 will be changing the face of American journalism, making us "frankly competitive with TV," said one AP photographer with whom I spoke.

According to PDN shooter MacMillan, 1994 will be remembered as the year American photojournalism really went digital. MacMillan, who concedes digital at first was "terrifying for a lot of photographers," is a whole-hearted convert now. The new system, whether it's all digital or still film-based, allows the photographer to spend more time in the street and less time in the darkroom. In addition, digital, which is expensive up front, pays for itself in the long run because it doesn't require film, paper and chemicals.

Early prototypes were heavy, clunky and required too much wiring and support equipment. But now, the latest model NC 2000 and AP PhotoLynx have solved much of those problems.

Philosophically, MacMillan observed that the digital learning curve lasted a long time. He says, "For about two years we were so wrapped up in the conversion to digital that we didn't talk about composition or content; all we were talking about was pixels and resolution ... now, we're getting back to it, and I for one am glad."

MacMillan almost got nostalgic when he said, sighing, "I miss printing ... but it's (digital) been a good trade-off." He conceded he hadn't been in a traditional "wet" darkroom in two years. Film that the PDN shoots is processed entirely by a dry-to-dry automatic processor.

Still, he notes, keeping up with the leading edge is all but impossible. Photographers are expected to stay current, and that's not easy. "From a shooter's perspective, now you're expected to be at home with Mission Control. But every time I go out, (on a shoot) it seems like I'm carrying something new and different." Risk taking and on-the-job training are an everyday thing for MacMillan. "You've got to be willing to crash and burn every once in a while … it's all worth it," he says.

Still, we shouldn't be tempted to abuse our privileges. Photoshop is a very powerful tool, and MacMillan warns photographers of the dangers of digital imaging manipulation: moving heads to different bodies, moving the Pyramids, erasing a Coke can. "We've always allowed for a certain degree of correction, burning and dodging and cropping; but this is pretty scary." MacMillan's rule: Don't change anything fundamental to how the photo was shot.

AP's product manager for editorial imaging, Jim Gerberich (who was part of the team responsible for developing the NC 2000), traced the development of digital photojournalism from the first shot transmitted at the 1988 George Bush inauguration with a fairly primitive low-resolution prototype that still beats film by 30 to 45 minutes, to the work done in the '92 election providing newsmagazines and newspapers with quick digital color from the presidential debates and Clinton's inauguration. However, color quality, particularly in the shadow detail and highlights, was not even close to film-based prints.

And so AP was not happy with the Kodak DCS 100 or 200, and set about to build an entirely new camera. The result was a Nikon N-90 mated to a Kodak-built system designed to AP specs. It can shoot two frames a second, or a six-shot burst every two seconds. With an effective ASA of 200 to 1600, it can hold up to 75 images on a disk or MobileMax hard drive. Also, the NC 2000 records on the spot dictated caption information with a microphone on the camera's back, allowing a shooter to keep working in the field, especially if he uses the "sneaker network"—a runner who can transmit his disk images while the photographer loads another disk and keeps shooting, for instance at a Super Bowl. In addition, you can shoot 700 images before recharging is needed. But in the field, a Quantum battery pack can solve that problem.

"The quality is completely up to speed," says Jim MacMillan, "good enough for newspaper reproduction." As to magazine-quality work, he notes, "We're on the way. We're not quite there, but for *newspapers*, we're there."

HIGH TECH—COMMUNITY SPIN

What's so new about what we're going to be shooting and recording with our amazing new equipment? We're still going to be dealing with living, breathing flesh and blood people. Young journalists enamored of All the Very Latest should consider Virginia Wesleyan College President William T. Greer's approach to the future.

He calls it "high tech with heart."

No computerized notepad or camera is going to help you get your foot in the door with prime sources if they don't like you as a person. In community journalism, if we lose sight that we are in the people business, then all the computers in the world won't save us. It's one thing to have Star Wars tools, but the reporter-photographer still has to have soul and an eye with heart behind that disk-camera or video "still" Nikon or liquid crystal notepad.

This, the human element, must still be modeled by great editors and teachers.

YOUR TOWN; YOUR TURN

1. Look in your own newsroom and backshop and catalog the technology, old and new.

2. How has the newest piece of equipment altered the dynamics of your workplace?

3. In what direction is your paper moving with regard to emerging tech. Ask your publisher what s/he thinks about the future of print.

4. Is your paper considering alternatives to ink-on-paper? If so, what? And what will be gained? What will be lost?

In the community setting, where high school major sports tend to dominate, it's easy to overlook the lesser sports that occur off the beaten
track. If you're beginning to feel that your sports coverage is becoming
too repetitious, you might look elsewhere too.

11

Community Sports:
It's Only a Game, Right?

OUT AT HOME

The venue was not exactly what Joe, the new photographer at the *News,* had had in mind. Not exactly Camden Yards, Fenway Park, Wrigley Field or Yankee Stadium.

The grass in center field at the Sandy Run School baseball field was over ankle deep. The scorekeeper sat on a folding metal chair using a collapsible card table to keep track of the game.

There were no lights. No dugout. No concessions. The field could only be described as marginal for sandlot. The bleachers, if you could call them that, consisted of a grassy hillside, now dotted with parents on quilts and blankets, cheering for a game between the Sandy Run Pirates and the Pleasant Gardens Phillies.

Joe was there on his first assignment with the *News* after graduating from a major university school of communications. He'd even won a Hearst Award his senior year. He was good. He knew it. His professors knew it. The Hearst people knew it. So why was he here today shooting Little League? Didn't they know who he was? And the final insult—his editor even expected him to write the game story. Imagine!

Joe wasn't at all convinced he'd done the right thing settling for this first job with this 8,000 circulation biweekly. He told himself it was the best

Great photos are everywhere, even at a "rural gig."

job he could find at the time. Joe figured he'd put in his time doing what he called "a rural gig," and make his jump as soon as possible to a big, impressive-sounding metro daily. Then he could forget he'd done time in Podunk, U.S.A.

Meanwhile, the game had started. The first batter had walked and was now attempting to steal second. Joe, bored already, watched with his state-of-the-art Nikon F-4 and 300 mm 2.8 lens hanging listlessly around his neck, as the runner arrived safely at second—only to have the looping throw from the catcher strike the boy directly on the top of the head and bounce off comically.

Joe had to keep from laughing out loud as he thought to himself,

152

Most times the sports feature photos you'll find at the community level are completely unique. Here, a Little League scorekeeper protects himself from a passing summer shower.

"These kids don't even know how to play baseball. If I was at a *real* ballgame, I could get some great sports shots."

Soon, a summer shower passed over the little ballpark, halting the game for the duration of the brief downpour, which prompted the scorekeeper to find shelter beneath the card table as he phoned the Rec Department to tell them the game was temporarily delayed. Joe was too busy packing up his cameras to notice. "Man! What a waste of my time," he grumbled to himself as he headed for his car.

WORK WHERE YOU WORK

The ancients have a wise saying that goes something like this: "Eat when you eat; breathe when you breathe; die when you die." It means life is now, in the present, not in the recalled past or the imagined future. You might even paraphrase that axiom to apply to community journalism: "Work where you work."

Right before his very eyes Joe had the makings of great human interest photos and an entertaining, worthwhile story. But his own attitude blinded him just as surely as if he had his personal lens cap on. And so long as that "badittude" persists, no fancy equipment made by Nikon, Canon or anyone else could have opened his vision to the value of sports coverage on the community journalism level.

What a waste indeed.

We'll say it once more: Before you go to *Sports Illustrated* or the *Sporting News,* you've got to show your stuff at the Butler *Eagle* or the Cary *News*—"little" papers you may think no one has ever heard of. But ask any great reporter or photographer with *SI* and they'll tell you they paid their dues and earned their stripes covering community sports.

So—heads up! In this journalistic ballpark you will be expected to be a utility infielder—able to hit, run, and field at many positions. In other words, the team needs a generalist. The young reporter or photographer on the community journalism scene will find out one of the major differences between the community paper and our big-city cousins on his/her first assignment.

It may happen when the managing editor sends you to your first high school game and expects you to take photos as well. Or if you're a shooter, they'll expects you to bring back a game story along with your photos. What may boggle and infuriate you is that the people at the paper will act as if this is normal.

So hear it right now. It is normal.

It makes no difference if the venue is an American Legion park in Altoona, Pa., or Camden Yards; the photographer must still capture peak action.

WHY IT'S IMPORTANT

Few things can ignite, divide, excite or unite a community more than the issues surrounding church, school and local sports.

And perhaps nowhere is the reciprocal relationship between the paper and the community more strongly evident than in the arena of sports. This is because sports coverage on the community level is so personal and immediate. It reaches into households that otherwise might not be touched by the paper.

Ken Byerly, a longtime community newspaper publisher and former professor, used to be fond of saying that successful newspapering had everything to do with printing lots of names and faces. He even went so far as to advocate the use of photos of large groups of people staring into the camera. "Trees full of owls," he jokingly called them. But there was a publisher's shrewd judgment behind this practice. To Byerly's way of thinking, for every name or face in his paper, there'd be at least eight people who that impacted directly—mom, dad, sisters and brothers, grandparents, aunts and uncles—not to mention friends.

Community sports coverage affords the paper a unique opportunity to get ample names and faces in the paper. And the more people in the paper, the more personal and vital the paper is to the community.

Think about your own childhood scrapbook. If you were raised in a small town with a community paper, you should have clips of yourself as a kid growing up, photos of you winning a Cub Scout birdhouse-building contest, of you getting an award in high school for civics, and surely a picture of you and your Little League team. Think about how you felt when you saw your picture in the paper for the first time, and you'll see that old Ken Byerly was right on target.

Your newspaper's mission statement should be to cover everything in your neighborhood—from Little League to area civic and church league teams to high school and college sports. This sort of highly inclusive community sports coverage provides "points of entry" for the community, and ultimately translates into more papers sold, which, can be only a win-win situation for everyone.

IT JUST TAKES COMMITMENT, COMMITMENT, COMMITMENT

Great local sports coverage can and should be one of your paper's most positive strengths. It doesn't even take particularly gifted writing or photography; it just takes a commitment to comprehensive, exhaustive and consistent coverage.

This is your turf. Nobody should be beating you here. TV can't give the Friday night high school football game much more than a 20-second blip on the 11 p.m. news. You should be running circles around the big-city dailies (if they chose to cover that high school game) because you've got fewer schools to cover. Plus, big-city shooters typically have to leave after the first quarter because of their assignment load and stringent deadlines.

You, on the other hand, don't have to leave after the first quarter like TV and big-city photographers who have five other games to cover and a deadline that night. You can stay for the whole game and get the complete story with all its subtleties and personal nuances. You, because you are known and trusted, can wander around behind the bench, and go to halftime locker rooms and post-game coaches' offices to get the details of the story. If you have friends working at big papers, they will tell you, that is a great luxury for which they envy you mightily. Imagine that; they envy you.

Then, after you've taken the necessary time to get the story and pictures, the great community paper can give them all the space they need and deserve. So what if the Nitwitness News scoops you on the score. When your paper comes out, you can give the story 30 inches and a slew of photos. And remember: Somebody's mama will be clipping that game story and sticking it between the pages of the family scrapbook, dictionary or even the Bible.

BALANCE, TONE AND EMPHASIS

The local junior college soccer team was getting beaten very badly by a clearly superior visiting team. Suddenly, the home team's Coach Don Scarborough leapt off the bench and began racing up and down the sidelines, cupping his hands over his mouth and shouting at each of his players—first one and then the other:

"George! I *believe* in you!"

"The good thing about community journalism is that it gives people something they can't get anywhere else—names and faces ... ," says Summerville (S.C.) editor Bill Collins. This swim meet action photo doubtless got clipped for some proud parent's scrapbook. Or maybe it stayed on the fridge door until it turned yellow. That would be the highest compliment we could receive.

"Billy! I *believe* in you!"

"David! I *believe* in you!"

Each individual affirmation floated faintly but distinctly across the field, as intimate and personal as a sweet memory.

The fans in the bleachers on the opposite side of the field couldn't help but hear Coach Don's rallying call to his players, and many were moved. It wasn't grandstanding; it wasn't intended for the crowd to hear; it wasn't a ploy or a gimmick; the coach meant it.

The home team lost anyway, but in the long run the score didn't matter. After the numbers would be forgotten, the unconditional testimony of the coach would be remembered and live on. Coach Don had put things in perspective—win or lose, he believed in his boys.

If a community newspaper has a mission statement for sports coverage, this is it. The underlying motivation, tone and perspective of the paper should be predominately a positive, benevolent, supportive voice for the efforts of local sports participants.

Put-down coverage of area teams, regardless of how inspired the writing is, can only result in justifiable community outrage. Does the depiction of a weeping high school athlete, in an unguarded moment after a major loss, serve the public's right to know?

On the other hand, solid yet positive coverage can benefit both the community and the paper in many ways. For one, the paper has a real chance to help build community pride. But maybe even more importantly, a paper can help teach undergirding core values that can help young athletes throughout life—values such as the sanctity of personkind and the intrinsic worth of participating—not so much winning at all costs. Coach Don used to tell his teams (some of which were extremely successful) that "more human growth occurs, and you learn more ultimately in defeat than you do from victory."

In sports especially, our American society tends to reward only winning. How the media handles losing is fundamentally formative for our youth. When we subject kids to the false paradigm of winning at all costs, a very destructive set of dynamics can be set in motion, and people become secondary to winning. Consider the two true scenarios from a community newspaper reporter's notebook:

The Little League coach watched as the opposition's batter hit a fly ball to the left fielder, who happened to be the coach's son. The little boy dropped the ball. The coach, in a towering rage, shrieked like a madman at his son, the left fielder. Everybody in the stands heard him bellow: "WHAT'S WRONG WITH YOU?"

At a Special Olympics 100-meter-run competition there were six contestants. When the race was over, the last runner cavorted from the field shouting gleefully, "I came in *sixth*! I came in *sixth*!"

Which one makes you want to lose your lunch and which one makes you want to cheer? Which one is constructive and which one is destructive? We are not in the business of tearing people down for the sake of clip contests and our own advancement, but building community through balanced, fair and positive coverage.

This does not mean you have to sell out when writing community sports, that everything has to be, in the words of media observer L.K. Redmond, "all sunshine, Care Bears and rainbows," or that you must be a shill or a flack for local teams. It does mean that the emphasis is different from that at the major metro daily; in a word—it's personal.

The personal approach means you apply this yardstick to every judgment call: How would I feel about this story or picture if it were about me, my kid, someone in my family, my best friend?

Our approach toward sports means we have to be more concerned, conscientious, precise, discerning and balanced. In short, just because they play sports doesn't mean we can chew people up and spit them out for the sake of a great story or picture. And yes, it does make it harder—especially when your home team loses badly.

There's a fine line between balanced reporting and giddy boosterism. The rule of thumb: You should know it when you see it.

Consider the lead from one community newspaper reporter, who, after his home team took a drubbing, wrote this euphemism: "It's possible that the 60-0 loss to South Point was a blessing in disguise for the East High Cavaliers."

If it sounds more like shameless PR than reporting, then you've probably crossed the line.

CRITICAL OR NOT? HOW MUCH TO SAY?

How judgmental or critical should community sports coverage be? A tried-and-true yardstick: The higher up the ladder of sports hierarchy, from T-Ball to NFL, the more critical a paper can be. Once a sporting event gets into the professional arena, then media scrutiny is more appropriate, the rationale is that people being paid to play must expect to be held accountable for their performance. A grayer area is how to handle coverage of college players on athletic scholarships. Are they not receiving remuneration for their services? The generally accepted practice is: The bigger the school, the more intense the coverage. But even here, the community paper should exercise judgment.

When in doubt, better to err on the side of restraint. Especially in the area of nonprofessional sports coverage. Remember, the kid you blast in the paper on Wednesday may be bagging your groceries that weekend. Could you look him or her in the eye?

By this set of guidelines, critical, judgmental coverage of individuals from the high school level on down is off-limits. At the extreme end of the spectrum, some community papers have an iron-clad "my town right or wrong" policy that will strike some energetic young sports reporters as unnecessarily restrictive.

However, you can tell the truth and give a fair and balanced account of the event without reducing to roadkill the hapless kid who dropped the pass. The key here is balance. Of course this isn't easy because on the surface sports seems to be about winning and losing. Amateurs tend always to lead with the score. But the seasoned community sports reporter is wise to search for other angles and de-emphasize the culpability of a single young athlete. Pointing a journalistic finger after the fact can only be destructive for athletes at that age and stage. For one thing, print is so permanent. Besides, overly critical coverage can make the paper look insensitive and even mean-spirited.

If there's to be a critical voice, which is appropriate, it should be one of authority, and that's the coach's, not the reporter's.

The high schooler at the town meeting (Chapter 14) is quite justified in asking the editor why the paper chose to run a photo of a classmate who had fallen on the final leg of the women's high school 4×100 race. The slip had cost the home team the state championship. Yes, the news had to be reported, the young man realized, but did the paper have to publish a large photo depicting the fallen runner in her anguish and shame? No, of course not. But someone at the paper had decided the photo was "too good" to not use.

So-called great newspapering, at the expense of human beings, is anti-ethical to what capital-C Community journalism is about. There is a way of telling the track story, but with compassion and empathy. Otherwise, we come off like the ghoulish voyeurs that media critics claim we are.

ABOUT TRUST AND A JUDGMENT CALL

Lucy was on assignment for her local paper covering her town's small-college track team as they participated in the national cross-country championship. Her paper had sent her all the way across the country for this event because the team was favored to win.

Instead, they came in a distant fourth—which to this team was like finishing dead last. The runners were humiliated and heartbroken, and at the end of the race, Lucy found herself the only reporter-photographer in the company of her team, as the young men collapsed on the grass in exhaustion and grief, weeping openly.

"What a great shot!" Lucy thought to herself. "Guys lying all over the ground crying! And it's a scoop! I'll sell it to AP! I'll be famous!"

Just then, the words of her community journalism instructor came back to her.

Some of your greatest pictures will be the ones you don't take.

She hadn't understood that enigmatic quote in the college classroom. But now she got it.

"Click," she told herself silently with an inward, ironic grin, before going over to comfort one of the runners.

Instead of becoming just another invasive, insensitive reporter/photographer getting in people's faces, she took all the energy of that highly charged scene and channeled it into a compassionate, thorough and thoughtful story, which earned her the respect, gratitude and trust of the team and the coach.

The following year when that same college team hosted and won the national championship, Lucy was right there in the thick of it, and then she got the exclusive story and pictures of a lifetime.

FAVORITISM AND WHO'S ON FIRST

If you've got multiple teams, and especially schools, which are intense rivals within your coverage area, how do you handle fair and balanced coverage, yet with the personal approach?

One upstart community newspaper with three rival high schools in its county solved the problem (and boggled the competition paper) by assigning one editor to each school and giving each school a full page of sports every week. No more. No less. It was a massive amount of coverage. People were bowled over; they'd never seen anything like it. And yet, after the newness of it wore off, they watched jealously to see that the other schools weren't getting more space. The paper even rotated the page order of the three schools' sports pages to prevent any claims of unfair emphasis and favoritism.

The equation "Rapport = Access = Success" is particularly true in the area of sports coverage. Master teacher and author Michael C.L. Thompson says success is a function of accretion. On the sports beat that would mean the same editor, reporter or photographer covering the same sports area, team, or beat. Coaches, players and parents, who see the same reporter week in and week out, get to know that reporter on a deeper, more personal level, and are certain to give him/her stories, angles, tips and photos that a hit-and-run itinerant sports reporter will find continually elusive.

ASSUMING YOU'VE GOT ACCESS MEANS TROUBLE

Not being known can be dangerous. Most community journalists rarely find themselves in the "pack journalism" situation, and are stunned by the impersonality when they do get caught in such a dehumanizing scenario:

The weekly newspaper sports editor/photographer secured a position in the back of the official pace truck for the prestigious Maggie Valley Moonlight Race, a grueling five-mile race that attracted world-class runners to the little mountain town each August.

Feeling pretty smug to be shoulder to shoulder with shooters from *SI* and *Runners World*, the community journalist took notes and pictures as the pace truck rolled along just ahead of the four lead runners—all world-class, potential Olympic runners.

Then, about 100 yards from the finish line, the truck pulled over and all the photographers were ordered out of the truck. Of course, they all wanted the finish line picture, and so everybody scrambled out and started sprinting for the finish line, arriving there just ahead of the runners.

What happened next would afterward remind the journalists of their early college days covering civil rights, anti-war demonstrations and campus riots—because the next thing they knew, the photographers were being grabbed from behind and wrestled to the ground by overzealous race marshals. One photographer got his shot off while being forcibly restrained—and then came up swinging at his assailant—until he realized the race marshal holding him down was about the size of a Mack truck.

Lesson: The bigger the sporting event, the more you should make sure you have iron-clad sideline access. Then pick your position and guard it like a junkyard dog.

TIPS FOR THE COMMUNITY SPORTS JOURNALIST

• If you're a newcomer to sports reporting, learn as much about each

As the winner hits the electronic tape, an overzealous race marshal tells the press to get back. The author shot this photo while being physically restrained. Not much fun. You can get hurt trying to take photos where you don't have proper access. Get your press credentials in order well in advance of shooting any major event.

sport before you attempt to cover an actual game. To do otherwise would be about as foolhardy as walking into a county commissioners' meeting without knowing the local politics, the names or the issues.

• If you have a college or university in your neighborhood, their SID (sports information director) should be feeding you with stories, photos and ideas. The trick here on a low budget is how to look different from the handouts and the competition: localize, personalize, visualize.

• Because they are often the major sports venue in many communities, high schools usually receive major attention from community papers. Popular sports vary from region to region. Some places it's football, some places it's wrestling, other places it's basketball. Whatever—your paper ought to be out-hustling everyone else for the story, the local angle, the color piece, the personality portrait, the athlete of the week, the play of the week, the scholar-athlete of the week, the coach's talk story, the pre-game and post-game stories, as well as every sort of human interest sidebar you can create.

• If one of your town's teams goes big time, your paper ought to go ballistic right along with the fans. Here's a unique opportunity for the community paper to outshine everyone else, regardless of publication frequency. When one community's Little League All-Stars went to the nationals, the innovative semiweekly paper sent the sports editor halfway across the country to get the story and pictures. The resulting double truck in the next paper created immense community goodwill, high reader interest and record single-copy sales. In addition, the exhaustive coverage stunned the competition which hadn't even bothered to send a reporter.

• To perform at their best, the athletes we cover have to get psyched up for each game. If them—why not us as well? The best sports reporters/photographers get pumped for each game. Everyone has his or her own method. There's one reporter who prior to each game does push ups in the press box. The more simple, less physical method is to get to the ballpark early and soak in the atmosphere to get you in the mood.

• "Luck is the residue of design," said Branch Rickey, manager of the then Brooklyn Dodgers. With apologies to the Boy Scouts, that means "Be Prepared." Before the game, get a team roster from the game program. Underline the numbers of key players. Take extra pens. Can you work in the rain? Carry a plastic grocery bag for your cameras, in case. Do you have your duct tape?

• Take copious notes. In sports as in any other reporting, you live or die by your notes. If you're shooting and reporting, shoot the play, then write what you saw on a reporter's notepad you keep stuffed in your belt. You'll soon develop your own personal shorthand. "45 OLT 4/50" means number 45 went off left tackle for four yards to the 50-yard line.

• Or better yet, train a volunteer high school kid to take the play-by-play for you. Many aspiring young journalists will be only too happy to help you for free—and for the experience and the thrill of being close to the action on the sidelines. It's a great deal for both of you.

• Want to increase your paper's sports coverage but can't afford another reporter? Form a network of community sports correspondents and stringers to feed your paper results and box scores. Enlist coaches, parents, wives, husbands. At the end of the year, take them to the Steak House. Or give them a free subscription.

• Think divergently. You don't always have to do it the same old way. One young sports editor, facing yet another pre-season high school football story, chose to take the George Plimpton approach. The journalist, who had never played a day of high school football in his life, convinced the local high school football coach to let him dress out and practice with the team for a couple of days. After one of the paper's photographers showed up to doc-

Not every editor should try this: see what football is like by dressing out for pre-season training in the August heat. The George Plimpton approach is good PR for the paper, but it can also be more work than you ever bargained for. (*Photo by Ron Paris*)

ument the nonsense, the resulting first-person story, "Pssst, the Linebacker is the Sports Editor," ran as a full-page spread, creating tremendous good will and community response, as well as winning first place in the state press association's feature-writing contest.

• Don't let the competition get you down. One weekly paper had its photos of the Friday night high school football games ready late that same night, but with a traditional Wednesday publication date found itself regularly scooped by the competition, a triweekly that came out on Mon.-Wed.-Fri. To get the jump, the weekly sports editor decided he wouldn't wait until Wednesday to show his best stuff. He found a local drug store owner who was willing to exhibit, in his main street store front, the paper's photos from the previous night's game. It turned into a win-win situation. The drug store owner was delighted by the increased business the pictures generated, the high school kids loved it, and the paper created a great public relations coup while confounding the competition.

YOUR TOWN; YOUR TURN

1. Rate your paper on its local sports coverage. What are its strong points? How could it improve?

2. Did your hometown paper cover your youth sports when you were a kid? Cite examples, good or bad.

3. Within your newspaper's coverage area are there high schools which are sports rivals? How does your paper attempt to balance its coverage?

12

It Used To Be Called
The Women's Page

VITAL INGREDIENTS

So, you're thinking of starting a community paper, or buying one, or taking one over. You go over your inventory of expertise and equipment: business manager, ad reps, news editor, reporters, computers, cameras, a press or someone to print the paper ... what else?

But wait, your paper is missing a vital ingredient. Without one of these you might as well not even turn on the press.

You need a Virginia.

Forgive the first person, but it would be impossible to talk about the growth, development and success of any community paper with which I've ever been involved—without saying up front that the old-fashioned "women's editor" can make all the difference.

When my partners and I started my first paper in 1969, we were blessed by great kind fortune to have secured the services of Virginia Rucker, the former "society editor" of our competition, the cross-town Forest City, N.C., *Courier*. I was a mere 24, and Virginia, at 55, seemed to me a virtual ancient. Looking at the situation, 25 years later, I can only imagine what she thought of the still wet-behind-the-ears kid trying desperately to act like a co-editor.

Virginia never let on. She gently guided me, celebrated my little creative triumphs, discussed spelling and grammar in a nonjudgmental fashion, and shared in the paper's dynamic growth. I can see now that much of the

Former "society editor" Virginia Rucker is flanked by (left to right) business manager Bill Blair, the author, and co-editor Ron Paris after a major sweep of the state press association contest. Twenty-five years later, Virginia is still at the paper which evolved into the *Daily Courier*. (*Photo by Maggie Lauterer*)

reason for *THIS WEEK*'s success was due to this wise woman's fine touch. Her grace under pressure provided us all with the lesson of her example. In short, she brought continuity and class to our paper. By the sheer dint of good work over time, she endeared herself—and by extension, the paper— to the community.

Twenty-five years later, she's still at that old golden oak desk, pecking away at a typewriter (never a computer) with that ever-present and never-ending sheaf of AP paper feeding up from a box on the floor. To my eye, Virginia doesn't look a day older than she did in March of 1969. The only thing different is that she's got the current Atlanta Braves poster and season schedule tacked to the wall behind her. Though *THIS WEEK* is now the *Daily Courier*, and Virginia is now called an associate editor, the old society editor is a die-hard Braves fan.

BUT THIS IS THE '90s, ISN'T IT?

You'll find places in these United States where they still call her that— the women's editor, or the society editor (as if men aren't members of that august body), and the page might be called something anachronistic such as the "Distaff Side."

Somewhere along in the '70s, most papers caught up with society and retooled these pages or sections under thinly-disguised monikers, such as "Lifestyle," "Style" or "Family."

Stories on weddings, engagements, anniversaries, fashion, child raising, women's health, home, food and cooking used to be the staple in an age that seems quaint and sexist to us now. While that lineup may still be true at many newspapers, others have expanded the vision to include stories on societal trends, the changing role of the sexes in general and women in particular, and issues in family life such as child abuse, father absenteeism, and issues of aging and health care.

Example: Virginia Rucker did a series of stories and photos depicting how local elderly on fixed incomes in a modest retirement community had gone about making their homes reflect their individual tastes and values. The overall effect of the series convincingly showed readers that they could do quite a lot at a minimal expenditure using mostly imagination and flair.

Also, you'll still find papers which haven't figured out what to do with community arts coverage, and so by default have given this beat to the "women's page," because historically manly men weren't supposed to be sensitive and artistic; that was a girl thing. So that coverage traditionally was relegated to women's editors. It wasn't until the late '60s that many community newspapers woke up to the silly imbalance. The resulting expansion of coverage has changed the face of community newspapers. However, weddings, club news, engagements and "society" still need and deserve coverage in community newspapers.

So how did the women's movement affect community journalism?

Ask Virginia. She's been in the business for 50 years.

OTHER VOICES; OTHER NEWSROOMS

When she started at the old Forest City Courier *in March of 1945, it wasn't even called "Women's News." Her page was called "Society."*

Before It Was Women's News It Was Society

By Virginia Rucker

Large papers didn't use all the stuff (I use the word advisedly) that I did: circle meetings, bridge club meetings, and personals—I phoned various women I knew and they told me of people from their neighborhood, or their relatives, who had been on trips—even to Charlotte or Spartanburg (30 to 50 miles away). A trip abroad was outstanding.

169

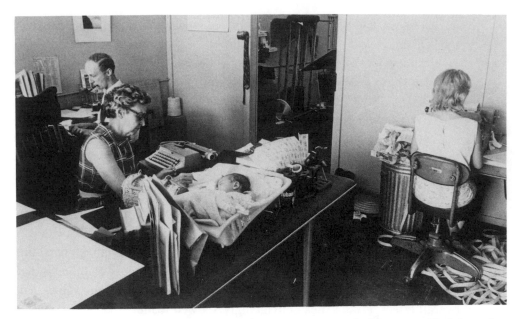

Handling the weddings, engagements and society news, Virginia works
in the tiny newsroom of *THIS WEEK* in 1969, sharing the space with
the typesetter, Co-Editor Paris and sleeping infant daughter of the other
co-editor.

And the Society Editor was a person to respect back in those days. It would be nice to
have a little bit of that nowadays.

Women phoned me, any day or time, to ask my advice. Usually, the caller did not identify herself but society was so much more structured in those days she did not want—heaven
forbid—to arrive at a party and find she was the only woman in the room wearing a hat.

Whether to wear a hat or carry gloves was the burning issue of the day. Where to seat
guests for a wedding rehearsal dinner was another. One of my favorites was the woman
(anonymous) who phoned to inquire if her daughter should be allowed to wear eye make-up
to high school.

I skirted that diplomatically until she finally asked: Would you? I told her I wouldn't
(back then it was worn only to dances or night parties) but if her friends were wearing it she
(the mother) might as well acquiesce. In a triumphant voice, she said: "I told her you
wouldn't wear it." Which gave another disgruntled young girl reason to dislike that Society
Editor.

Gradually times changed and women changed. The cleanest house, the highest risen
cake on the block became unimportant and the word Society fell into disrepute. And, in this
area at least, old families, proper manners gave way to Money and show of same.

And at age 80, I have reached the point in life where I can sit back and observe the
foibles and changes with amusement, acceptance and, finally, have gotten off my charger
ready to change the world. It's been a relief but a lot less fun.

Writing in 1992, Virginia Rucker contemplated how the changing times
had impacted on the society editor. Here are her observations:

If you read many newspapers you're sure to notice the change in reporting over the years. Nowhere does it show up more vividly that in wedding write-ups.

Forty years ago we described the potted palms in great detail, what music was played and what the bride's and groom's mothers wore.

Somebody must have decided back then that no wedding was legal unless "O Promise Me" was sung. I welcomed the day when that changed, but surely using "We've Only Just Begun" in a religious ceremony was no improvement.

Some papers (not ours) wrote about the "radiant" bride and every detail of the ceremony—anything the bride's mother wanted, even if it included saying the wedding dress was trimmed in one thousand pearls. And mothers threatened the "society editor" with disaster if she didn't use the picture above the fold of the newspaper.

Excerpted from one of Virginia's 1948 wedding write-ups, material which is omitted these days:

Seven branched candelabra holding white tapers, fern balls, fancy leaf caladiums and white gladioli formed a background for the ceremony. Before the ceremony Miss Ola Johnson of Shelby, pianist, played "Ave Maria" by Schubert, "My Heart At Thy Sweet Voice" by Saint-Saens and "Sweetest Story Every Told" by Stults ... (This paragraph goes on for 16 more lines of musical and floral details.)

The bride's mother wore a dress of black bemberg and black and white accessories. The bridegroom's mother wore a grey crepe dress with black accessories. Both wore shoulder bouquets of red roses. ... After the ceremony the couple left for a wedding trip and upon their return, will make their home in Pendleton, S.C. For traveling the bride wore a luggage tan suit with brown and white accessories and the orchid from her bouquet. ... Out-of-town guests included Miss Rachel Swan of Mars Hill, Miss Wilda Ellis, Hickory, Thomas Swann, Greensboro and Faulton Hodge, Rutherfordton. (15 more out-of-town guests and their hometowns are listed.)

In 1994, going on 50 years, Virginia finally confronted the fact that she's been writing for four generations. In one weekly column she observed:

I've made a fool of myself—again.

Sometimes I'm able to hide it, but this time it was in print—and I surely should have learned better even 22 years ago.

This is how it happened: In today's paper, I wrote about Gina Harrill who wore her grandmother's wedding dress last month when Gina and Thad were married in the same church where her grandparents wed in 1948.

At my request, Carolyn brought the account of her wedding which I had written for the old *Courier* in August 1948. And she also had a picture and story about her mother, Mrs. H.C. Vess, published in 1954.

That story was one of a series I wrote and then-editor Frank Jeter took pictures of Cook of the Week. So that made two generations in that family.

In 1971, I was with *THIS WEEK* newspaper, predecessor of *The Daily Courier* since its inception in 1969, and wrote Glenda Bradley's wedding to Chester Melton, held in Alexander Baptist Church, like her parents'.

Then, nine years ago, I had written and had pictures of the Meltons' lovely home, decorated so beautifully for Christmas.

Before I wrote about Glenda's wedding in June 1971, I wrote a column about brides,

That was then, this is now: Associate Editor Rucker at work in 1994 has provided the paper with 25 years of continuity. Her one concession to time: She replaced her manual with an electric typewriter because slinging the old carriage return began to wear on her. Note the ever-present roll of AP paper. (*Photo by Jane Alexander*)

their mothers, and my experience with some of them and their weddings. Here are the last three paragraphs:

> *So, this weekend, when I write Glenda Bradley's wedding to Chester Melton it will be an extra-pleasant chore because I'll recall writing her mother's wedding, too.*
>
> *That, and the fact that this is the first occasion that I'm aware I'm writing the second generation wedding.*
>
> *Before the write-ups begin coming in for the third generation, I'll retire, I promise.*

So, what am I doing 22 years later? Writing about Gina, Glenda's daughter and Carolyn's granddaughter, who happens to be fourth generation.

I should have listened years ago when someone advised me: Never say never. Perhaps I should have known, though, that as long as I was having fun working I'd continue as long as I was able.

And renewing contact with these delightful women is just another reason that the job is pleasurable and that I've stayed this long.

CONCLUSION: YOU GOTTA HAVE IT

The reporting of some lifestyle stories may not seem to vary so much between large metropolitan dailies and community papers. But when it comes to old-fashioned women's news, there is a vast difference in the two types of newspapers.

In community journalism, reporting of weddings and the like, though, as Virginia observes, pared down over the years, is still vital and given ample spread. The two-column photo and 14-inch story is common. By contrast many major big-city papers, which, if they even run weddings at all, either give them the short shrift by comparison (a three-inch story wrapped around a photo not much larger than some postage stamps) or charge money for running the couple's photo.

Virginia notes, "Now, city papers often have a standard report, using only the couple's name, when and where the ceremony was held and parents' names. And some metropolitan papers, surprisingly, report on the parents' occupations."

From a sheer common-sense standpoint, there's the paper's reason for supporting a strong lifestyle section. The enlightened publisher will realize that a great lifestyle section is another way the community paper can distance and distinguish itself from any big-city dailies trying to compete—either directly or indirectly (with Neighbors editions). If your paper doesn't already have such an editor, it ought to be looking for someone like Virginia Rucker, who can provide the community paper with a valuable perspective, years of continuity and quality reporting with the personal touch.

YOUR TOWN; YOUR TURN

1. Examine the lifestyle section in your selected community newspaper. Does your paper have a Virginia? In your estimation, how could that section be improved?

2. Compare its style of wedding coverage (size of picture, length of story, etc.) with that of the nearby large metropolitan daily.

3. Talk to the lifestyle editor at your community paper about the changes in that field. If there are men working on that section, ask them about their feelings.

13

Whose Paper Is It Anyway?

HAVING A PAPER MUST BE LIKE OWNING A COW

The old farmer, stopping by the paper office to renew his subscription, noted that the young editor seemed to be there working at all hours. "Son," he observed with characteristic folk wisdom, "having a newspaper must be like having a cow." And seeing the editor's puzzlement, he explained, "Well, y' gotta milk 'er twice a day, and you can't go off."

Nowhere is the difference between the community paper and the big daily more apparent than in the area of ownership. We're not talking about corporate ownership here, but the community's emotional and philosophical ownership.

Up until now we've been talking about how you and your paper relate to the community; now we're turning the mirror on ourselves. How does the community look at us? How do our readers regard the paper?

First and most importantly, it's not *the* paper. It's *their* paper. Everything about community journalism is personal, even the way the readers regard their paper.

Repeat. It's *their* paper. Or more personally, you're likely to hear "MY paper." Even if *you're* the owner, it's THEIR paper. Lose sight of that fact and fail; recognize and capitalize on that attitude and soar.

175

POSSESSION IS THREE-FIFTHS OF THE WAY THERE

Your readers are possessive about their paper because that's the nature of small-town people. They're also possessive about their high school football team, the school marching band, Little League, the way the church is run, what happens in the county courthouse, borough council, planning board and town hall. It's their town; it's their paper.

Miss a delivery, do something they don't like in the paper, or change something that's been long-standing—and you'll hear from the readers.

"Where's MY paper?"

"What have you gone and done to MY paper?"

By now, some of you are shaking your heads. But big-city daily papers and TV stations hire ad agencies and PR firms to try and figure out how to get their readers and viewers so committed, involved, possessive and even jealous. That's not a problem for us in community journalism. Half the time the readers act like we work for *them*.

A constructive way of looking at that makes the publisher more of a public servant than an entrepreneur out for a fast buck. Nothing wrong with a buck. Nothing wrong at all. Fact is, the more you recognize, accept and buy into your paper's unique relationship with the community, the more bucks you'll have.

And the rest of you—editors, reporters, photographers, ad people—listen up. While your highest calling may be to the principles of journalism or the bottom line, you too work for the reader.

Coach Dave Rinker of Brevard College, whose men's running team had twice won the national junior college cross country championships, often called the sports information director "Boss." And when asked why, Rinker replied with a grin, "because I work for everybody." As it turns out, that's not true at all, but it's the generous, non-ego attitude of a proven winner.

PERSONALITIES AND COMMUNITIES

Just as surely as people have vastly different personalities, towns also possess varied personalities. Cosmopolitan, cultured, open-minded, forward-thinking—or ingrown and rootbound, suspicious of new things, outsiders and change. Financially busting at the seams, holding its own, or in decline. Is the town friendly and optimistic or grumpy and grim? Some communities welcome strangers and newcomers with genuine charm and early acts of friendship. Others take pride in studiously ignoring newcomers. Some communities make you prove yourself before they'll take you in— then once accepted, you're blood kin. Others will never accept you no matter how long you live and work there.

Where does a community get its collective personality? Study the area's ethnic, cultural, religious, commercial/financial and historical background, and the answers will reveal themselves to you.

A played-out Pennsylvania coal town dominated by a central and eastern European culture is going to have a very different personality than a culturally-thriving, tourist-oriented, vacation community in the Smokies of western North Carolina with a Scots-Irish population base.

PERSONALITIES AND COMMUNITY NEWSPAPERS

Newspapers are individuals, too, with distinct personalities. The longer you're at a paper, the more you'll recognize the paper's true nature. A paper's personality is usually the function of two factors: ownership and the community itself.

The Community

It stands to reason that newspapers reflect the personalities of their communities. Grumpy town, grumpy paper. And conversely, a thriving town with high livability is likely to have an enlightened, creative, involved and high-quality paper.

This is important to know if you are soon to be a college graduate and are considering a first job in community journalism, or if you are already at a community paper and seeking a change, or if you are a community journalism vet ready to move on and perhaps buy (or start) "your" own paper.

Mark these words: Save yourself a lot of time, bucks and stomach lining by researching the target community before you commit to a move. Because if you don't find out these personality factors first, you'll surely find them out later, when it will be too late to avert a bad move.

Where do the people come from? Are newcomers and change welcomed or shunned? What is their attitude toward themselves? Do they like their town or look down on themselves? There's nothing worse than a place filled with self-hate and loathing. Do they all shop 30 miles away in the big city? If they do, you probably don't have an ad base.

What do they think of their government, their schools, their hospital, their social services? What's the local governmental picture like? Who's who in the zoo? Is there a political machine that runs the town? If there is, you better know about this up front.

Is there a college in town or nearby? What's the state of the arts in this town? What kind of social action programs exist? What is the dominant ethnic background? What churches predominate and how does that affect behavior and attitude? Where do people work? Is the town and area's population growing or shrinking?

The Paper's Ownership

In addition to being a reflection of the community, a newspaper tends to be a mirror image of its ownership and the publisher's attitude. While there are several forward-thinking, community-involved chains across America, there are many more that take as much out of the community as possible, while putting back as little as possible. These are the bottom-feeders of community journalism. They're not fooling their community; folks usually openly hate these papers. It stands to reason it's not much fun to work at one of these rags.

A recent outstanding college graduate from a major northeastern university took his first job at a small community daily whose chain ownership imposed a quota of six stories a day (they didn't care about the quality, just the quantity) without overtime pay. Additionally, on any given assignment, a reporter-photographer only received a 10-shot roll of film and was told not to take more than one negative per separate picture. For instance, when our man wanted to do a photo page on a disaster drill, they gave him one 10-shot roll. Also, the chain banned border tape and screens because they were too expensive. After six months of teeth-gnashing and hair-pulling, our cub reporter found employment at a nearby progressive, enlightened community paper (also chain-owned) where the publishers are committed to quality and journalistic excellence.

Before you take a job at a paper, do some research on the ownership. If it's a family-owned paper, what is the family like? What do people in town think of the paper and the owners? Do reporters like working there? What's the turnover like? What's the newsroom dynamics like? Does it seem like a happy shop? The same goes for a chain paper, but also you need to determine the chain's reputation and direction. Compared to other papers, how do they pay and treat their people?

You will have an uphill struggle imposing your personality on the town's personality, or the personality of the existing paper. The wiser route is to find a community and a paper that already matches your personality.

You'll live longer, and your stomach lining—not to mention your loved ones—will thank you.

COMMUNITY NEWSPAPER PERSONALITIES AND AGING

Like people, newspapers have lifespans. They age. A bumptious new community weekly run by a bunch of enthusiastic whippersnappers may evolve into a larger weekly, then be forced to go semi- or triweekly, or even five-day-a-week afternoon daily; "semidaily" some call this.

Why do newspapers change?

Change can come from within or without.

Sometimes owners, publishers and editors see opportunity for growth in changing the format and printing schedules. More often, it's because the paper has grown along with the community's commercial areas, and must respond or lose out to competition. A newspaper that doesn't keep pace with the needs of its advertising community is no longer growing. And if it isn't growing, then it's in decline, and may be even dying a slow death.

When a community newspaper dies, or folds, it's usually the result these days of the decline of the community. But sometimes internal mismanagement plays a part. If a chain closes a community paper, there can be a variety of reasons at work, but usually it has to do with declining revenues and lackluster prospects for any future growth.

The important thing for the professional to do is to determine what age your paper is. Is it a dowdy old gray mare out to pasture? A frolicking teenager afraid of nothing? A settled and conservative middle-aged business-as-usual type? Is your target paper on the brink of a personality identity crisis? Is it about to change publication schedule? Identifying all these character traits of the paper will save you needless grief, and it will enhance your working there and empower you with your relationships.

OTHER VOICES; OTHER NEWSROOMS

William E. Shaw, fifth-generation publisher of the Dixon, Ill., Telegraph, says it took him years to realize who really owned the paper. The following is excerpted from his presentation to a symposium titled "Community Newspapers and Community-Building," co-sponsored by Kansas State University's Huck Boyd National Center for Community Media, held in conjunction with the 1994 National Newspaper Association Convention in Orlando, Fla.

Our Republican

by William E. Shaw

Each morning I re-assume my role as publisher of *The Telegraph*, Dixon, Illinois' daily newspaper. It is a job and a title that has been held in my family for many years. My father and his father before him were newspaper publishers their whole lives. This unbroken string goes back 143 years to my great-great grandfather who joined *The Dixon Telegraph* in its first year of publication.

Folks in town know the Shaw family well. Our name is synonymous with this newspaper. My original newspaper ancestor greeted Abraham Lincoln as he passed through town on his way to debate Douglas. Not only greeted him, but helped Lincoln plan his debate strategy. My grandfather gave Ronald Reagan his first job, as carrier boy for his hometown newspaper.

Through the years we have continuously published *The Telegraph,* never missing an issue or episode. The chain of events that has shaped our community has been faithfully chronicled in our pages over our five generations of family stewardship. *The Telegraph* embodies the past history of Dixon as well as it channels the energies that will lead the community ahead toward an uncertain future.

Each day brings with it new stories and headlines for *The Telegraph*. When we come to work in the morning, we have no inkling about what news will be bannered across our front page. However, when the day is done, the spontaneous events of the day will be permanently recorded in our official record.

In this era of newspaper chains and publicly-held newspaper, the ownership of most newspapers has become far-removed from their constituency. Most people no longer know who owns the local newspaper published in their community. Some newspaper owners do not even know anything about the communities served by their newspapers.

But even in our case, where our family has operated this newspaper in this town for so many years, I wonder about the essence of ownership. An incident happened about seven years ago that challenged my notions regarding a newspaper's investor's role respective to newspaper ownership.

In an effort to expand our family business, to keep pace with an expanding family, we have purchased several newspapers in communities of Illinois, Iowa and Wisconsin. One such newspaper, *The Bureau County Republican*, is located in the town of Princeton, Illinois, scarcely 30 miles south of Dixon. I held the position of publisher of that newspaper for five years, immediately preceding my return to Dixon in 1986.

A few months after I left Princeton a fire broke out in the same block as our newspaper plant. The gas explosion quickly consumed the building next to ours and flames leapt onto our roof.

Afterwards, our publisher, Bob Sorensen, who succeeded me in Princeton, reported the disaster in which our newspaper almost changed from a news object to a news subject.

Bob rushed to the scene in the early evening and began removing computers and valuables from our building. When the fire began threatening our plant, he could do nothing but watch the firemen conduct the valiant fight. While watching in terror, Bob heard a lady shriek in a loud voice:

"There goes our *Republican!*"

It's funny how, in a moment of panic, a thought can crystallize in one's mind. When Bob shared that comment with me, we both realized that the lady sincerely believed that *her* newspaper was about to burn down. In fact, the whole community probably felt that way. *The Bureau County Republican* belonged to the people of the community. We merely owned the rights to manage the company that published it.

For four years that comment haunted me. Even back in Dixon, where our family had been plying its trade for nearly a century and a half, did we really own the newspaper? Of course we did. Our newspaper holds the record for continuous family ownership in Illinois. We have toiled, sacrificed, saved and invested our blood, sweat and tears for all that time.

But in a larger sense, the newspaper has always belonged to the people of the greater Dixon community. If we are to be a healthy newspaper, we must hope our local citizens perceive that *they* own *Telegraph*. It is *their* newspaper.

Fortunately, the firefighters put out the blaze on the roof before *The Republican* was destroyed. But the distraught woman's cry—"there goes our *Republican*!"—burned in Shaw's mind, all the same. In 1993 the lesson of the trial by fire inspired publisher Shaw to put together an "Owner's Manual" for *The Telegraph*, which is distributed to new and old subscribers as well as advertisers. In the intro, Shaw opens with these words: "In the larger sense, you readers own this newspaper. By subscribing to *The Telegraph* you

At the community level, you are accessible to your readers in a most open-door sort of way. If someone wants to send you a dead opossum wrapped in floral greenery, they can and will. The author ponders how to run this "possum to the editor." (We didn't; it was unsigned.) (*Photo by Ron Paris*)

181

have hired us to produce a newspaper that lives up to your standards. We have prepared this Owner's Manual for you to better utilize 'your' newspaper. … We are also eager to hear from you about how we can improve 'your' *Telegraph*. Feel free to give me a call or write me a note with your ideas."

FROM THE TRENCHES

Years ago I was embroiled in a tooth-and-nail shoot-out with a chain paper with an unlovely reputation. On the occasion of the paper's first birthday, we received a bouquet of yellow carnations spray-painted black.

Whether it was from a prankster or the competition newspaper across town, we could only guess. However, in the spirit of battle, we placed that death bouquet proudly in a vase in the front office, so that everybody coming in that day could see and be as shocked as we were.

You never know what your readers are thinking about you. And you never know what they're going to send you.

At another paper I once received a large, flat, rather heavy box, wrapped in bright ribbons. Opening it, I found a fresh-killed opossum, grinning up at me from its bower of florist's ferns and greenery. A practical joke? A reader's comment about my work or the paper's editorial stance? I'll never know. But what I do know is, at a community paper, life is never boring.

YOUR TOWN; YOUR TURN

1. Define in as many ways as you can, the factors that contribute to the personality of your community. Then, in a 30-word lead, define your community: Boogersburg is …

2. Do the same thing with your newspaper. What kind of a paper is it? Does it have a happy shop? What's the attitude of the owner-publishers toward the community?

3. Where is your newspaper in its life span? Is it on the verge of a midlife crisis?

14

Ethics and Community Newspapers: A Different Way of Looking at Things

ETHICS AND THE COMMUNITY NEWSPAPER

Most community newspapers orient themselves ethically toward their communities in a fundamentally different way than their big-city cousins, according to a former Maine weekly newspaper editor and now professor and editor of the recent book, *The Journalist's Moral Compass.*

While the community paper, like the large metro paper, serves in the vital role of public watchdog of the governmental affairs, Steven R. Knowlton of Penn State says the similarities end there.

"At many large metro papers, when a bad guy is caught with his hand in the public till, they report it almost with a sense of triumphant glee," Knowlton says. "But at the community paper, when the bad guy is caught," he notes, "it is still reported, with a certain sense of sadness."

The very nature of a community's shared physical geography and common social landscape makes it highly likely that people at the paper will know the accused or guilty party in more than just an abstract, detached manner. The accused will be a neighbor, someone from church, the Lions Club, the elementary school PTA.

Community newspapers do not enjoy the luxury of issuing detached, abstract editorial and news judgments. When it comes down to making

183

tough ethical decisions, the community newspaper editor better have a moral compass that is locked unswervingly on magnetic north, because his or her reasons whether and how to publish will be tested and questioned with almost every issue that comes along and every issue of the paper that comes out.

NEWS IS NEWS—OR IS IT?

Community journalism has been around for a long time. Even before this country *was* a country, our first papers were concerned with intensely local political coverage. It's nothing new. It's just what works because it suits the way we're made.

Call it whatever you will—community journalism, public journalism, relentlessly local coverage—it's not a new idea; it's just one whose time has come again. Now in the '90s, largely in response to cities out of control, we've finally started to embrace the concept of *the human scale*, neighborhoods in the truest sense, and the realization that people can only relate to so many other people at any given time. Communities only work to the extent that they're personal. Large aggregates come unglued because they never were adhered to start with.

And yet, there are a lot of people who don't get it.

Witness the following real conversation that occurred between two friends recently, one a self-proclaimed enlightened but openly cynical media critic, and the other, a young but dedicated community journalist:

"News is news. It's all the same, isn't it?" demands the devil's advocate. "What differentiates what happens in Harrisburg and what happens in Danville?"

Comes the quick reply from the journalist, who, just a couple of years out of college, often subs as managing editor: "About 50 freakin' miles."

"Are you a Democrat or a Republican?" the critic demands.

The reply comes quickly and with surety. "I'm a reporter."

Rejoins the skeptic: "Why would I believe and trust the story in your paper as opposed to the other paper?"

"Because you can trust me," says the reporter.

"And why is that?" laughs the other, who has seen too much tabloid television and not enough of great community papers like the Dixon (Ill.) *Telegraph* or the *N'West Iowa REVIEW* or the *Bugle*.

The community man doesn't even pause to think before saying, "Because I've got a track record. Because of accretion. Because you know me."

BECAUSE THEY KNOW YOU

The gemstone of accountability is perhaps the heaviest burden for a community journalist to carry, but yet is the most precious lode one can possess. If invested wisely, it can earn you a lifetime of satisfaction.

In short, if people know you (you shop at Food Mart, you attend the Methodist church, your kid plays for the West High Comets, and yet your coverage seems balanced and fair) they will trust and believe your word in print or the images you portray on your pages. And why shouldn't they? You know this is a trusteeship, not to be entered into lightly. Think of your reader as a good neighbor or best friend, someone you would never knowingly deceive. And if you erred, you would make it right quickly, wouldn't you? You bet you would.

That is the kernel, the "nut graph" of community journalism ethics; never deceive knowingly. And when a mistake is made, correct it promptly, and with equal weight. In other words, front-page errors should be corrected in the same space. After a blaring P-1 story that was flat wrong, the readers will pick up on how grudging and mean-spirited the paper was to bury the correction among the classifieds.

Public Service/ The Public Interest

What is the role of the community newspaper in serving its community?

First off, you must accept—no, that verb is not a strong enough—*commit* to the first law of community journalism: that there exists a fundamental and reciprocal relationship between the paper and its town. It's a perspective as possessive and affectionate and all-seeing as that of Thornton Wilder's *Our Town*.

A community newspaper cares about its community in a supportive, positive, nurturing way. The paper's own birth, history, development, welfare and future is inextricably bound up with that of its community.

How could it be otherwise? The community paper, by its very name and description, is a creature of service. It's not called just a newspaper; it's a COMMUNITY newspaper. That's why knowing what you are and staying on message, as the politicians say, is so vital.

The role of the enlightened community newspaper is far more demanding and complex than that of the big city paper, which can afford to be detached, remote, critical, aloof, cynical and at times, elite.

On the other hand, the work of the great community newspaper is made more complex by its difficult multiple and conflicting roles as fair and balanced reporter of the news while also serving as advocate for all it finds good and worthwhile in the community, a consistently positive force for community-building and appropriate growth.

We are also cheerleader, encourager, adviser, booster, supporter, advocate—and above all, an accurate, unflinching yet benevolent mirror to the community. At times the paper must function as a "tough love" counselor and say things the community may not want to hear but needs to be exposed to. This is where, as they say, the rubber meets the road. Without putting down our brothers and sisters at the big-city papers, theirs is a relatively simple role when it comes to public service—report the news fairly and completely, and don't get involved.

For us in community journalism, it's much more likely to be a matter of intense involvement on many levels of the community. Your pressman may belong to the American Legion. The sports editor may play on a church softball team. The news editor may coach a Little League team. The M.E. may be active in the local arts council. The executive ed may be on the board of trustees of the community college. The publisher may be in the Rotary Club or on the county's economic development task force.

So—I hear you thinking—what about conflict of interest? What happens when Joe the M.E.'s rival Little League coach complains that the paper's coverage of the big game was slanted in Joe's team's favor? Is this improper for the staff to have outside involvement with the coverage area? Doesn't that set you up for charges of favoritism and biased coverage?

But what are you going to do? Restrict your staff to live in a biosphere called "The Newsroom"? If you live in a small town, you can't help but get involved with community life. It's one of the things that makes community life so rich, fulfilling and worthwhile.

The question begs to be answered. And that's what this book is all about and that's why the study of community newspapering is so enduring. There are no simple answers, friends. The newspaper's role in a community setting is complex, ever-changing and downright difficult. When it comes to the ethics of how you serve your community, how you handle news judgment and community involvement, you take each issue on a case-by-case basis. There are no formulas in community journalism, except that people are what really matter. And that is "on message."

A TOWN MEETING

The complexity of community newspaper/community relationships became the focus of a recent town meeting between one paper and representative members of its constituency.

The roundtable between community leaders and newspaper executives was co-sponsored by the College of Communications of the Pennsylvania State University and the local newspaper, *Centre Daily Times*, a 20,000 circulation Knight-Ridder daily. The timing was right for this event. Encouraged by Knight-Ridder and local readers, the *Times* was beginning to take a noticeable shift toward more community coverage. In addition, the *Times* had just named a new executive editor who was a strong advocate for community journalism.

Moderating the televised event, the dean of the Penn State College of Communications, Terri Brooks, opened the forum. "Newspapers are wrestling with the issue of how they can best serve their communities," she said. "This provides an opportunity for a valuable exchange of views and perhaps some redefining of what constitutes *news*."

Under the broad umbrella of "Journalism and the Public Interest" the roundtable's format featured a panel which included the newspaper's publisher and new exec ed, the president of the downtown merchants association, the chairman of the university's board of trustees and downtown *Town & Gown* magazine publisher, the high school public information officer, the chairwoman of the League of Women Voters, a county commissioner, the immediate past mayor who had just retired after a 20-year tenure, the head of the local public television station, a woman in a wheelchair who declared herself to be an activist for social and community causes and who served on the local human relations group, and a university professor specializing in community journalism.

The studio audience of about 25 had been selected to represent a broad cross section from the community. In it were a diverse sampling of people; young and old, men and women, including the local police chief, an AP reporter, an African-American university staff member, AIDS and gay awareness activists, a member of the ACLU, an Evangelical church leader, a former newspaper publisher and church minister, a township supervisor, a farmer, several high school students, as well as people with outspoken liberal and conservative political views.

From the outset, this first-of-its-kind event for this community took on a very specific focus. In the words of the moderator: "How can a community newspaper serve its public? Its community? How can the local newspaper do a better job?"

The unspoken question: Was this going to turn into a gripe session about the *Times*?

The importance of the occasion and the gravity of the subject was underscored by the glare of the TV lights and under the unblinking eyes of the two TV cameras. The irony of being in the artificial and very controlled environment of a television studio while talking about print journalism was not lost on many of the participants, many of whom clearly had never done anything like this before.

Indeed, the session began with a TV tape created by Gannett Co. for its employees on the subject of public interest. The main points: American newspapers existed under First Amendment rights with the moral imperative to cover the activities of the government; newspapers represent the free exchange of information; newspapers should represent all facets of a community with diversity on the pages and in the staff; the newspaper's presentation should be appealing; newspapers should provide information that people need; and that "news is about you and the things that affect your life."

So, how can we design "the ideal newspaper for our town"? the moderator began.

The paper's new exec ed, Cecil L. Bentley, took up the cudgel, responding that he planned for the paper to be more "intensely local" in the future, and that if the *Times* didn't cover its own community well, then what good was it? The editor emphasized that as a newcomer from another region of the country, he was at the forum to listen and learn.

The university trustee said she thought the community paper was a second-read.

The high school publicist said she thought the paper should reflect the readers' shared sensibilities.

The downtown-merchants' leader said he was excited about the local news getting front-page treatment for there is a "glaring need for the paper to report in-depth local issues." He emphasized that the many complex local issues deserve quality coverage.

The retired mayor noted that he was troubled by young, flip reporters seeking simple answers to complex local problems, reporters who wouldn't take the time to do in-depth work. He called for experienced writers on the news side, and "someone to direct the newspaper staff to go back (historically) and provide context."

The League of Women Voters rep said the town itself was "a conundrum." The difference between town and gown in a university community is peculiar to this setting. She thought the paper had an identity problem because it was not able to please everyone all the time.

The *Times* publisher, James A. Moss, conceded "we are wrestling with issues" that keep shifting, not the least of which is information technology that made him wonder when we speak of community, are we talking about the area within 25 miles or are we talking about the world. "It's difficult to find the right formula," Moss said, adding that the paper was committed first to covering its own "immediate backyard."

The journalism professor praised that sentiment, calling on the paper to be, in Charles Kuralt's words, "relentlessly local."

The local public television leader challenged the paper to "lead as well as listen." He thought it was the role of the paper to "give them (the readers) what they need, which may not be necessarily what they want."

The retired mayor added that he thought "the media" needed to "establish better relationships with their sources"—to which the journalism professor requested that a distinction be made between community newspapers and "the media"—otherwise, he said community papers might be lumped in with the likes of Geraldo and supermarket tabs.

The local police chief said that the role of the newspaper was to communicate a benevolent perspective, one reflecting the attitude that "we're all in this together."

A local minister called on the paper to hire or develop reporters who are willing to stay at the paper long enough to understand the community's core values. "We need reporters who have depth," he said.

The ACLU member noted that there were "many truths" and that he wondered if the paper wasn't becoming "too local" while sacrificing national and international coverage. Another audience member disagreed, saying he thought he got enough national and international news from CNN and *USA Today*.

A mid-20s man who managed a local bookstore said he thought the paper's university coverage needed improving, that he had to read the campus student daily to get complete coverage of the university community. Had the paper ever considered separate pages devoted to such coverage?

The publisher responded, saying that he understood about six years ago a separate *Campus Times* edition was launched, but had not succeeded because it was not supported (by the business community). He said he thought the paper did a reasonably good job of folding university news into the mainstream of the paper, but the audience member clearly remained unconvinced.

An African American reader who works at the university noted that a community newspaper should be "tying the national and international stories into the region" and that there was "a dearth of hard-core investigative reporting" at the local paper, and he challenged them to go underneath the press releases.

The downtown-merchants' leader said he realized young reporters usually got their first jobs at places like the *Times*, and it caused him to wonder, "What kind of instruction are these young reporters getting? What is the College of Communications doing?"

A columnist from an alternative liberal local magazine, citing the need for more in-depth background stories on local issues, criticized the paper for shallow, event-oriented reporting.

The local high school public information officer responded, saying that the local paper had missed the mark and blown things out of proportion when covering a recent incident in which a student was found to have a gun at school. "The reporter didn't go deep enough," she said. "He focused just on the 5 W's."

A local Evangelical minister said he was concerned with "core values" of the community and that it was very important to teach these to young reporters.

The county commissioner charged that "when a newspaper drives an issue, the newspaper doesn't stimulate both positions." She said when the newspaper has an agenda, politicians tend to play to the paper because they know the paper will back that position.

A high school student said that the paper needs to "connect what's happening nationally to what's going on here," and she wondered why non-sports high school news didn't receive more coverage.

The journalism professor suggested that this could be solved if the paper instituted a separate monthly high-school-news page generated by the high school journalism class.

Another high school student said he was under the impression that "you're hurting in this community for a large issue," and he charged the paper with sensationalism when covering the "gun in school" story. In a related issue, he was critical of the paper's running a large photo of a member of the high school track team who had fallen on the last lap. Her collapse had caused the team to lose the event. But publishing the photo needlessly embarrassed the girl. "Should you have published that?" the student asked the newspaper leaders on the panel. There was no response.

The high school publicist picked up the thread, saying, "One of the jobs of a community newspaper is to help create a sense of community."

A local PR executive said that the paper should embark on a "thorough research study of the community—what does the community want and need." And he asked that more township news be included.

A local AIDS and gay activist said she thought the community paper tends to leave out the extreme voices, and that she encouraged publishing voices from these perspectives.

The retired mayor said he thought the practice of community newspapers endorsing political candidates was useless and counterproductive. Of letters to the editors and especially their responses, he said he thought the paper should publish them more promptly.

At this point in the roundtable, the moderator introduced a tape on the studio monitor outlining a proposed draft statement of journalism ethics by the Associated Press Managing Editors. The statement tied press responsibility to its historical Constitutional protection, and in addition made the following points:

Relevance—a newspaper's primary obligation is to provide information to help an informed citizenry make better decisions.

Vigilance—that newspapers are the watchdogs of society and government.

Timeliness—that newspapers provide a prompt dissemination of this information.

But that broad-brush outline was too vague for one of the audience members, a township supervisor, who called on the paper to "be the glue, the bridge" of the community, and he stressed that he'd like to see the press pay more attention to their First Amendment *responsibilities* as opposed to their *rights*. He concluded that there exists a shared responsibility between elected officials and the press.

But what use is a specific code of ethics? The local AP reporter said he thought he was objective and that, "every situation is different," and that he tried to judge each issue on a case-by-case basis.

The local county commissioner again charged the paper with bias, and this time she got a response. "If I wanted to be the darling of the print media, all I had to do was to get on the same side as the paper in order to get great coverage," and that people who didn't agree with the paper's agenda got their stories cut.

Times Editor Bentley responded with conviction that if a story got cut, it was only because of space considerations, and that as far as the charge of agenda-setting and political favoritism, as far as he knew, that was completely false. Otherwise, he said, "we get into a serious credibility problem."

A visiting Knight-Ridder assistant to the vice-president for news, Steven A. Smith, said that the paper ought to be pushing what he called "the public agenda" for that specific community. He called this "an effort to restore public life … to bring parties together to discuss basic core values."

A WAKE-UP CALL

The two-hour session ended with the moderator summarizing the salient points: The session was a wake-up call for the paper to better know its community, to listen more carefully to its readers. The audience was practically unanimous in its desire for more intense, local, in-depth coverage, with particular attention paid to fair and balanced reporting and presentation.

Finally, one of the unspoken themes that ran throughout the session: The readers clearly wanted to understand the process by which news judgment is arrived at—and where practical, be a part of it.

Afterward, participants generally agreed more community forums should be held in the future; that this should be just the start of an ongoing dialogue, a series of town meetings on the role of the paper and the community. Several panel and audience members suggested a more informal, uninhibited setting to encourage a spontaneous exchange. They felt the TV studio atmosphere was too intimidating and that the format actually suppressed a free verbal exchange.

In the studio's green room after the cameras were turned off and the microphones unplugged, the publisher lamented to a circle of friends that the paper's best efforts seemed to have gone unrecognized.

Would he give any credence to the call to arms his constituency had tried so politely to give him on camera? Or would the *Times* fall into the oldest trap of our trade: elitism and the ensuing cynicism that blinds our vision, a defensive mechanism that robs us of the possibility for novelty?

The question seemed to hang in the air for weeks. And then, slowly at first, but then more and more, the *Times* appeared to be evolving.

Over a space of three months, the entire emphasis of the *Times* shifted noticeably to local coverage. The management must have heard and heeded the wake-up call. In fact, the community coverage increased dramatically.

Just three weeks after the town meeting, *Times* Editor Bentley announced the new direction in his Sunday column, writing that he and Publisher Moss had heard the readers "loud and clear. You want local news and views. You want more depth in our reporting. You want us to cover issues, not just events. And you want us to show how news from around the world relates to residents of Centre County ... you should notice a stronger local presence each day on Page 1A. But we're also interested in similar improvement on the Opinion Page. For us to be relentlessly local and provide greater debate and depth on issues, we need your help."

The paper solicited and secured the services of local columnists who wrote on local issues and topics. Every section of the paper became noticeably more locally driven. A local story or photograph dominated every section front. And finally, the paper undertook a redesign that reflected the "relentlessly local" emphasis by mainstreaming the local news throughout each issue. Local school, sports and religion coverage became prodigious. As this book was going to press, the *Times* appeared well on its way to transforming itself into a dedicated community newspaper. Even though the *Time*'s management may have been heading the paper toward a more public journalism emphasis, the town meeting had served as a positive vote for the shift. For the *Centre Daily Times,* the town meeting appeared to be a defining moment in the paper's growth and development. Readers who wanted a national and international news emphasis were openly critical of the change, while readers who wanted more local emphasis and community news said they were pleased with the new *Times.*

THORNY PROBLEMS

What are some of the ethical dilemmas a community paper editor is likely to encounter in the course of an average week?

Accusations of conflict of interest, whether to depict dead bodies and human suffering, how to handle obscenity and good/poor taste in relation to community standards, to name a few.

The following are all true stories.

Dead Bodies or Not?

The scanner went off in the newsroom two hours before final photo deadline for the twice-weekly paper. It sounded bad; a tractor had overturned on someone out plowing. According to the emergency broadcast over the scanner in the newsroom, a man was pinned beneath the tractor and presumed in critical condition at best. Ed, the news editor, grabbed his Pentax K-1000 and raced out of the main street office, heading toward the site, just north of town. Who is it? he wondered. When he got there, he was greeted by a most unsettling scene. No one was rushing about, as they would do ordinarily. The emergency workers were milling about despondently or standing around the tractor in a circle, looking down. The news editor suspected the worst. The poor tractor driver was dead. Approaching the scene slowly and with decorum, Ed quietly inquired of an EMS worker he knew, who was the victim? The reply came back as a shock. It was the chairman of the county commissioners.

Just then, as the news editor was formulating his decisions about what to shoot and how to deal with the story, a reporter from the competition tri-weekly appeared on the scene, and without any preamble, pushed his way through the emergency workers to the crushed body beneath the tractor and began shooting pictures, obviously very close up and very graphic. After a few quick questions, the reporter left the scene, headed back for the paper's office and the scoop—but not before he was overheard saying, "Wow, this is great stuff."

This is not a parable about a small community paper gutting it out hero-ically against a giant metro daily. This is about two community papers with diametrically opposed ethical standards; one reporter thought the gore "great stuff," the other found it tragic, yet realized the long-range significance of the unexpected death of the community's most important political leader. His pictures showed no mangled corpse, in keeping with his paper's policy of no dead bodies, just the overturned tractor and workers standing around, looking down helplessly. The strength of Ed's coverage lay in the in-depth reporting and backgrounding, explanatory journalism that tried to make some sense of the tragedy as it related to both the affected family and county political dynamics.

The competition, predictably concentrated on depicting the death scene in multiple, large, lurid photos beneath shrieking headlines. It doesn't take a rocket scientist to know whose papers sold out quickest on the newsstands.

To Cover or to Aid?

Ken Irby, now deputy director of photography for the prestigious Long Island newspaper *Newsday*, recalls a pivotal event in his young career. Working at a community paper in Michigan, he raced to cover a 10-50 with PI, the scanner alarm for a traffic accident with personal injury. Arriving on the scene before anyone else, Irby says he found a woman pinned in the crushed wreckage of her car, and without thinking, he got a blanket out of his car and comforted the woman until the ambulance arrived.

Only then did Irby go to work as a photojournalist, taking photos of the emergency workers getting the woman out of her mangled car. By then, other photographers had arrived to shoot the scene too.

Back at the newsroom, Irby was confronted by an editor who de-manded to see the exclusive photos of the wreck in its earliest stages. He wasn't interested in shots of the rescue. "But you had the scoop! You were the first one there!" the irate editor exclaimed, "*Where's that photo?*"

Irby replied, "There aren't any, because I didn't take any."

Later, Irby realized, "I did what I had to do, and I made up my mind right there, that was the right thing to do."

194

Hartford, Conn., *Courant* chief photographer John Long agrees. Addressing a recent National Press Photographers Association session on ethics, he said, "After a day's shooting, you've got to be able to go home and sleep with yourself."

When Do You Print Foul Language?

The assignment had been to do a color story on the outdoor fish market down by the wharf. Marge, a reporter-photographer for the *Bugle*, returned to the newsroom excited about the contents of her notebook and her camera bag. This was going to be a neat story.

Once the color film was out of the darkroom, negatives edited and scanned, the photo page started to take shape. "Hey, got something we can use for a pull quote?" asked the young layout editor.

"Well," Marge said, laughing, pointing to a fishing boat captain in one of her photos, "this guy told me, *'They're selling the shit out of them fish this morning.'*"

"Hey, that's great!" the layout editor said, "that really catches the excitement of the event." And she put quote right beside the photo of the fisherman.

"Well now, wait a minute," Marge wasn't so sure, "do you really think we ought have this guy cussing in the paper?"

"Aw, it's OK," the layout editor responded. "He said it, didn't he? And besides, he knew you worked for the *Bugle*, right?"

"Yeah, but I'd still feel better if we asked the M.E.," Marge said.

"OK by me," shrugged the layout editor. "But it's still a cool quote."

It didn't take Brenda, the M.E., long to give them her answer. "Do you really want to do that to this guy?" she asked Marge and the layout editor. "In this community that man would never live down that quote. If we print him cursing in the paper, he's going to catch it at church, his kids will be teased at school, his wife will be the article of ridicule and he himself will be publicly embarrassed. Unless there's a compelling reason for this newspaper to print a curse word in a direct quote, we shouldn't do it."

"Yeah, but the quote makes the page and the story so much better," the layout editor urged.

But the M.E. had the final word. "Look, I'm sure that's true. But this is community journalism and not a stage play. We're dealing with living, breathing people here, not a bunch of fictitious characters we've dreamed up. These people have to live their lives in the context of this community's standards. If we go around quoting their every verbal indiscretion for the sake of a zingy or lively quote, not only will we wound our sources by wrecking their standing in the community, but we'll also offend many readers, and eventually no one will be willing to talk to us on the record."

Community Standards

When it comes to issues of taste, every community has a shared sense of what is acceptable and what is over the line. Nudity, expletives, cursing, and bathroom humor may have their places in some publications, but less so in community journalism—unless there is a compelling reason to use something objectionable.

While the fishing captain story provides an example of an offensive quote for which the paper has no compelling reason to print, what about the following? At a volatile public hearing, the chairman of the county commissioners shouts at long-winded citizen, "Sit down sir, you're starting to *piss me off.*"

Now we have an elected official cursing at a member of his constituency at a public meeting. Now there's compelling reason. How can the paper not use the quote?

Still, this isn't an easy call for a community newspaper. It's not just a matter of whether to print or not, but how to handle the fallout. With the county commissioner's gaffe, for instance, a community-savvy editor might take the occasion to write an explanatory editorial outlining the paper's guidelines for printing offensive language in direct quotes, and why in this instance, the paper chose to print it verbatim.

When it comes to matters of good taste and community standards, most community papers think of themselves broadly as "family newspapers." That old term means that the newspaper will be "safe" for everyone to read, from innocent children right on up to granny. But different communities have different standards, and the papers that serve those places reflect those different community standards.

When an art student at Yaleanova College staged an exhibit which included his AIDS awareness posters employing used condoms, it made the news. The story was politically topical, the art was unique, and people all over campus were talking about it.

After publication, the newspaper serving the large, culturally sophisticated northeastern college community received a blistering letter to the editor from a parent living in a rural area of the state. The older woman said she was highly offended by the material both in the photos and in the story.

Writing back, the editor responded in part,

Thank you for your frank and candid letter regarding "Grad Student Creates Art with

Used Condoms." I agree with you, the story did contain some objectionable material. However, I think it was well within the tolerance level of our readers. Our editorial news judgment was based on *the matter of audience*. That audience, a college town at a major university, is mainly students. The community's standards are different at a college town than they are elsewhere. More tolerant, certainly less apt to be shocked. Even so, we carefully weighed whether or not to run the story. We decided our main audience, while finding some of the material distasteful, would want to know about the story. Also, our paper merely covered the story—a story which other area papers covered as well—we didn't create the art you found distasteful.

Finally, had this same story broken in a different kind of community with different standards, and if I were editor of that paper, I would have handled it otherwise. Perhaps a simple announcement of the show's opening without any photos.

GRIP 'N' GRINS—JUST SAY NO?

We've all seen this photo: one person handing another a check while they shake hands. Such a static picture of a staged check presentation and deadpan handshake is called a "Grip 'n' Grin." They are the community journalism equivalent of the "Photo Opportunity" or "Photo Op," in which a political person stages an event designed to make him or her look good, and then invites the press to witness this supposedly heartfelt and touching moment. Photographers loathe such assignments; editors hate running these pictures. So it's not surprising, the larger the paper, the less they run "check presentations." Many larger community dailies simply refuse to shoot or print Grip 'n' Grins at all.

Good riddance. They're a bunch of hooey.

Or are they?

If the local Lions Club has raised $5,000 with their pancake suppers to help inner-city kids have eye checkups and new glasses, don't they deserve a photo of that check presentation?

If a women's church group has held bake sales to raise money for Habitat for Humanity, don't they get a check presentation photo in the *Bugle* too?

How can you say no to these and other worthy causes that deserve coverage? You don't have to say no, but you do have to do some creative thinking. Try coming at the story from a different angle. You cover the event or the result, and thus avoid the eye-glazing Grip 'n' Grin.

For instance, send a photographer to the Lions pancake supper or the church group's bake sale. That way, you can encourage the worthy works as they are occurring, and the caption can give credit while there's still time to help the groups raise more money.

Another tack: Do an in-depth, follow-up story on one of the inner-city kids who was actually helped by your local Lions Club money. Do a photo spread on Habitat for Humanity and find the connection between the women's church group and that worthy effort. Maybe one of the women is on the construction team. Bingo, there's your angle.

For every potential Grip 'n' Grin there's a creative solution and a good story behind the boring check presentation. It just takes work on the paper's part. The problem (or challenge) is the same year in and year out. Whether it's the annual Girl Scout cookie sales or Red Cross blood drive, the *Bugle* will be called upon to supply deserved coverage. The trick is to find new and fresh angles on repetitive stories.

Yet another solution used by some papers: Buy some basic point-and-shoot cameras and pass them around the community to civic clubs and businesses and let them take their own Grip 'n' Grins, which you run on a community salute page or business round-up page once a month, or in a quarterly business publication loaded with ads they've bought.

GRIP 'N' GRINS AND THE BIGGO MART

The manager of the local Biggo Mart phones and says she wants you to start running photos of her Employees of the Month, and that means one for each of the six separate departments in your hometown store.

When you tell her it's against your paper's policy to run employee-of-the-month (or, of-the-week, or day) photos, she grows belligerent and threatens, "Do you know how much advertising we place in the *Bugle*?"

Is this fight worth a fight? What do you do?

Here are some creative solutions offered by other community newspaper folk under the gun.

✓ Tell the manager you'll do a story on her honored employees, simply listing their names. Then at the end of the year, say you'll do a photo and feature on the winner of the store's annual employee-of-the-year contest.

✓ Suggest to the manager a group shot of all the honored employees and limit it to once a month. Explain to her that whatever the *Bugle* does for Biggo Mart, the people down at Bleck's Department Store will demand the same coverage. Point out to her that the paper's photographer can do only so much.

OTHER VOICES, OTHER NEWSROOMS

Community journalist Loren Ghiglione, editor of the Southbridge, Mass., News, *won a Mellett Citation from Penn State's University College of Communications for excellence in media criticism. In this column he wrote in a December 1992 paper, Ghiglione grapples with the issue of how community newspapers should report suicide.*

How Can You Not Report Suicides?

by Loren Ghiglione

The day after Thanksgiving, a funeral director at a local funeral home called *News* reporter Michele Morse with an obituary about a 24-year-old Sturbridge man.

Morse, who had gone to high school with the man, asked the funeral director the cause of death. She replied, "Just say that he died."

"As soon as she said that," Morse recalls, "I knew it was suicide." Though a medical examiner ruled a self-inflicted gunshot the cause of death, *The News* reported only that the young man had "died early yesterday morning."

"People always lie about suicide," a newspaper editor instructs the cub reporter in Benjamin Cheever's "The Plagiarist." The family lies. The police lie. Even the medical examiner will lie if he has to."

The newspaper, too, lies. Or it unquestioningly reports the lie or dissemblance of the victim's funeral home.

The review of death certificates from area towns for the past 15 years reveals that medical examiners have ruled almost 100 of the region's deaths to be suicides. But, with few exceptions, those self-inflicted deaths have not been described by *The News* as suicides.

News obituaries, based on information provided by funeral homes, often have misled readers. A 65-year-old Southbridge man who shot himself in the head with a .22 caliber rifle, *The News* reported, "died today in his home." A 79-year-old Southbridge man who hanged himself, the newspaper wrote, "died Saturday in Harrington Memorial Hospital."

In other instances, *The News* has hinted at suicide but has failed to report the medical examiner's ruling. A Charlton man, 26, was "found dead in his car near his home." A 20-year-old Woodstock man "died of carbon monoxide poisoning at his home."

Debate rages over press coverage of suicide. "It should not be reported," says one funeral home director. "Word gets passed around. It doesn't have to be printed for the archive. The family doesn't have to pick up a clipping 10 years from now and read that somebody blew his head off."

Another funeral home owner says, "When it's suicide, I refrain" from telling reporters. "It's for the survivors—if it is 10 people that don't know about the suicide, that's 10 less people they have to deal with."

But Stanton C. Kessler, acting chief medical examiner for the Commonwealth of Massachusetts, believes accurate disclosure—not grisly, gory reporting—"is really important. I would report fully. The more the news gets out, the better things are. How can you not report suicides?"

What should a small-town newspaper—any newspaper—do about reporting suicides?" The local standard has changed over the last century. In 1888, when the weekly *Southbridge Journal* deemed Sylvanus Davis' purchase of two cows newsworthy, a suicide guaranteed front-page coverage.

The *Journal* detailed the suicide of a Charlton farmer who stood on an old chair and hanged himself in his barn. "When found the chair was overturned and his palmleaf hat, with a red bandanna handkerchief in it, was lying near the chair," noted the Journal.

Suicide began to be reported more discreetly at the beginning of the 20th century. The humiliation felt by surviving family members, the false belief that suicide "runs in the family," the religious attitude of condemnation—all worked to encourage understatement, if not non-statement.

George Grant, owner of the weekly *Southbridge Press* between 1891 and 1938, never reported suicide. "He ignored it because he was an old-fashioned type who didn't believe in a certain kind of news," recalled Andrew Tully, who got his start in journalism as a $7-a-week *Journal* sportswriter and proofreader. "Of course everyone loved him."

The News, founded in 1923 and published by Virgil McNitt and Frank McNitt between 1931 and 1969, downplayed suicide. A suicide at home "was left up to the readers," Tully said. In 1957, a 64-year-old optical worker hanged himself. *The News* merely noted that he "died at his home yesterday morning."

A prominent person's suicide in a public place might result in a tiny article, recalled George A. Anderson, *News* managing editor during 1945-50 and 1964-69. In 1953, an automobile dealer, missing for six days, was found dead in his car on a cart path off Eastford Road.

The News kept the word suicide out of both the headline and the lead of the two-paragraph news brief. But the second paragraph listed the medical examiner's finding and concluded, "A hose had been run from the exhaust pipe of the car into a rear window."

The News of 1976, by then under ownership of this editor, announced a policy change in reporting suicide: The newspaper would describe the medical examiner's finding—for example, "suicide by carbon monoxide asphyxiation"—even if its reporters could not learn that finding until after publication of the victim's obituary.

To remain silent, *The News* editorialized, threatens the newspaper's credibility and "risks making suicide into an invisible death." Suicide patterns that deserve public scrutiny, the newspaper warned, would otherwise go undetected and undiscussed.

The new policy failed on four fronts.

First, more than three-fourths of suicides still went unreported. Of 17 deaths termed self-inflicted by medical examiners in the next four years, 1977-1980, *The News* reported only four as suicides. Medical examiners and funeral directors often kept the cause of death from *The News*.

Second, the ethics of the newspaper, which spoke of its duty to try to tell the truth, ran into the ethics of the readers. Some attacked the new policy as, in the words of Sally Kalis, a 1980 letter-to-the-editor writer, "tasteless and totally lacking in compassion." Others criticized it as an invasion of privacy that threatened the victim's right to a Christian burial.

The harder *The News* tried to track the cause of death, the louder readers protested. In 1982 *The News* reported that a 17-year-old student had died "in Worcester City Hospital." The funeral director and medical examiner refused to tell *The News* the cause of death. *The News* spent two weeks locating the death certificate, which confirmed suicide.

Without mentioning the student's name, *The News* editorialized about the need to provide the facts that would encourage readers' understanding of adolescent suicide locally. "A newspaper shouldn't seek to sensationalize suicide," *The News* said, "but it should at least report the truth."

A letter signed by three residents of the victim's hometown sided with the medical examiner and funeral director: "They realize the family involved has to live with the hurt every day of their lives. After weeks have gone by you just had to let your readers know the truth about (the young woman's) unpleasant death. For what purpose?"

Third, *The News* began to worry about the impact of reporting suicide on those who might themselves be considering suicide. Dr. Richard L. Fowler, then medical examiner for the region, said, "I personally would prefer that suicides wouldn't be reported. When a prominent person commits suicide, usually two or three others follow. Apparently it stirs people thinking of something of that sort."

The notion of an account of one suicide causing—through suggestion or imitation—another suicide dates from at least 1774. Johann Wolfgang von Goethe, inspired by a diplomat's suicide, wrote a novel, *The Sorrows of Young Werther.* Goethe declined to discourage reports, since refuted, that his novel's publication led to a wave of suicides. In studies between 1974 and 1979 sociologist David P. Phillips found what is called the Werther effect: Newspaper's suicide stories were followed by statistically relevant "excess suicides."

Fourth, the manner in which an understaffed newsroom tried to carry out *News* policy encouraged the newspaper, like most media, to focus its feature reporting on certain suicide patterns while ignoring others.

If a young person's cause of death was not made available, *The News* staff, logically pushed for the cause. But the death of a 70-year-old failed to attract as much staff attention. Aware of teenagers killing themselves, *The News* devoted lengthy articles to local teenage suicides and the response of the health establishment.

Suicides of older people, however, went unreported. A review of local death certificates suggests *The News* missed an important story. Of the region's 21 suicide victims between 1976 and 1980, for instance, none was a teenager. But 11—more than 52 percent—were men between the ages of 50 and 79.

Since 1985, *The News* has returned to reporting the cause of death as provided by the person's family or funeral home. In effect, suicides have gone unreported for the past seven years. Of 11 Southbridge deaths that medical examiners have ruled self-inflicted, not one has been reported by *The News* as suicide.

Reporting policies by New England's major metropolitan newspapers provide no simple answer as to what the policy of *The News* should have been or should be. Newspapers everywhere find it virtually impossible to report suicides evenhandedly. Some families, doctors and undertakers go beyond hiding the truth.

Daniel Warner, editor of the *Lawrence Eagle-Tribune*, caught a police captain—aided by a coroner—falsifying the death certificate of his father-in-law, a suicide victim. Edward Patenaude, veteran Webster reporter for the *Worcester Telegram & Gazette*, remembers a millworker's obituary submitted by an undertaker. "(He) said the man died 'after a short illness.' He had hanged himself."

But reporting of suicide by *The News* and other media suggests a "do" and "don't" list.

I. Don't report suicide as entertainment, glamorizing or glorifying suicide as the ultimate flight from life, the great getaway for eternity.

If Shakespeare had his Romeo and Juliet, newspapers and magazines have their leaping suicides. The *Worcester Telegram & Gazette* publishes a large photo atop Page One of a man in Toledo, Ohio, swinging from a 200-foot-high bridge girder threatening to jump. *New York Magazine* features "a remarkable woman," who sees her solution to life's problems as a leap to her death from a ninth floor midtown Manhattan apartment.

The New York Times profile of the 900th suicide off the Golden Gate Bridge romanticizes the jump from "the beautiful span that is San Francisco's signature." The article ends with a quote from the dead man's sister. His leap, she says, "has eloquence to it, and maybe that's what he wanted to say."

II. In a society fixated on the young, don't suggest by the frequency and quantity of prominent coverage that suicide almost exclusively befalls people—especially bright people—in their teens and twenties.

Suicide "epidemics" and "copycat suicides" among the young are staples of press coverage. But even the staid *New York Times* gives Page One tabloid treatment to adolescent suicides: "4 Jersey Teen-Agers Kill Themselves in Death Pact."

Reporters, who are often young and who often see themselves as brilliant, write there-but-for-the-grace-of-God-go-I profiles of young, brilliant suicide victims. John Doe, "a brilliant" Harvard Phi Beta Kappa; Jane Doe, "a brilliant girl who entered Michigan State at 16."

III. In reporting the news of suicide, don't appear to sell so-called "rational suicide," and "assisted suicide" as ultimate civil rights appropriate for all.

Headlines from a major metropolitan newspaper like "In Matters of Life and Death: the

Dying Take Control" may suggest suicide is a simple, rational act. Media attention focuses on Derek Humphry's best-selling suicide manual, "Final Exit," on Dr. Jack Kervorkian, the Michigan doctor who has helped people commit suicide, and on initiatives in California and Washington state that would have authorized doctors to assist in suicides.

But most suicides, say psychiatrists, are far from rational. They are desperate, often irrational, acts of depressed, despairing people. The hopelessness that leads to those suicides often can be reversed through medications, hospitalization, therapy and support. But, in a statistic that the press should take to heart, two of three Americans with serious depression will not seek help. They do not see treatment, which receives little coverage, as a choice.

IV. Do demand that vital sources of information about suicides—autopsies and the state's annual cause of death survey—are continued, and do be sure to study them.

Budget cuts and staff reductions statewide threaten the compilation and publication of death data. The area's primary medical examiner for the past years, warns, "For the past one and a half years (1990-91) we were not autopsying all suicide cases." When asked about annual Massachusetts reports on causes of death, the state's acting chief medical examiner says, "We haven't been doing them."

Of significance locally, perhaps, a federal survey last year (1991) showed that suicides among the elderly, which dropped between 1950 and 1980, have risen in recent years. Indeed, the rate of suicide for people ages 75-84 is almost double the rate among young people—in 1990, 26.1 suicides per 100,000 vs. 13.6 per 100,000 for people ages 15-24.

The state's acting medical examiner reinforces the data's message by repeating an acronym he uses when lecturing medical students about suicides—MA'S SALAD. The letters, he says, stand for middle-aged and older people with previous suicide attempts, males who are single, alcohol users and abusers—lonely, alone and divorced.

V. In reporting suicides, do put the emphasis on the living—on those who might be able to help a suicidal person, or on the bereaved who are trying to cope with their loss.

Two articles earlier this year by Jane E. Brody of the *New York Times*—"Suicide myths cloud efforts to save children" and "Recognizing and rescuing suicidal youths"—deftly described signs of depression, suicidal triggers and overlooked hints to recognize the seriously suicidal. Such reporting is all too rare.

The media need to make the public aware of sources of help: The American Suicide Foundation and a national survivor's referral line, 1-800-531-4477; the National Institute of Mental Health Depression Awareness, Recognition, Treatment program, 1-800-421-4211; Samaritans hotlines and the Samariteens hotline, 1-800-252-TEEN.

VI. Do acknowledge the possibility that reports of suicide—possibly even this column—may encourage people at risk to question their shaky hold on life.

Caution should push newspapers to question photos, extensive page one coverage, headlines that use the word suicide, detailed accounts that suggest suicide is easy, and intimate, romanticized reconstructions that invite readers to identify with heroic victims eulogized by their communities.

However hard-nosed the self-image that journalists wish to perpetuate, they need to recognize that emotion—the anger, even terror—that surrounds suicide. It symbolizes society's failure. Parents, ministers, counselors and other safety nets have not worked. That "frightens the horses in the street," as Virginia Woolf wrote before killing herself.

Painful for survivors, suicide, nevertheless, remains newsworthy. It should not be allowed to disappear, slipping silently back into the community's closet. It may be most usefully as well as most sensitively reported but not in a details-and-drama profile about a victim. And not in a medical examiner's one-sentence finding or in an obituary code phrased like "died suddenly."

It may be best reported in an annual review of the region's suicides that, without identifying victims by name, draws attention to patterns and issues that should concern us.

So this scribbler will add one item to his list of New Year's resolutions: to report at the end of each year on those in the area who killed themselves. Perhaps those who died can provide a lesson or two for those who live.

YOUR TOWN; YOUR TURN

1. Does your newspaper have guidelines for ethically challenging dilemmas? Are they written down or just implied? What's the paper's policy on reporting suicides?

2. Does your paper have a "dead body" rule? What would you have done in the case of the tractor wreck?

3. The local Ruritan Club has raised $500 for new playground equipment at the town park. They want the *Bugle* to take a photo of the check presentation. What do you tell them?

Young journalists tend to overlook good story and picture potential if
they think the setting is beneath them. But human interest stories are
everywhere. Even a kindergarten graduation can produce memorable
moments.

15

About That Little Old Lady from Dubuque

THE *NEW YORKER* WE AIN'T

When the svelte and urbane *New Yorker* started up in 1925, its editor, Harold Ross, wrote grandly in his opening essay, "*The New Yorker ...* will not be edited for the old lady from Dubuque."

Well, friends, in case you haven't figured it out, we *are* writing for the little old lady from Dubuque. Or Tryon. Or Winetka. If you want to do esoteric and urbane stuff, you'll have to wait. Maybe that comes later after you've earned your stripes in our shop. For now, you'd better remember that little old lady; she's your reader.

REALITY CHECK ABOARD FLIGHT 1041

High over the eastern seaboard, the Washington to Miami USAir flight 1041 cruised at 37,000 feet, the passengers enjoying their drinks, taking in the views, dozing or reading newspapers. Even the flight attendants had time on their hands.

"Excuse me, sir," said a young flight attendant to a businessman, who had put his large Northeastern metro daily down and was gazing out the window. "Is that your paper?" she asked politely.

"Yes," he replied.

"Can I read it?" she asked.

"Well, I need it back," he noted.

"That's OK," she replied brightly, "I just want 'Calvin and Hobbes' and the front page."

And she said it in exactly that order. As in, entertainment first, a little news second.

The young flight attendant was as good as her word, returning the *News* in under *five minutes*, having summarily dispensed with a weighty 68-page broadsheet newspaper with a 68-page tab weekend insert!

Ouch.

Sometimes your reader might not be just the little old lady from Dubuque; she might be a young flight attendant.

CANARY IN THE COAL MINE

Deep within that same edition of the *News,* a letter to the editor noted that 25 years ago 60 percent of the people between ages 18 and 29 read newspapers every day. Today the figure is 30 percent and falling. The letter writer then presented reasons she thought many readers have stopped turning to newspapers:

It is not the readers who have changed but the newspapers. Twenty-five years ago, you could read in most papers how to bake a cake and fix a car, as well as news of your community. Youngsters would eagerly scan the paper looking for their names and photos.

Today, newspapers everywhere blame TV and our education system for eroding readership. Some sponsor newspaper-in-the-classroom projects in a bid for younger readers, while others opt for mindless contests to increase circulation. Glitzy and expensive graphics and color are also employed to heighten reader interest. Meanwhile when average readers send heartfelt but amateurish letters to the editor, the letters are trashed. When a schoolteacher asks if someone from the newspaper can cover a Columbus Day play, she gets the brush-off. Church news is relegated to the religion page. Press releases must arrive three or four weeks in advance (absolutely no phone calls), and there is no guarantee of publication.

Today's editors and reporters are more sophisticated and better educated than those of yesteryear. They rarely grow up in the cities and towns they cover, and they keep their bags packed as they hop from paper to paper in their quest for a career on a large daily. They do not share the values, lifestyles or history of their average readers.

If newspapers are serious about recapturing readership, then they should become reacquainted with their readers. While TV, time-starved lifestyles and lower SAT scores do play a role in declining readership, the elitist approach taken by more and more newspapers is what's really turning people off.

Boom. There you have it. The canary in the coal mine has dropped dead. What more of a warning do we need? That concise critical analysis of what's wrong with newspapers today came not from a media specialist, not from a professor of journalism and mass communications, but—you guessed it—from the little old lady from Dubuque!

READ AND WEEP

Community newspapers are a part of that monster word, the *media*. People tend to lump us together with all the other weird family members. Do we deserve the blanket condemnations? Maybe, maybe not. But we'd better know what people are thinking and saying out there. Here are the points most often heard from people—readers—complaining about the media:

• The media are not involved with the community. They project a holier-than-thou attitude. As the letter writer noted, reporters are like free agents: keeping their bags packed, selfishly advancing their own careers, always looking for that big move to the next big market. They have no roots, no links to the community, and no intention of making any.

• Attitude toward the smaller and disenfranchised or minority communities is detached and condescending. The major media companies cover small towns only when there's a disaster or bad news. In the aftermath of the LA riots of May 1992, critics charged that the media came in to do stories on South LA only during and after the conflagration.

• The major media are sensation-driven. TV news especially is "angst-pandering," as singer/songwriter Bill Byers puts it. The adage is still the rule: "If it bleeds, it leads." TV example from 8 p.m. teaser: "Boy struck by javelin at track meet. Details and film at 11." We have to wait till 11 to find out if the kid lived? *Who* is the kid? Is that serving the public's right and need to know? No, it's prurient ghoulish titillation and the worst of info-tainment. It is *not* news.

• The media are arrogant and self-righteous, overlaying events with opinion when given the slightest chance. When the press declared Clinton an early winner well before the 1992 fall elections, many readers and viewers were turned off yet again.

• The media sometimes act as if they care about people and the community but really they don't. "Neighbors" editions are disingenuous attempts to win over outlying areas surrounding the center city, thinly disguised maneuvers designed mainly to sell ads, expand circulation and insinuate themselves into someone else's market, or to prevent competition from entering what they see as their turf. Neighbors editions have proved to be a good way to head off or at least compete with shoppers. That's their real reason for existence; the community news value is of little concern to the paper.

• The media are impersonal, inaccessible, unaccountable, uncaring. Remember the example of the big daily that gets 400 letters to the editor a day and runs only about six. That's fairly understandable for a big-city daily;

they are overwhelmed by the sheer numbers and limited by their editorial news hole. Less forgivable is the story of the former big-city newspaperman, an experienced veteran from a major northeastern daily, who bought a small coastal Southern weekly, and who, within six months of coming to town, had alienated most all of his readers and every single one of his advertisers. He was brusque, perceived as unfriendly, business-first, openly arrogant, inaccessible and condescending to the natives. He may have had peerless credentials and stunning clips from New York or Washington, but along the way he had failed to develop that fine talent they don't teach in big newsrooms or J-schools—how to be neighborly. As every experienced community journalist knows, in a small town there's only so many people to alienate until you've pretty much touched every household. So it didn't take long for word to get around town; the new man was a self-inflated, stuffed shirt who looked down on the locals as mere groundlings, hardly worth his eminent editorial brainpower. How different it might have turned out for the new editor-publisher had he treated everyone as if they mattered—be they bankers or bagboys, cooks or county commissioners. They're all readers and advertisers or *potential* advertisers and readers—in other words, his customers.

A NO-BRAINER FOR COMMUNITY JOURNALISM

We don't have to hire expensive media consultants to help us figure this one out; it's a no-brainer for community journalism. The cries of discontent with the media are everywhere. And the handwriting on the wall is in our own pages.

All this adds up to a damning indictment of the media. Elitism, that is, projecting a superior, somehow "we're above and better than you" attitude, is probably the single worst charge a newspaper could ever hear.

Community newspapers should project the opposite image. The level of involvement with community should be total. We should reflect the lines from another famous community document and be: "of the people, for the people, by the people." The moment we in community journalism get puffy, we're done for. We might as well hang up the old green eye shade.

There's no room for arrogance and elitism in community journalism. There is room for caring, accountable, responsible individuals with community vision, human compassion, a desire to communicate about the changing human condition. In the words of a Century 21 commercial, "People don't care about how much you know until they know how much you care."

YOUR TOWN, YOUR TURN

1. Talk to the reporters in your newsroom. What is their attitude toward the paper? Do they see it as just a rung on their professional ladder? A place to learn and grow? Their dream job?

2. How is the staff of your newspaper involved with the community beyond their professional contacts? How many of them consider the community their hometown?

3. Find an example of angst-pandering news presentation. Is it coming from your newspaper or some other media source?

Don't discount the possibility for novelty. A series of personality profiles on area business leaders sounded routine at first, until the series led
off with an old insurance man whose legendary sense of humor brought
the story and photo to life.

16

We Mean Business, Too

SUPER MARIO VS. REALITY

Mario had always wanted his own paper. At eight, he'd put out a neighborhood newsletter. In high school, he started an underground newsletter of his own; he'd never gotten over the thrill.

Now he was in his mid-20s and had a couple of years under his belt at a mediocre chain-owned afternoon daily with a circulation of about 14,000. Mario told himself he wasn't totally miserable at the paper, but he wasn't inspired either. Nobody cared much about quality journalism or community growth. It was time to do one of two things: Find a job at a better paper where he could get expert editorial guidance—or look into getting a paper of his own.

The very thought of his own paper left him sleepless with excitement for several nights. Then one day making his rounds in a neighboring town, he got his break. A local commercial printer had recently bought a thriving print-shop business that included the *Sun*, an old, white-elephant sort of community newspaper. The paper had been started by the former owner's grandfather, and for sentimental reason, the old rag had been kept afloat by the commercial printing part of the business.

Now, the new owner wanted to unload the white elephant and keep the cash cow. He quoted a price that sounded unbelievable to Mario. For less than a new car, he would have his own paper.

But something kept nibbling at the edges of his consciousness. A question begged to be answered: If the old *Sun* hadn't been a success in this town, would it be a success just because of Mario's presence? Mario had to admit, he was a newsie, and didn't know much about the business of running a paper. Back at the J-school at State U he hadn't thought of taking advertising, business or a newspaper management course. Now he realized, he could have used that knowledge.

But he did have a name. His old college newspaper's faculty adviser was a former community newspaperman who'd had his own paper. Mario decided to call Professor Bolton.

"I was about your age when I helped start my first paper," Bolton told Mario when the young man phoned. Mario's spirits soared, and then plummeted when Bolton warned, "You've got to realize two things: A newspaper is a business first. And secondly, if there's not enough advertising in your area, it doesn't matter what a hotshot writer you are, the paper won't make it."

Mario responded, "But Professor Bolton, "The *Sun* has *lots* of ads."

"Yes, Mario," Bolton replied, "But who are they from, how big are they? And what percentage of the paper generates income?"

Mario had to admit he'd been mainly concerned with that nice big juicy news hole. He didn't know about the ads, just that it seemed like there were ads on most pages.

Bolton advised Mario to select four random issues of the *Sun,* and catalog the ads: the name of each business, the size of each ad, and did the ad or that business reappear in subsequent issues. Mario was to compile the total column inches (multiply columns times vertical inches) of the entire paper, compute the ad inches in the same way, and figure out the percentage of ads.

Finally, Bolton told Mario to multiply the number of ad inches in each paper times the paper's open-column inch rate. That way, Mario could tell fairly accurately just how much money each issue of the *Sun* generated. Doing that would give Mario a fair idea of how much advertising revenue each issue generated. Using that number as a benchmark, Mario needed only simple math to figure out the *Sun*'s monthly advertising income.

Mario's research revealed that an average issue of the *Sun* carried 24 ads, all local, ranging in size from one column by one inch to the largest at three columns by 10 inches deep. The average size was a two by four (two columns wide by four inches deep). There were no full-page ads, no big department stores, and not a single large grocery-store chain in town. The *Sun* was under 20 percent ads. In addition, Mario discovered that the full page of classified the *Sun* carried turned out to all be freebies.

When Mario compared his projected ad-generated income to his projected expenses, he was shocked. The *Sun* would be lucky just to come close to breaking even every month—and that was if Mario did it all himself. He'd have to get a day job to support his habit. And hiring a staff was out of the question.

Not surprisingly, Mario didn't need Bolton's advice to save him from crashing into the *Sun*. Mario could see for himself: Little wonder the paper had been carried by the print shop all these years. Mario conceded that Bolton had been right when he'd said, "If your ad base is nothing but mom 'n' pop places (unless you're independently wealthy), your paper is going to be a mom 'n' pop weekly."

Sadder but wiser, Mario resolved to hunker down at his old job, keep his counsel, and bide his time until another opportunity presented itself. He knew that it was just a matter of time.

IT'S NONE OF YOUR BUSINESS?

When Joan spotted the movie ad on the paste-up board in the backshop, she felt her temperature rise; how could Ralph, the *Bugle*'s veteran advertising director, let such a piece of trash get in the paper? The ad for the Bijou theater displayed a mostly naked young woman on her knees, hands tied behind her, about to be abused by a leering male standing over her. It didn't help that the submissive figure in the ad was about Joan's age.

As the young M.E. glared at the lurid Bijou ad, she tried to reason beyond her growing indignation: Ralph's on vacation this week; we're about to go to press; what harm can come if I jerk this ad? It's clearly prurient, designed to titillate; and furthermore, it's way beyond the acceptable limit of taste according to our community's standards.

Without telling anyone, Joan removed the 2×10 movie ad from the paste-up, replacing it with a standing house ad, one that urged readers to use the *Bugle* classifieds. Then she promptly put the incident out of her mind and went about the business of running the news department.

"How could you do that?!" Ralph was practically shouting.

"Do what?" Joan barely looked up from her terminal. She was concentrating on the end of a really complex zoning ordinance story for that day's deadline. She didn't usually have to talk to people on the business side.

"You know very well what I'm talking about!" Ralph said hotly. Then the ad director, trying to keep his anger in check, lowered his voice with visible effort, "Look Joan, I know you're the M.E., but I get back from my vacation only to find that last week's Bijou ad got pulled. Did anyone ask me first? Did anyone even bother to warn the Bijou manager? No! And now he's pulled all his ads from us, and going to the competition. Can't you see where that puts me?"

Joan was fully engaged now. "Yes, Ralph, but that movie ad was down-right obscene," she said.

"It may have been," Ralph responded reasonably. "But it was *my* call. What you did was the same as if I came over and jerked a story off the front page without telling you—just because the subject matter offended me."

"Well, you're right about that," she said, "That would light my fuse."

"And not only that," Ralph went on, "but the Bijou manager is so mad he's talking it up with all his business buddies, and the whole incident has damaged my and the *Bugle*'s credibility in the advertising community."

"But it's just one little ad," Joan said without thinking.

Ralph had to sit down and take a deep breath before telling his young M.E. the facts of community journalism business life.

"You just don't get it, do you? Look Joan, the entire paper is built on such little ads. One little ad after another; each one the result of a carefully crafted relationship between me and the store owner. From the mom 'n' pop fruit stand that runs a one column by two inch ad to the big supermarket with its full-page ad—to me, to you, and to the *Bugle,* they're all equally impor-tant.

"At the risk of sounding like I'm preaching, let me remind you what pays the bills around here and what makes your paycheck possible. In my years I've seen editors and reporters come and go, and you newsies are all alike. You think you're so almighty powerful and important. You look down your noses at us ad people as mercenary bean-counters. But let me tell you, without us, without the ads, you'd have nothing to print your news on. News doesn't make money; advertising does." Ralph was clearly on a tear.

Joan held up both hands and laughed, "OK, Ralph, OK, down boy, I'm starting to get it. I admit it—I've never thought about the newspaper busi-ness like that. But hey, what about subscriptions? What about street sales, news racks and circulation? I thought that made money. People buy papers for the news more than for the ads."

Ralph took another deep breath. "Welcome to Community Journalism Business 101," he began. "First of all, you'd be surprised at how many peo-ple buy the paper mainly for the ads, and just give the news a glance. Sec-ondly, yes, circulation does bring in revenue, but only about 10 percent of our gross comes from subscriptions and street sales. In other words, circula-tion about pays for itself. Remember the postal rates aren't cheap, and we pay our route carriers to deliver those *Bugle*s all over the county every afternoon. It's advertising—*local advertising*—that carries the freight."

Joan sat there a minute thinking, then: "You know Ralph, in one sense I'm sorry I pulled that ad; you're right, I shouldn't have done that, and I see your point. On the other hand, I don't think the *Bugle* has any business portraying women the way that ad did. That was soft porn and this is a family newspaper. And I'm just as serious as I can be about that.

"But I also think I owe the Bijou manager an apology and an explanation. What do you think about me going out to the Mall and speaking with him? Maybe I can get your ads back and at the same time, get him to start running ads that are more in keeping with this community's standards. How does all that sit with you?" Joan finished.

Ralph exhaled in relief, "Joan, that'd be great. And you're right, that ad was over the line; I really didn't even look at it when it came in, I was in such a hurry to get done and get on vacation."

Then an idea struck Ralph. "Say, Joan, maybe you and I could sit down some time with the publisher and think about this notion of community standards as it relates to advertising. It would help me and my staff, as well as the advertisers, if we had a written set of guidelines."

ABOUT THAT BOTTOM LINE

Those two true stories underscore a critical fact of community journalism that most young, dewy-eyed reporters don't want to hear.

No matter how altruistic our values, we on the news side can't escape the fact. A newspaper is a business. It is a business first, and it is a business in the end. When a newspaper folds, it fails because the advertising didn't happen. When a paper succeeds, though the news side may want to take all the credit, it is a business success. Advertising—*local* display advertising— makes the news possible. If you want to survive in this arena, give the folks on the business side the respect and support they deserve.

A community newspaper must be prospering financially in order for it to fulfill its destiny as a positive and effective factor in community growth. Frank E. Gannett, the founder of the immensely successful Gannett chain, realized that when in 1948 he said, "The independent community newspaper has two incentives: To promote the general welfare and to make money. Like the physician, it must be more concerned with the good that it does."

WEALTHY ENOUGH TO BE HONEST?

Mark, a dedicated journalism student, was mystified when he heard

Community Journalism Professor Ken Byerly say, "You've got to be wealthy enough to be honest."

Only two years later, Mark found himself running the *Bugle*, a struggling but quality 5,000 circulation weekly. It wasn't long before he would hear Byerly's words resonate. The son of the manager of Bleck's department store had been arrested for suspected DUI and marijuana possession. The father called the paper, threatening, "If you run that story, I'll pull my ad. And as you know, I'm your biggest advertiser."

Mark now realized just how right his old professor had been. He'd have to stand up to the manager of Bleck's. Do it politely and with respect. To do otherwise—to kill the story to keep the advertising—would have been reprehensible. The *Bugle* had to be wealthy enough to allow Mark to be honest.

That meant, the *Bugle* had to be able to ride out the storm of the lost revenues. Yes, it would hurt everybody on the paper, but to cave in to the demands of the big advertiser would be to sacrifice his and his paper's integrity and credibility on the alter of just staying alive financially.

Mark learned that the father feared a front-page banner-headline story of his son's arrest. So the editor calmly explained how the *Bugle* handled such stories, that it would receive no special treatment, yet be placed inside the paper, down among the police blotter stories in small type. Mark tried to help the distraught father realize the *Bugle*'s obligations to complete, fair and accurate coverage. "If *my* son was busted," Mark explained, "I'd have to report that, just the same."

The Bleck's manager would not be placated. He left Mark's office, making good on his threat, he pulled his full-page ad from that week's *Bugle*.

For a whole month, nothing changed. Mark held his breath while the *Bugle*'s ad director went about the office ashen-faced. He supported Mark's decision, and on the streets put on the courageous face. But all the same he was privately shaken by the course of events.

And then, miraculously, Bleck's came back, along with a note from the manager. In it, the father wrote: "I was surprised at two things: How many people told me they respected the *Bugle* for doing what it had to do, and at how many people told me, 'We missed your ad in the *Bugle*.'"

Mark breathed a silent thanks to his old journalism professor.

WHEN TOO MUCH ADVERTISING IS TOO MUCH

If a publisher is interested in only making money, then that publisher might as well be putting out a "shopper," of which there are plenty. The shopper carries nothing but ads—or if there is a news hole, it's tiny, or filled with canned copy and superfluous filler. This type of paper makes no pretense at covering the news; its sole reason for being is to make money. Typically, you'll find the shopper as a freebie tabloid in supermarket racks. Such a publication makes no claims to being a true newspaper; they're in it for the bucks.

More insidious is the mock community paper disguised as a shopper. These papers claim "total market coverage" (TMC) and so, armed with the impressive circulation numbers, are able to convince local advertisers of their market penetration. By itself there's nothing ethically wrong with that. However, some such closet shoppers fill their news hole with retro-fitted "news" from other papers, or worse, replate a local front page, and fill most of the rest of the news hole with canned stuffing they get by subscribing to the feature services. Such publications do a vast disservice to the name of quality community journalism.

WHAT REALLY MATTERS

When newspaper consultant Bill Fuller says for a paper to succeed it must be *vital*, he means more than just vital to the community as a source of news. He means business, too.

A community newspaper must be vital to the reader as a source for business information, sales, product reinforcement, business identity—in other words, advertising.

Just as clearly, Fuller stresses that the paper must be vital to its advertisers, providing a platform for timely messages, significant circulation, and market penetration.

The Telegraph publisher William Shaw of Dixon, Ill., understands that reciprocal relationship between advertiser and newspaper. In a unique, award-winning publication called the Owner's Manual of *The Telegraph*, Shaw says, "The readers are the real owners of this newspaper. ... It is not enough for us to convince people to buy the newspaper. They must buy into it. Only then can we claim to have a healthy partnership with our owners."

The Owner's Manual further underscores the paper's vital role in the community: "From the publisher's desk to the mail room, there is one overriding philosophy *The Telegraph* subscribes to. Give the readers a full-service newspaper, one that is filled with information which will make their lives more meaningful, more rewarding and more interesting."

The ad staff's stated goal is "to help businesses prosper." The Owner's Manual explains: "Calvin Coolidge once said, 'The chief business of America is business.' That's something *The Telegraph*'s Display Advertising Department can relate to. Because, to paraphrase the 30th president, the chief business of the Display Advertising Department is to help businesses."

After emphasizing that the six sales reps "are all LOCAL and have a good insight into the communities we cover," the Owner's Manual demonstrates just how vital *The Telegraph*'s advertising is with the following blurb: "If you were to mail a 3×5 postcard to each one of *The Telegraph*'s nearly 11,000 subscribers, it would cost you $2,090. But if you were to place a FULL PAGE AD in *The Telegraph* and cover the same number of people, that would cost you $737. A full page ad would have a much larger impact than the postcard, and look at the cost savings."

YOU SCRATCH HERE, AND I'LL SCRATCH THERE

Bob and Peg Allen have spent 42 years building their high-quality family newspaper, *The Wake Weekly* of Wake Forest, N.C. Their son Jimmy is news editor. His wife, Ginger, covers local government and does features. Peg is the editor and Bob is advertising manager. (For how they manage it, see Chapter 17.)

Peg observes, "Bob says advertising now has become a science. It is no longer enough to say you have a good paper with strong readership. Advertisers want demographics. They need cold hard facts."

Bob's advice is to consult good books on newspaper advertising, attend area seminars on advertising, and seek outside help. Peg says, "Bob found it particularly useful to organize an all-day Saturday advertising seminar with an expert from Georgia. Area weeklies attended, and it proved to be a helpful event."

Peg explains that all community newspapers "are struggling with direct-mail, big dailies who want to move back into the communities they have been ignoring. Some (big metro dailies) publish free tabs to squeeze in to the markets traditionally held by community papers.

"Perhaps the biggest competition is the circular ads in the big dailies. In our county, chains (stores) think they don't need to be in the local papers." Peg says this is occurring despite a survey that shows *The Wake Weekly* has more circulation in the local ZIP code than the major metro daily from the nearby city.

To counter this, the Allens stress local advertising. "Bob tries to get his ad people to realize they must know their advertisers," Peg observes. The Allens know shopping at home helps. On one Saturday jaunt to a local strawberry farm, Bob picked up an ad, took photos of the owner for a future feature, and then proceeded to purchase armloads of strawberries, which he distributed to his staff back at the paper.

Peg and Bob Allen, far right, holding copies of their prize-winning community paper, *The Wake Weekly*, are joined by staff members outside their office (a newly renovated old house) in downtown Wake Forest, N.C. Son Jimmy, the news editor, took this picture and notes that in 1947 "Mom and Dad's first newspaper office was a tin building with a pot-bellied stove for heat."

Bob may not have needed those strawberries, but in this business, if we don't shop at home, how can we expect our advertisers to do the same when it comes to us?

YOUR TOWN, YOUR TURN

1. How would you characterize the relationship at your paper between the business people and the newsroom? If there's resentment and bad feelings, see if you can determine from where they come.

2. Determine to the best of your ability who really "owns" your paper.

3. Does your newspaper have business competition? Who is it and what is your paper doing about it?

4. Ask your publisher what the biggest business problem or challenge facing your newspaper is right now. What is he/she doing about it?

5. Does your paper have "good taste" rules for the advertising it will accept or reject? If so, what are the guidelines? If the paper doesn't have such standards, why doesn't it?

17

Newsroom Management: The *Personnel* Approach

WHY THIS MATTERS TO YOU

If you are a college student or a newcomer to the field contemplating a career in community journalism, you may think you're years away from becoming an editor or publisher. But in community journalism, things can happen quickly and without much warning. Sooner than you might imagine you could find yourself in a management position where your personnel abilities will be tested. Some come by their people skills naturally; others must learn the hard way. Usually, it's an acquired skill. At a community newspaper, where in many cases the newsroom resembles a goldfish bowl, personnel work can be a demanding and time-consuming task. Many papers can't afford the luxury of personnel managers; it's just part of the editors' many duties.

So how does a successful editor inspire the paper's staff to consistent levels of quality work while dealing with an individual's problems? One key is to look at and understand the various relationships that exist under one roof. Consider the following single relationship in microcosm, and then how it relates to the big picture.

OUR RELT IS IN TRBLE

Kathy loved her work, no question about that. As the chief photogra-

221

When people tell you there's a family atmosphere to smaller community papers, this is what they mean. Keys sticky with baby food are not unusual. Though this shot is dated by the old faithful black manual typewriter, the human conditions remain unchanged, thankfully.

pher for the *Bugle*, she found personal fulfillment, professional rewards and enough creative satisfaction to keep her going eight days a week and far into the nights.

Never turning down an assignment opportunity and gladly taking on weekend darkroom duties, Kathy was the model employee—cheerful and bright at work. People wondered how she did it.

Her husband, Brian, thought he knew. She brought it all home—what little time she *was* home. She'd come in from another 12-hour day, fall on the bed and inevitably start complaining about whatever had ticked her off that day. Or she'd unload on him—or even worse—on their five-year-old, Seth, for some trivial misdeed.

Brian, a quiet, thoughtful accountant, was trying to make this relationship work. After all, he reasoned, hadn't Kathy supported him by working at the local paper while he'd finished college? Now he was keeping his part of the silent bargain, helping with Seth while Kathy was out shooting evening sports, city council, Boy Scout field days, farmers markets, Special Olympics, the arts festival, the college's theater group in rehearsal. ... There seemed to be no end to the events that took Kathy away from her family.

In short, Brian was starting to feel as if he were raising the kindergartner by himself while Kathy was out covering what he was coming to regard as petty events. It was a good thing he could cook, too, he told himself with growing bitterness, or else he and Seth would have starved long ago. He tried to remember, when *was* the last time the three of them had sat down at the dinner table together?

Brian realized he was starting to openly resent Kathy's work schedule. But every time he mentioned the problem to Kathy, she either blew up or dissolved in tears. He'd even hinted at their going to a marriage counselor. But Kathy had dismissed that notion with the typical, "You know how busy I am." He never mentioned it again.

And the worst part of it, little Seth could feel the tension between them.

It all blew up on the day of Seth's class play. Brian had even made the little boy's costume (the program listed Seth as a Rock in the environmental play). But when Kathy failed to show up for the play—and hours later explained in a hurried phone call that there'd been a bad wreck out on the four-lane, the patient, loyal Brian knew his long fuse was about burned down.

He decided he'd try writing it all out for Kathy. But once Brian started, he found he couldn't write fast enough to record the flood of pent-up anger spewing out on the page. In his haste, he began condensing words and leaving out letters.

One sentence read: "Our relt is in trble." and from then on, in the letter, every time Brian wanted to use the word *relationship*, he simply scrawled the abbreviation "relt."

When Kathy read the letter, she couldn't understand—first of all why he was mad at her at all—and second, what was this goofy word "relt"?

"It's short for relationship!" Brian exploded at last, "and short is what our relationship is! Don't you see? What kind of relationship is this? We don't even see each other enough to *have* a relationship. All we've got is a— *RELT*."

WE'RE ALL IN THIS TOGETHER, AGAIN

That story could have been written about a journalist and her spouse on a large metro daily as well, but when the above scenario occurs at a community paper the fallout is much more widespread.

The theorem goes like this: Because everything on a community paper is more concentrated—fewer people to do the job all packed in a smaller space—relationships can't help but be intensely personal. It's all the same, whether it's between colleagues, editors and staffers, business and news, word people and picture people, backshop and newsroom.

It boils down to a basic nut graf: We're all in this together.

If that sounds familiar, it's because the same statement has been made about the paper's relationship to the community. That philosophy applies equally to the internal workings of the paper, too. Contrary to many large metro daily papers where some reporters don't even know each other, on the community paper it's like the old country expression: If Mama Ain't Happy, Ain't Nobody Happy. In this line of work, everything touches everybody.

Small newspaper staffs resemble families much more than their counterparts at the big-city dailies where journalists can live in the luxury of anonymity if they so choose. As with a family, community newspaper staffers are thrown together in close proximity with people they did not chose to be with, and basically have to live with each other's faults, foibles and bad habits. To the extent a newspaper staff thrives is a function of how well they have come to terms with each other's individualities.

Whether you want to or not, you will come to know each other's weaknesses, strengths, personal lives, husbands, wives, kids, significant others, histories, hopes, dreams, hobbies, fetishes, phobias, pets, pet peeves, drinking habits and whether you like your coffee black and your hot dogs with relish. You may not even like each other, but you must learn to work and survive together.

Then, consider the nature of the beast. We're not talking about running a shoe store here. Take this goulash of egos patched together and throw them into a high-stress, deadline-driven, high-profile, production-oriented enterprise that never seems to take a holiday—and what do you expect?

There's going to be fireworks.

When personnel problems ignite, the most common problem areas are conflicts between the community newspaper staffer and a non-media spouse and/or SO; between staffers themselves, in and across department lines; and between labor and management.

It's another truism of our business, every facet of our work is more personal, even personnel work.

If a community paper's chief photographer is having marital problems, it's going to be felt in the newsroom. Once Brian confronted Kathy about their non-relt, it was bound to show up in her work. Not only is the conflict going to impact Kathy and her attitude when she's in the newsroom or darkroom, but it could start to have a negative impact on the look of the entire newspaper as well.

CAN THIS MARRIAGE BE SAVED?

How do you stay married to a non-media partner (or have a real relationship) and still be a good community newsperson? What do you do about a non-media spouse who doesn't understand your devotion to your craft and your calling, and who resents the time it takes for you to do the job?

Work comes first, doesn't it?

Not ... exactly.

Every couple has to work out for themselves what matters. It comes down to *balancing a constellation of priorities*. Perhaps the bright spots in one couple's constellation might be work/career, family, lifestyle, location—not necessarily in that order. Depending on individual needs and situations, the priorities are always shifting between elements in the constellation.

The media spouse, however, must make it plain to the non-media partner that because this work is time-driven, the professional life may seem all-enveloping. Understandably, this is a business that is rough on marriages. However, you can make it work, but you have to be aware of and understand the speedbumps.

A couple of common sense guidelines for Relts:

"Newsies" tend to be big egos. It's a common mistake to assume your mate automatically thinks of your work as a divine calling; more likely your partner will not share your enthusiasm for your coverage of city council or Little League. Share, don't preach. Try to get your significant other involved with your work. Explain the issues and your perspectives on each story you're working on.

Give equal time; what's going on in your partner's world? Listen well, and don't swing the conversation back around to you and your work. Establish time for creative conversations when there's no talking shop allowed, times when you both agree that talking about work is off-limits.

On the topic of Relts in the Newsroom—you've heard that old expression, "Don't get your honey where you get your money." But it's no accident there are so many media relationships, simply because of proximity, common interest, and just plain chemistry. Still, such a relationship has no guarantee of working out any better than the media/non-media mix. There are pitfalls aplenty for the couple that works together, including natural competition for headlines and bylines, conflicts over career direction, salary, promotion, conflict of interest, and possibly even who works for whom. Some papers have strict guidelines about spouses working together; some forbid it outright, and others not only allow it but actually encourage it, figuring such a union guarantees staff permanence.

OTHER NEWSROOMS

A Family Paper

Everyone knows of the declining number of family-owned newspapers and the rise of the chain-owned community papers. No other single change has so dominated the American community journalism landscape over the last quarter century. But it would be a mistake to read the eulogy for the family-owned paper; far from it.

There are thriving, quality, family-owned papers out there. The question for now is, how do they do it? How do they get along, brothers and sisters, wives and husbands, moms and dads working together? Do they bring it home each night? Are they happy? How do they keep winning press contests? What's the secret?

For the last 42 years, Bob and Peggy Allen of Wake Forest, N.C., have been putting out *The Wake Weekly*. The paper is regularly ranked among the very best of the state's weekly newspapers. But it took a long haul for Bob and Peg to get the *WW* to the coveted first place in the general excellence category.

It's been a family operation from the get-go. Bob, only 22, bought into the paper with his older brother in the early '50s and by '56 Bob and Peg bought *The Wake Weekly* outright. For years, Bob was in charge of selling ads and Peg managed the news side. Peg recalls, "Bob was the only ad salesman until Greg (our) second son was old enough to help out. ... News coverage, including meetings, was shared by the two (parents), with the one not attending a meeting tending to the kids."

When asked if they took the business home, you can almost hear Peg chuckle. "Through the years (we) didn't take the business home as much as the business kept (us) at the office. As the boys grew—there are four—they helped out around the office, cleaning ... pulling proofs. Mostly, they did homework in the spare office and slept on the floor (4 a.m. Tuesdays not being unusual) until it was time to go home. That was one way to keep them away from TV."

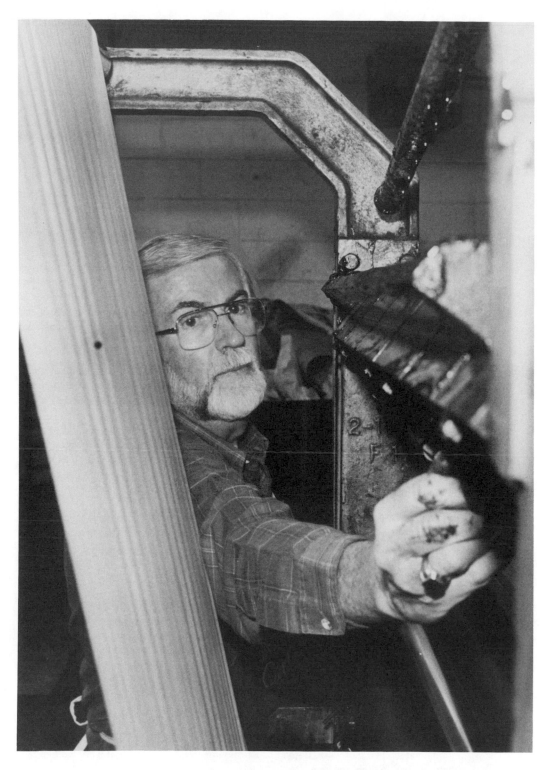

Every week Bob Allen of *The Wake Weekly* turns part-time pressman, adjusting the ink on the Goss Community press at the neighboring Henderson *Daily Dispatch*. (*Photo by Jimmy Allen*)

The Allens consider themselves "fortunate to have four sons who are or have been in-volved in the business. Jimmy is news editor. He is a serious and diplomatic reporter who does all of the editorials now," Peg says. "Wife Ginger—a bright University of North Car-olina at Chapel Hill intern from a few summers ago—covers school and county government, does features and is a whiz on the Macs.

"Bobby, the oldest son, works in the front office, helps with proofing, classifieds and goes to Henderson (to get the paper printed)."

Son Greg, after graduating from the University of North Carolina at Chapel Hill, be-came the *Weekly*'s ad manager, a position he held for several years, until he decided to sell for an Ohio-based graphics company supplying newspaper-related copiers. Peg observes that "his experience in the newspaper business has been helpful and his newspaper contacts have been great for him."

Todd, the youngest, also finished at UNC-CH, and took up the reins as ad manager for a time. Peg explains that Todd's "interests for several years have been in the religious field of missions," but that with Todd living in town, he is occasionally called upon to "pull the fam-ily out of the ditch now and then." Peg adds, "Even though Greg and Todd are no longer in-volved on a day-to-day basis (with the paper), they are just as apt to be taking pictures at some event as Bob and Jimmy. Both are always free with their advice as to how the paper can be improved. It's like the old adage, you can take the boys out of the paper, but you can't take the paper out of the boys."

The Allens, as they contemplate thoughts of retirement, realize they have a rare thing in a family newspaper. Peg says, "Everyone will help out when another is in a bind. Family is more apt to volunteer than employees, it seems. The family is also a good sounding board about all kinds of problems from editorials to ads."

She concedes there is a certain prestige "—whether the family would admit it or not—to being the town newspaper folks." But that status has not come without its own demands. Through the years the family has been highly active in the community. Peg observes that "Bob and two of the boys served on the Chamber (of Commerce) board, Fourth of July com-mittee and about everything that comes along." And just recently, Peg "volunteered" the en-tire family to organize the local CROP Walk.

But the Allens made sure their boys knew the light of justice and print shone equally on all. They believe raising the boys in the community news business "has helped the boys become good citizens. A family newspaper business is a good one for bringing up children as law-abiding, involved citizens. They always knew if they got in trouble, they would see their names in the paper."

The Allens have built *The Wake Weekly* from a struggling paper with barely 700 sub-scribers (many of whom back in '52 didn't even pay to receive the paper) to a prosperous, successful, respected, home-owned weekly with about 7300 paid subscribers.

Peg asks herself, "Would (we) do it again? Of course. In fact (we) are having a hard time thinking of retirement." The Allens say they would like nothing better than to have the sons or some of them continue running the paper. ...

It is 3 a.m., the night before pressday, and Peg admits she's having trouble staying awake. But she's got the energy to say, "I guess all this says we love the business. We've been through hard times, but we never thought about it as hard then. It is such a part of us we can-not imagine not being at work. It gives us a feeling of satisfaction when it's printed that few others can feel in their vocation."

Then she asks herself a final time, "Would (we) do it again?

"Yes. Journalism, especially community journalism consumes you like kudzu covers the trees. It is a vocation where you can work as hard as you want, know you will never get done, and yet, you don't want to give it up."

WELCOME TO THE ORCHESTRA

A newspaper is like an orchestra, and every orchestra is different.

The publisher, perhaps the executive editor or even the managing editor is the conductor contending with the fractious sections. The subtle woodwinds look down on the ego-driven high brass who look down on the plodding lower brass who resent the flashy percussionists who wonder why anyone would want to waste their time in the string section—and so it goes.

The effective conductor must take all this potential, personal and professional cacophony and make music. In the end, if an orchestra is to succeed, various sections must lay aside technical and philosophical differences for the sake of the product, which, in their case is sound.

If you could be a fly on the wall at almost any newspaper, you'd see that the business side doesn't get along with—much less like—the news side. Their attitude will be that the "news hole" is a waste of space better spent on ads that produce money. Additionally, they are resentful that the news side gets all the romance and glory. (When was the last time you saw a TV show or a movie about a newspaper ad person?)

But even within the news department, traditional divisions run deep. Word people vs. picture people. News vs. editorial. Sports vs. everybody.

Following this very extended orchestra metaphor—why do people become flute players vs. tuba players, drummers vs. clarinetists? Or for that matter, reporters vs. ad reps, editorial writers vs. circulation managers, copy editors vs. sports writers?

Most people tend to self-select, that is, gravitate toward the type of work that suits their personality, meaning that you've got an orchestra or staff in which people find themselves where they are best-suited to play their part, so to speak.

BOSSING 101

For a newspaper to work well, something has got to be there that makes all these diverse factions play the same tune with such harmony, fluidity and clarity that the audience gets the message without any communications disorders.

Sometimes it's a great editor. Sometimes it's a great tradition of excellence. Other times it's the influence of all that plus a great community where readers demand such quality. But make no mistake about it—ultimately for a newspaper to work well it takes a publisher/editor with a vision far beyond merely the bottom line. The wise editor/publisher recognizes and yet cherishes these natural differences in his/her orchestra and knows how to draw the finest out of each player, each section.

In community journalism, where turnover is typically high, and staffs tend to be young people starting their careers, the editor is often the first real-world teacher. To know that is to recognize the fundamentally different nature of newspaper management at the community level. If you are that editor, your role is far larger and more demanding than that of your big-city counterparts; you are model and mentor for young reporters who will never forget you. For better or for worse, your impression will be indelible.

But to be fair here, sometimes the green, overzealous reporter deserves the upbraiding they never got in college. "Community newspapers serve as grad school for kids right out of J-school, hotshot cub reporters who haven't yet learned the rules of the road," says one battle-hardened photo chief of a 30,000 circulation daily, "so it's up to us to 'educate' them."

Sometimes that finishing education takes on a hands-on approach. "These kids rush right in at a spot news event and begin firing questions without surveying or scoping out the hard news scene," says the community newspaper veteran. If the young reporter gets in the way of emergency personnel at the scene, they might get off with a mild warning. But heaven help the reporter who gets in the way of our grizzled chief photog at a hard news event. It's called upstaging, and it can result in your early demise.

"I grab 'em by the back of the neck," he allows with a fatherly grin, "and tell 'em calmly, 'If you *ever* get between me and a person I'm shooting—*ever*—I'll kill you.' "

Dale Carnegie, who knew nothing of the concept of tough love, would not endorse this approach. Still, the gentle admonition usually makes a lasting impression. Coming from the crusty old shooter with an inside as gooey as a melted marshmallow, call it "tough love."

COMMUNITY PAPERS AS GRASS-ROOTS GRAD SCHOOLS

In this business, every year or so editors are going to get new people in the newsroom, perhaps right out of J-school. They are going to make mistakes; that's a given. Since we learn and grow most substantively not through our successes but rather our mistakes, what matters is how the editor handles the gaffe. It can make all the difference between a hell hole and a happy shop.

Peter Cook, editor of the Jackson Hole, Wyo., *Guide*, welcomes the role of editor-as-teacher, and seeks out quality university graduates to staff his tabloid-sized, national award-winning daily, where the average age of his newsroom is under 30.

"Ours is a great place to start," he says, "To get anywhere in Yellowstone, you have to drive through Jackson. The town has 4,500 permanent residents, but in the summer we've got 30,000 vehicles coming through town every day. Naturally, the community is a mecca for environmentalists and a mecca for developers. On top of that, 96 percent of the land is public and only 4 percent is private; so you can just imagine the land-use issues."

Cook is a man clearly at home with his dual position of editor-as-coach/educator. He says he enjoys seeing the journalistic and personal development of his young charges. Is it any surprise the Jackson Hole *Guide* is a reflection of his generous and buoyant spirit? "We may not make a lot of money, but we have a good time and put out a good product," he says.

Contrast that example with the editor/publisher who marches into the newsroom and summarily begins shouting a tirade of verbal abuse at the offending reporter—right in front of the entire staff—is courting disaster.

Whoa. Instead of motivating the newsroom, an odd things happens. Work ceases. Everybody gets their resumés updated. If the editor/publisher does this regularly, the word gets out. Furthermore, s/he will have destroyed the staff's sense of drive and purpose. If there is any unity, it will be against the Psychoboss. There will be little possibility for quality work on the paper, except by accident. Staffers will plod through their daily work as if in prison.

This "Newspaper from Hell" scenario is real and all-too-often repeated. Employees don't just leave papers like this, they evacuate. And afterward, when they laugh about it, they speak of themselves as refugees or survivors.

Is that any way to run a railroad?

MANAGEMENT STYLES

Every newspaper has a management style, whether it's stated or only implied.

At smaller papers, the management style is usually reflected in the highly personal style of one or two individuals. At larger community papers, defining and identifying management style becomes more complex. The most successful papers are the ones which have taken the initiative and time to craft a coherent credo or mission statement of management style. Finally, to be effective, guidelines must be written down, shared, emulated and practiced as a model for management behavior.

If a newspaper doesn't have a mission statement for its management style, then that very nonstyle becomes its style. The newspaper lurches forward, propelled by the inertia of nothing more than its own production schedule and publication frequency—without direction, guidance, or any sense of self, calling, purpose or mission.

You will find a variety of management styles in various newsrooms. Listing just a sampling will sound suspiciously like Matt Groening's "Nine Types of Bosses" cartoon essay from the inimitable *Work Is Hell* cartoon book; however, management styles do tend to be easy to type.

You've already met the Psychoboss several pages ago. S/he's the one whom you know better than to even approach because you know s/he's like Khrushchev with his shoe; you know s/he's going to bury you. Other types:

2. **The Unapproachables.** The upper-level people keep their doors closed. The message they're sending is: Don't bother me; I'm too busy and important.

3. **Zombies on the March.** Not really a living thing at all. The paper has no effective leadership. It just muddles on without a clue. Of course, the reading public is aware they're getting the Chronicles of the Dead.

4. **Bottom Feeders.** A paper dominated by a leadership dedicated only to the bottom line. The result is a tiny news hole, an unhappy newsroom and a predictably uninspired news product. The paper, in fact, is a closet shopper.

5. **Cutthroats.** Where everybody is watching out for their own necks and advancing only their own careers. See No. 3.

6. **Fiefdoms.** When a paper has ineffective leadership, individual clan chiefs arise and lead tiny insurrections. Like an orchestra without a conductor, the result is corporate cacophony. See Nos. 3 and 5.

7. **Mom 'n' Pop.** Family-owned operation dominated by a single family or patriarchal/matriarchal figure. Going to work here can be like marrying into the family. Working at this kind of paper can be wonderful if you like the family and they like you. However, if you fall out of favor, you can fall very quickly.

8. **The "10".** The enlightened, quality journalism-conscious community paper with a benevolent, nurturing management style. A young reporter who finds him- or herself at such a paper is blessed indeed. Working there is like going to journalism graduate school tuition-free. This paper likely has a heightened sense of internal corporate community. Employees feel more like team members than just numbers. Everyone knows about and shares in the paper's mission, the core values, load and rewards.

THE FIVE-MINUTE EDITOR

So, what are community newspaper management tactics that have been proven effective in dealing with employees, especially young ones? To borrow from the title of a highly successful management book, let's look at how to better "boss." Points to ponder:

Zen and the Art of Newspaper Management. As far back as the sixth century B.C., the wise men of China have studied the qualities of great leadership. Lao Tsu advises, "No fight; no blame." In other words, never angrily confront a young reporter and denounce him or her publicly.

The Aretha Franklin Factor. Lessons are best taught one-on-one. When a reporter stumbles, give them R-E-S-P-E-C-T. If you have guidance to give, talk to the offending reporter in private to preserve his or her dignity. Craft your constructive comments so that reporters come away from the discussion with something they can use. If they've screwed up, they're liable to already feel bad enough as is. Your firm but nurturing treatment reinforces the community journalism mantra within your own staff, "people are what really matter."

The No-Fault Policy. To borrow from the automotive insurance industry, try this policy. There are no mistakes, only lessons.

High Tech with the Human Touch. Just because your shop is going digital and sprouting computers like dandelions, don't let that high tech override the personal nature which has been one of the traditional strengths of our business. E-mail does not replace eye-to-eye or a pat on the back.

The Gospel According to the Boy Scout Patrol Leader's Handbook. Instead of ordering your staff around, you might follow the dictum from an old *Boy Scout Patrol Leader's Handbook:* "Lets go do it!" beats "you better do it or else" every time. An involved, active editor gets far better results by participating in projects as opposed to issuing flat orders. In fact, the editor who demonstrates that he or she is enthusiastic about sharing the load generates respect and loyalty, which in turn, motivates a staff to produce quality work far beyond anything you could order from them.

The Ben Franklin Dictum. "We must all hang together, or surely we will all hang separately," this nation's great revolutionary publisher told his Continental Congress brethren. The same goes for community papers, where the product is infinitely improved when reporters and photographers and editors talk to each other about projects and stories beforehand. At the larger metro papers this is being treated as a novel concept. Admittedly, it is a welcome change for the large daily, one that requires quite a bit of logistical reorganization and long-range planning. For the smaller papers, where editors, reporters and photographers should have easy access to each other on an informal daily basis, if we aren't already talking to each other a lot, then something is dreadfully wrong with our newsrooms.

No Mo' Memos. Does anybody out there actually *like* memos? If you have a small shop, the overuse of the memo is the quickest way to alienate someone who you could otherwise talk to like a human being. Memos—those terse little impersonal statements issued to save time in large institutions—are officious and demeaning in a small setting. Here, the subtext of the boss's memo may be this message: I'm so big and important and busy that I don't have the time to walk down the hall to speak with lowly little you.

The Peripatetic Editor. The "management by wandering" technique has proven highly effective. If you're an editor, take a moment, just walk the halls, chat with whom you run into. Or, if you have something to say to someone, do it by visiting the reporter in her office or at his desk. Talk about something else first—like how their kids are doing in Little League—then slide into the issue about which you really want to address. Studies on effective leadership show that the least-effective bosses are those who never leave their offices, but who issue all their decrees through e-mail and memos. If you're in community journalism, get out of your office, mix it up. And that goes for the entire town and community as well as your newsroom. Wander mainstreet. Drop in at the local Greasy Spoon, hit the backroads with a clear mind, your camera and a notepad. You don't have time? Make time. It will add years to your life and zest to your paper.

GRIEVANCE PROCEDURES

At large corporations and institutions, the employee with a gripe knows what to do. There's usually a personnel officer to go to, or a formal grievance procedure through which the employee can state his or her case without fear of job reprisal.

However, at many smaller papers, no such grievance procedure exists, and in many cases, it would be somewhat silly. Ideally, with the open-door access typical to many community papers, if you've got a beef, you go see the editor or the publisher and have your say. The downside of this informality lies in the absolute authority of that manager. If the management thinks your concern is trivial, the editor or publisher can deep-six it as if it had never been mentioned. And then what is your recourse? To bring it up again might make you appear to be a whiner, a constant complainer.

Two young women reporters, one white and the other African American, approached the executive editor about what they perceived as unconscious bias on the part of the managing editor, an older white male. According to the women reporters, the M.E. gave all the good story assignments to the men reporters. They were also convinced the M.E. wasn't doing this maliciously, but just behaving along the good-old-boy lines of traditional male management styles. After the conference with the executive ed, the two women said they felt better, but after six months, the situation in the newsroom hadn't improved one bit. They became convinced the executive ed "just didn't get it." Within a year, both had found better jobs at more enlightened community papers.

On the other hand, if you are that manager, you should listen patiently to the concern of the employee, make note of the nature of the complaint, and then either do something about it, or explain and clarify why the situation is the way it is.

For a paper to have a happy shop, employees must feel that the management is accessible, supportive, sympathetic, eager to listen, and most importantly, flexible enough to change policy when it's needed. Such a creative and dynamic atmosphere can be achieved by taking the personal approach to personnel work.

YOUR TOWN; YOUR TURN

1. What are the orchestra sections at your paper? How do they get along? What is the glue that cements them? Or are they unglued?

2. Does your paper's leadership appear to have a coherent and consistent management style? Can you identify it? Does it work, in your opinion?

3. Does your newspaper have a grievance procedure? How does it work? If there's not such a formal process, what options exist for an employee with a concern?

When the photographer asked the avid coupon-clipper what it felt like
to get a grocery cart of food practically for free—the woman began
laughing and tossing her coupons in the air like confetti—and there's
your picture. The Boy Scouts have got it right: Be Prepared.

18

A Day in the Life of a Community Newspaper

IT'S A BRAVE NEW WORLD FOR THE WORLD'S SMALLEST DAILY

When publisher Jeff Byrd arrived at the main street offices of the *Tryon Daily Bulletin* at 8 a.m. Thursday, assistant pressman Tony Elder already had printed three runs of the Friday paper. But then, at the *Bulletin*, a run is an 8½-by-11-inch, four-page flat sheet. It's a 66-year-old, sheet-fed, letter-sized operation, and notably, the *Bulletin* is the self-proclaimed "World's Smallest Daily Newspaper."

Scated at a computer, working on getting accounts squared away, Byrd observes, "Basically, we're a weekly that comes out five times a week. We don't carry any wire copy or national news (or photos). It's all local. It's a community paper. That's what people want here."

Byrd, at 37 already a veteran community newspaperman, bought the paper in 1989 and has recharged the *Bulletin*'s batteries with youthful vigor, but for the most part has run it with an if-it-ain't-broke-don't-fix-it attitude.

Prudently, he hasn't tinkered much with the formula for success pioneered by Seth "Pop" Vining, who started the *Bulletin* in the retirement village of Tryon, N.C., in '28. Back then, the paper was printed from hand-set type on an old Kluge and about half its present-day size—hence the hyperbole.

Folks still think of Byrd as the "new kid," but his boyish charm and head for numbers are paying off. The 4,300, five-day-a-week daily (3,450 mail, approximately 850 street sales) *Bulletin* seems to be thriving—and what's more, "Everybody in town reads every single word," Jeff says proudly but not boastfully, turning back to his work.

Meanwhile, the *Bulletin* seems to run itself with the familiarity of an old team that has been together a very long time—as indeed they have been. The average tenure of any staffer there is a dozen years.

Here's how it works for them: Jeff tried being the news editor (in addi-

Kate Larken, one of the *Tryon Daily Bulletin* news editors, takes a dictated letter from an elderly reader over the phone. She works three days a week, and her counterpart works two.

Tryon Daily Bulletin owner and editor Jeff Byrd tries to get accounts straight but is interrupted by a phone call.

tion to his duties as editor-publisher) at first, and then took over the business side a year ago, and initiated an unusual job-share arrangement. He hired two news editors (managing editors, basically) and assigned them to different days. Claire Wharton takes Monday and Friday, while Kate Larken does Tuesday, Wednesday and Thursday. It's an unorthodox system, but the editors dovetail smoothly, are compatible, and mostly, it works. In addition, Reen Smith serves as associate editor-reporter to round out the writing staff.

The Gemini editor system works because Jeff has a rock-solid backshop. He bought into a dependable, stable and cheery production crew—a factor not to be taken lightly by would-be buyers. Jeff will be the first person to acknowledge that he was plain lucky.

That the *Bulletin* is a happy shop is easy to see. On entering, you are greeted by Robin Lawter who's "been here forever and knows everything," Jeff says thankfully. The spacious front office is dominated by an immense window and high ceilings. The first-timer is immediately struck with the sense that here is a place of solidity, continuity and grace under pressure. Indeed, the turn-of-the-century office is a former bank. A faded blue and white banner from the 1942 Duke University Rose Bowl season hangs prominently on one wall; on another is a primitive wood-burned sign proclaiming *"The Tryon Daily Bulletin."*

There is an unpretentious homey feel to the place. The brown carpet is stained comfortably with printer's ink and the detritus of comings and goings in all weather. Down the hall to the left, the news editor du jour has a cubbyhole. Immediately to the right across the hall is Jeff's office, not the least bit grand or ostentatious. The darkroom opens right into his place, allowing the sweet, unmistakable smell of offset developing chemicals to waft through the publisher's office. Jeff's only concession to status is a large, golden-oak desk left by the former publisher, who they all call reverentially "ol' man Vining" or *"Mister* Vining."

Down the hall and to the right across from the coffee machine and snack table, the composing room is busy. By 9 a.m. Bobbie Briggs, the typesetter and computer whiz, and Joyce Jones, the ad composer and paste-up czar, are in the thick of it, talking to themselves in concentration as their monochrome computers respond to Pagemaker 4.0. "Real news for real people, OK," mutters Bobbie with a wry sense of humor that will be best understood by community journalism folk in the business for a long time.

A bank of two layout tables dominates one wall. Between the tables sits a worn, once-white waxer, years of heat having turned its plastic surface to shades of yellow. The pungent odor of printer's wax permeates the room like something cooking. To the left, one wall is festooned with local advertising logos. Joyce, who's been there 18 years, knows her personal filing system inside and out. Beside that, more logos and "standing art" are plastered to a giant, heavy steel door. Upon closer inspection, it is a vault, *the* vault of the old turn-of-the-century bank. Scrolls and a roaring lion dominate the lintel. On the other wall, no less than 80 styles of border tape hang on nails.

The *Bulletin* has been computerized for only one year now. Bobbie taught them all. Now Joyce says, "I love it, I don't know how we did it before."

In fact, they did it like everyone else: Compugraphic Justowriters,

7200's for headlines, and a lot of scissors and wax. Now, they do it with a combination of Pagemaker and news galleys. But on Fridays, just to ease into total pagination, they experiment and do it all on Pagemaker.

It's a brave new world for the world's smallest daily.

Still, the flag remains from the old days, as with the standing art sig from a local calendar and news item roundup, "The Curb Reporter," both of which Friday's news editor Kate says "have been a part of this paper for a ka-*jillion* years."

Farther back down the main narrow hall, Jeff is found working on paying accounts. Over his head hangs a faded Norman Rockwell painting from

Joyce Jones puts pages together using a combination of Pagemaker and old fashioned wax-and-scissors stripping-in. On the wall is her personal filing system for ad logos. She's been at the *Bulletin* for 18 years and knows where everything is.

the *Saturday Evening Post* depicting the Country Editor at work, circa 1937. Except for the computers, things don't look much different outside the frame. While he toys with the computer, Jeff is talking to a local columnist about a rural neighborhood's problems with a broken water system that resulted from a mudslide down the mountain.

He is interrupted by Kate who wants to know how to handle a sticky situation: On the phone she's got an elderly woman who's so old she can't write but who wants to run a letter to the editor. Will Kate just help her write it over the phone? Kate agrees, but after she has taken the time and effort to compose the woman's letter on the computer, she discovers the old woman doesn't want to sign the letter. Now she asks Jeff, what to do? Jeff tells Kate unequivocally, no signature, no letter. Kate nods, and goes back to the phone. The old woman declines to sign the letter.

10 a.m. Kate opens the morning mail, sorting through the pile, laying possible news copy to the left and "money stuff" to the right for Jeff and bookkeeping. Watching her would make any PR wo/man quail. Some of the mountain of mail she trashes almost immediately upon opening. "I doubt if the retirement community of Tryon cares about the Coneheads coming to Carowinds," she quips, flipping a PR release and photo into the recycling bin.

Letters to the editor, which typically begin with "Dear Jeff," are run under the identical 14-point head, "Communication." Many stories come from club secretaries and volunteers. These are tagged at the end of these stories in italics—*Community Reporter*.

Kate, clad in shorts, sockless tennis shoes, blue denim workshirt, hair back in a pony tail, returns to her office, scans the area dailies for local news they might have missed, as well as local obits.

The phone rings, she talks to the caller and takes notes. Hanging up, she exults "I *love* this place," mimicking the Burger King baseball-hat-backward-dude. The call had come from the local golf course where someone had just hit a hole-in-one. Turning to the computer, Kate knocks out a two paragraph bright. Before she is finished, she is interrupted by Joyce with another set of galleys to be proofed. She quickly scans the stories, makes corrections and returns them to composing.

Every time *any four pages* are ready at the *Bulletin,* they are put together, shot and run on the little press. The paper is thus built from four page runs. Production has only a rough idea how many pages any given paper will contain. Because of this inherited, unorthodox and yet effective system, the *Bulletin* contains no page numbers or jumps, with the exception of front to back. Basically, everything has to fit on each page; it makes for a dicey puzzle in layout. The *Bulletin* doesn't win awards for design and graphics. But

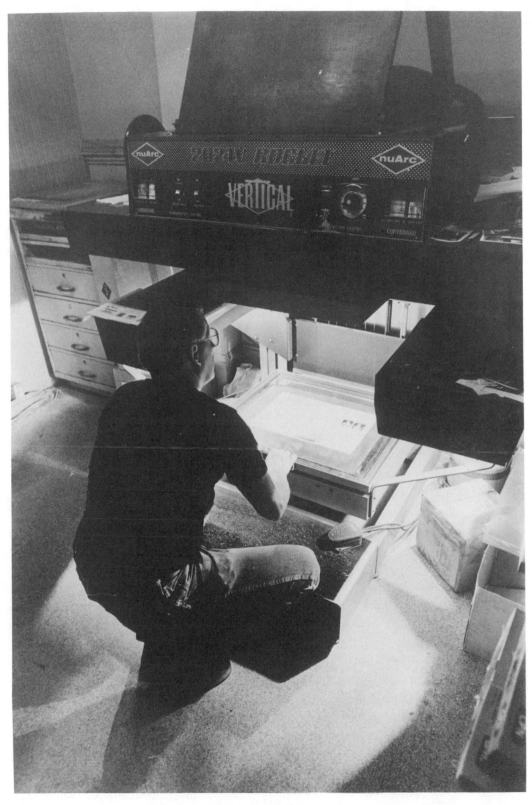

When any four pages are ready, they are put together (no page number, no page jumps) and shot by Charles Barnett, here setting the copy camera.

while it may not be pretty, it works. And, more importantly, it's what people in Tryon are used to.

Just ahead of 11 a.m. copy deadline, associate editor Reen arrives with an envelope containing a story and photo about the Bi-Lo 24-hour grocery store's opening. Inside the envelope are a Polaroid shot and a 3½-inch disk. Waving the disk gleefully, Kate says, "This is the only way to go."

Ad deadline, 11 a.m. A local merchant rushes in, as the second hand swings up to 12. She snakes her way back through the hall, past *Bulletin* staffers to find Jeff beneath the Norman Rockwell.

11: 15 a.m. Four more pages are ready. Charles Barnett, the pressman and copy camera operator, takes the two flats through Jeff's office into the darkroom. There squats an old faithful NuArc vertical "Rocket" which has been the paper's copy camera since the *Bulletin* went offset in '72. Loading the pages into the easel, Charles turns out the white lights, plunging the room into red safelights, activates the vacuum, loads the page film on the vacuum back, slides it shut, and hits the start button. The room is flooded with arc lamps for 18 seconds. And then he flips open the back of the copy camera, and slides the exposed film into an open tray full of developer, rocking the deeply-stained tray back and forth to keep fresh developer on the negative. In the eerie red safelights, Charles looks like something out of a submarine warfare movie. Then in about 30 seconds, the page begins to "come up" and develop fully. He reaches in the solution with one bare hand, grabs a corner and holds the dripping negative in front of the safelight for close inspection—then satisfied, plops it into the second tray containing fixer (which makes the negative light-safe). He repeats the operation until the other two pages are done. Then, he washes them briefly in water, and laughs. "Our negative dryer is out … I just use a hair dryer."

He isn't joking. Carrying the two new page negatives into the backshop, Charles lays them on the light table, goes over each with a paper towel and pulls out a Clairol women's hair dryer and begins a back-and-forth motion over the page negs. "Well, it works," he says matter-of-factly, "and sometime we even use it for hair!"

He makes the two plates, and takes these to Tony, who loads them on the daffodil yellow Solna flat sheet-fed press. As soon as a sheaf of several hundred pages has run off, Charles loads them on the folder. Meanwhile, as each man runs his respective machine, they are both hand-inserting the sections that have been run. Flap-flap, flap-flap goes the methodical papery sound of inserting sections as Charles and Tony rock back and forth on their feet.

They each work on old layout tables that appear to date from the paper's genesis in 1928; built of solid oak, the tables are now smooth with time and printers ink. The surfaces are heavy slabs of ink-stained marble or granite. Talk of the table reminds Charles, a 27-year veteran at the *Bulletin*, about old hot-type days. Before about 1972, the paper still used Linotype to set type. Charles laughs and says he's got that wonderfully clattering old machine at the house, and he's trying to get it running again, sort of as a hobby.

The shushing and whooshing sound of the press and the folder resounds through the high-ceilinged pressroom, spilling over into the hall that leads down to the main offices, filling the building with a sense of purpose and urgency. Charles has to holler to talk. Yes, the air conditioner sure makes a difference. With a grin, he shouts, "I don't remember when it was they put in the air conditioning, but I remember when it *wasn't*."

It was so hot they'd have to open those two large back windows and hope for a breeze. Except for the presses and AC, it appears that very little has changed in the pressroom in 66 years. The walls can only be described as once-beige, and the plaster is cracked, peeled and eroded in a most artful

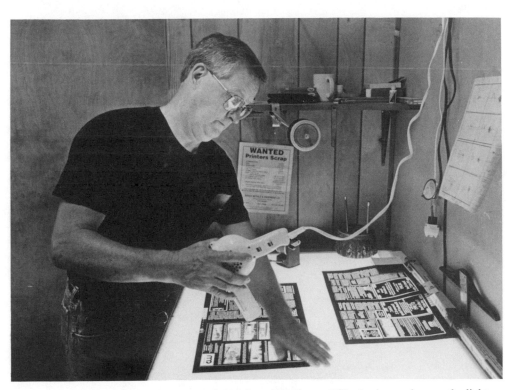

The page negative dryer is broken, so Charles improvises on the light table with a hand-held hair dryer. It works just fine.

state of decay. The large windows are framed by catalpa and ivy growing outside.

Today's paper will require eight to ten runs. Five have been done already. It takes about 35 minutes per run. Between runs there is about one hour per run of make-ready. Charles calculates mentally, "At this rate we might just make the PO by 5 p.m. If we're later than 5, we take 'em down to Landrum and Campobello ourselves. And sometimes on Thursday, our biggest night, we're here into the night."

Maybe someday Jeff will think about converting to a web press, Charles hopes.

Joyce sticks her head in the pressroom and hollers, "Alright, ya'll 're having too much fun back here!"

Noon. Jeff must run to Spartanburg, 45 minutes away, to pick up a 2×4 ad that has to run in the Friday paper. They could fax it, but they need the clean ad slick. Along the way, Jeff muses on how he came to be the editor-publisher of the world's smallest daily. A northern Virginia native, he grad-

In the pressroom, Tony Elder prints, left, while Charles Barnett operates
the folder, right, and inserts the freshly printed four-page section.

uated from the University of Colorado with a bachelor's degree in journalism, then came back East and worked as a reporter and then editor of a half-a-dozen weeklies in Virginia and Maryland, fell in love and got married along the way, did a stint as a reporter at the daily Roanoke *Times-World*, and then got picked up by the *Charlotte Observer* for his community journalism expertise to start their Neighbors edition and a bureau in Statesville, N.C. It sounded like a good idea at the time, somewhere in the decade that Jeff calls "the eighty-somethings."

He liked the idea of having his own paper. Maybe the Iredell bureau would be something like that. "I've always liked community journalism. I've always liked it that you had to be one part reporter and about two parts being *involved*. You got to be involved with the community; you gotta be *out* there"; he says it with a conviction that comes from experience.

Jeff thinks most reporters either don't want to do that, or don't care, or maybe don't know about community journalism. Either way, the experience was "the worst of both worlds," he says.

"At the bureau, there were two types of people working for me: They were either on their way up or on their way out. The ones on their way up hated it (being in the bureau, and thought they deserved to be *downtown* where all the action was). The ones on their way out hated it, hated me, and saw their posting there as a demotion."

After three years there as bureau chief, Jeff decided it was time to take his dad up on an old standing offer to help him buy his own paper. Jeff says it was during the annual family beach trip, he and his father were out in the ocean. "Hey Dad," he said, out of the blue, "remember you said maybe someday you'd help me buy a paper ... how about *now*?"

And when the answer was yes, they started scouting around, settling on a weekly in Henrico County outside Richmond, Va. But after three years, Jeff could see it wasn't working, sold out, but continued to work there for the new owners.

Mid-story, real time Thursday, July 8, 1993, Jeff arrives at Southern Advertising Agency in Spartanburg and picks up the ad. But it's a 2×7, not a 2×4. He calls Joyce to tell her of the change and to leave more space than what they had originally allotted, and that he'll see her in 45 minutes. They're literally holding the presses for a 2×7 ad.

Back on the road heading back to the *Bulletin*, Jeff resumes the story. In 1989, almost by fluke, a broker friend told him about Tryon, flew Jeff down to see the place with only a vague interest. But when he walked in the office, Jeff says he was immediately impressed with the homey feeling.

"Hey!" he recalls saying to himself, "this is like I'm back in my grand-mother's parlor. I like that window. I like that view. I like this light, I like this counter ... this would be cool."

Looking around town he couldn't help noticing the cultural enlighten-ment of the population. "I've worked at cruddy little weeklies in the rural South," Jeff says, "but this place is different. We could be happy here."

In November 1989, the Vinings accepted Jeff's offer, and a deal was struck.

His wife, Helen, at first reluctant to leave Virginia because she liked Richmond, had fallen in love with the Tryon area too. Besides, it was a great place to raise two children, ages 3 and 5.

"We bought an old house. Helen's got a good job, we've got good friends. It's just worked out real great. It's the lifestyle we really like."

By the time Jeff gets back to the paper at 1 p.m., 28 pages (seven four-page runs) have been printed and inserted. He gives the ad to Joyce, who lays it on the page, and takes it to Charles to shoot, and the day's last press-run is soon underway.

While Jeff was gone, news editor Kate ran the front office so Robin could go to lunch. "Jeez," Kate exclaims later, "I couldn't do that job. Peo-ple were coming in asking me all sorts of questions I didn't know anything about."

By around 2 p.m., the last run of the day's paper is done. The staff hud-dles around the layout table looking at it. There doesn't really seem to be a lead story. The standing column, "Curb Reporter," anchors the top left of the four-column front, as it has for 66 years. Five stories on the front all carry identical weight 14-point heads. What catches your eye are two mugshots of sisters in a summer theater production of "BARNUM"! The only hard news on today's front page is a two-inch story about a stolen pickup truck's re-covery. The other three stories are about bridge club results, herbs in bloom at a local nature center and the Class of '73 reunion plans. The paper really does look like its namesake, a bulletin board, with notices tacked up in ran-dom fashion and with no particular weight given to news judgment.

Who decides what goes where?

They all look at each other. Joyce shrugs. "I guess I do. Mr. Vining liked children; he always liked to put them on the front."

"It's community news," says Jeff, adding, "besides, it doesn't matter where a story goes. We put classifieds right in there with the news because we know that's what this community is used to, and they read it cover to cover."

2nd Class Postage at Tryon, North Carolina 28782 and additional post offices. Postmaster send address changes to The Tryon Daily Bulletin, P.O. Box 790, Tryon, N.C. 28782

The Tryon Daily Bulletin (USPS 643-360) is published daily except Sat. and Sun. for $35 per year by the Tryon Daily Bulletin, Inc. 106 N. Trade St., P.O. Box 790, Tryon, N.C. 28782

THE WORLD'S SMALLEST DAILY NEWSPAPER
Founded Jan. 31, 1928 by Seth M. Vining
(Consolidated with the Polk County News 1955)
Jeffrey A. Byrd, Editor and Publisher

The Tryon Daily Bulletin

Phone 859-9151   Printed in the Thermal Belt of Western North Carolina   **32 Pages Today**

Vol. 66 - No. 111   Tryon, N.C. 28782   **FRIDAY, JULY 9, 1993**   25¢ Per Copy

The weather: Wednesday, high 102, low 65, humidity 39 percent.

These days, it's not the humidity; it's the heat.

They're calling it a drought and a heat wave. Counties are enacting burning bans effective until a full day of rain has fallen.

Fireworks caused some burn damage last weekend.

Meanwhile, farmers and gardeners are having a tough time of it. At least one well has dried up.

Health precautions should be taken seriously, for extreme heat can do the body some real damage. And don't forget the pets!

The Thermal Belt Outreach Ministry has managed to help some of the people in need who are suffering from the heat.

Just this week, someone donated an air conditioner. The Ministry placed it in a home, then found someone in the Polk County sheriff's department to help install it.

People care.

This place may be hot as a firecracker right now, but it's still a cool place to live.

Here's what is happening:

Annual Coon Dog Day festivities will be Saturday, July 10, in Saluda. The day's events begin at 7:15 a.m. and go until midnight.

The parent support group will meet Monday from 7 to 8:30 p.m. at the Columbus Presbyterian Church. Free child care is available.

(Continued On Back Page)

Columbus Police Report Recovery Of Stolen Pickup Truck

Chief Billy Stepp of the Columbus Police Department reported Thursday that the truck stolen this week from the home of Fred Lindsey has been recovered in Anderson, S.C.

Earlier this week, a stolen Anderson truck had been found in Columbus.

Law enforcement agencies investigating the crimes believe the two auto thefts are linked to each other and to robberies in Columbus and Anderson. Drugstores in both cities were robbed.

Police have identified suspects, but no arrests have been made at this time.

Tryon Class Of '73 Looks For Alumni

The Class of 1973 of Tryon High School, which will hold its 20-year reunion on Saturday, August 21, is seeking the addresses of four of its classmates.

If you know how to get in touch with any of these four individuals - Ernest Doughty, Laura Joseph, Keith Starling or Jennifer Trainor - please contact either Dexter Williams at (803) 225-5821, Grant Vosburgh at (803) 984-0610 or (803) 833-8280, or June Williams in Tryon at 859-5675.

The reunion will be held at Tryon Youth Center beginning at 7:30 p.m.

Red Fox Bridge Club

Results of the Red Fox Bridge Club played on Tuesday, July 7, are: 1st - Eloise Harris; 2nd - Martha Graves; 3rd - Agatha Crawford.

Amy Grochowski

Robin Grochowski

Grochowski Family Involved In BARNUM!

The Tryon Youth Center and the cast of BARNUM! have quite a few Grochowski's involved with the summer musical.

Amy, who plays the barker bringing in our audience, is a 14-year-old freshman at Polk County High School. She is a theatrical veteran, having performed in "Grease," "Guys and Dolls" and numerous dance productions including "The Nutcracker" with the Carolina Ballet Theatre. She is a dancer, pianist and cheerleader.

Amy's 7-year-old sister Robin, a third grader at Tryon Elementary School, plays the building inspector and doubles as a clown. Robin is also a veteran of the Carolina Ballet Theater's "Nutcracker" and loves dancing and art.

The two sisters exclaim: "BARNUM! is fun! It's going to be a great show! You have to come see it!"

They seem to be enjoying the rehearsals, despite the fact that their mother is there. That's right - one more Grochowski! Patty's nimble fingers are busy creating marvelously colored clown costumes, brilliant jackets and extra-long pants for the stilt walkers.

BARNUM! will be presented at the Tryon Fine Arts Center July 15-18. Look elsewhere in *The Bulletin* for ticket information.

— *Community Reporter*

Herb Garden In Full Flower At FENCE

The new culinary Herb Garden at FENCE is growing rapidly under the care of the FENCE herb group. The design has included many different herbs, all of which can be used in the kitchen.

At least five types of basil have grown in to full leaf and oreganos, marjorams and savories line the raised borders. If you have never tasted the cucumber-like freshness of salad burnet or the perfume of rose-scented geranium, take an hour to visit the herb garden to explore the world of culinary herbs.

For more information call FENCE at 704-859-9021.

— *Community Reporter*

The average American drinks over 19 gallons of milk a year.
— *N.C. Dept. of Agriculture*

The day's front page of the *Tryon Daily Bulletin.*

Joyce agrees, "People read every single line." And they catch everything.

Charles laughs about the most famous typo of the paper's history, back in hot-type days when part of the flag broke off and the day's paper came out with "*The Tryon Daily Bull*" across the top.

More recently, after the snowstorm of the century in March of 1993, Jeff good-naturedly took flak from friends for a headline describing Tryon's survival and clean-up efforts during "The BIZZARD of '93."

3 p.m. Jeff interviews a new radio personality in town, then talks with Kate about doing some kind of weather-related burning story. If it's 102 degrees, aren't the forestry people worried? How about a fire tower story? Kate tells him they don't staff the towers in the summer. Jeff and Kate brainstorm. OK, we'll find another angle.

Reen, the associate editor, stops by to pick up a copy of a local author's new book she wants to review for next week. Bobbie and Joyce are already at work on the next day's paper.

From the back, the sound of the press and folder thrum and shush busily. For Charles and Tony, the rest of the day is spent inserting and mailing. With the aid of a Star Trek new labeling and mailing machine, they'll easily make the PO by 5.

For the editor-publisher, the day is far from over. At 4:15 p.m. Jeff still has the payroll to cut and five school board stories to write. "I guess I'll do the stories tomorrow morning." He concedes the stories will be late by *Bulletin* standards, but will still scoop the weekly from the next town. "We're just as timely as we can be with what we've got," he notes.

Jeff Byrd sees the handwriting on the wall and knows its on newsprint. "I'm building for the future," he explains thoughtfully, and then says it again: "We're a little daily paper, but we're really a weekly that comes out five times a week. ... We carry all the little chicken-dinner-news. No national stuff. It's what people want.

"But someday some medium is going serve this area—why shouldn't it be the one that's locally owned and operated?"

THE *TRYON DAILY BULLETIN*—REVISITED

Four months after that day in July, publisher Jeff Byrd went to an American Press Institute (API) seminar in Reston, Va., and after doing some cost comparisons between sheet paper and web newsprint, had something of an epiphany. He decided to start looking for a good used web press. It didn't take him long to find a King Press out of Nashville, Tenn.

To make room for the double-unit stacked web press, Byrd had the building's old basement renovated. Two months later, the sleek green press was in place, and printing 32 pages at a time.

Pressmen and owner Jeff Byrd at the *Tryon Daily Bulletin* admire the "new" web press.

In addition to saving on paper, the new web press saves on time and work. The day's paper used to take eight hours to run, fold and hand-insert. Now it's all done in one hour, with no folding or inserting. And how do they like their new press? Tony Elder says with satisfaction, "It runs like a Cadillac."

Ya' gotta want it bad. In some areas of community newspaper work there's very little separation between front- and backshop. *THIS WEEK* co-founder and co-editor Ron Paris bends to the task of press installation.

19

Two Case Studies of Community Newspaper Start-ups: One Home Run, One Sacrifice Fly

YA' GOTTA WANT IT BAD

For years the Black Knights of Robbinsville High School have been a football powerhouse. It remains something of a mystery how a tiny mountain community in the Blue Ridge Mountains can consistently generate great teams. Sure, the coaches can and should get a lot of credit, but something else is at work here too.

Right after the Big Game with their arch-rivals at the end of the regular season, one unremarkable looking split end was telling a reporter why he thought Robbinsville won. The kid said, "I guess we wanted it bad'er'n they did."

You could shake a stick at every big city newsroom across this nation, and out of each would fall a sprinkling of midlevel editors, reporters, photographers, business and ad people harboring the secret dream of having their own paper. "To have your own little weekly someday" is a standard newsroom cliché. And for good reason. Having one's own paper is something of the manifest destiny of journalism. It's what a marathon is to a runner: the ultimate achievement, even if it is a cliché.

But sometimes clichés come true. So, how do you break out and get your own paper? Should you get a broker? Hock the farm and buy a paper? Or should you throw in with some crazed buddies and start a paper from scratch? Where to start? How to find partners? Isn't that risky? Maybe you'd better just plod along here where you know you'll get a regular paycheck.

Whatever you do, remember the Black Knights of Robbinsville.

You've got to want it *bad*. Yes, even bad'er'n they do.

Who's they? The competition. And you will have competition.

A TALE OF TWO CITIES

This chapter alone is worth the price you paid for this entire book. It may save you from yourself; save you from flushing bucks down the commode. And on the other hand, it may turn you on so badly you won't be able to sleep; might even get you off that fence you've been straddling. What follows are case studies of two community newspaper start-ups with which I was intimately associated. One, a grand-slam homer, and the other a towering hit that turned into a sacrifice fly. The run scored but we were out.

But, to the story ...

I always knew I wanted my own paper. I was lucky. Sitting in Ken Byerly's Community Journalism class my junior year at the University of North Carolina at Chapel Hill in 1967, I had a revelation. This is what I would do. This is what I already *was*.

I'd been raised in the *Chapel Hill Weekly* backshop, doing everything from setting heads on the hot-type Ludlow to running the copy camera, in addition to regular black-and-white photography darkroom. I worked my way through college doing paste-up, layout, and all the copy camera work at the *Weekly*.

As far back as my high school days, *Weekly* editor Jim Shumaker had told me: "You're going to Carolina to major in journalism and then come back and work for me."

My junior year summer I interned at the semiweekly *Transylvania Times* in Brevard, N.C., and was smitten by western North Carolina and the mountains. I'd found my region. Back at college I fell in love with a mountain girl who shared my dream of having a paper back home.

Following graduation and a year with Shu on the *Weekly*, I found my first mountain weekly—a one-man job in Sparta, N.C. But the eight-page *Alleghany News* was stifling. The publisher, who lived in the next town over the mountain where we printed, wouldn't let me run my photos big, as I was accustomed to doing with Shu's *Weekly*. Many pointless hollering matches ensued. Within three months of taking the job I was plotting to start my own paper in Sparta.

Then events took over. Sitting there at the publisher's Christmas party dinner at Ron and Eddy's Restaurant in Forest City, I found myself seated by the crew from the Forest City *Courier*. When I told them of my plans, they said, in so many words: No, you're *not* going to start a paper in Sparta; you're going to come down here and start a paper with *us*. I saw the logic of joining in with these guys; they were spark plugs. And Forest City I knew to be ripe for a competition paper. It was worth the gamble. Besides, it was less of a gamble because Bill was from Rutherford County. He was the existing business/ad manager of the *Courier*, and Ron was the existing editor and had been there two years. In other words, they were *dug in* and had done the re-search. I was simply the icing, the element that would add spark to an al-ready great idea.

Along with the help of a local "silent partner," we pulled together about $10,000, a ludicrously low figure by today's standards, and started putting together the makings of our own paper.

What happened over the next three months was something of a running miracle. Ron Paris, in my estimation a genius on the news side, and Bill Blair, the solid rock of the business side, left the *Courier*, and set up shop literally across the street. They found bargain used equipment, purchased what we needed new, and either built or had layout tables built. By the time I got there on March 1, they had everything ready except the darkroom, which I supervised. As the photographer, I brought cameras, enlarger and the darkroom equipment, and we added a small vertical copy camera and PMT processor.

As the rest of the country leaned into the summer of love, down on Mill Street in Forest City it was the spring of dreams. We had set up shop in a for-mer beauty parlor. There was no space for individual offices, so Ron, Bill and I all crowded in the front of the place with used desks and old manual typewriters. For years I used a Smith-Corona portable. The tiny hole-in-the-wall newsroom also included a very old Addressograph machine, a slow but serviceable Morisawa (Morris) headline machine, and the loudest punch tape typesetting system ever invented. At first, we didn't even have air con-ditioning, except in the darkroom. Our 8×12-foot backshop consisted of a homemade light table, a waxer on a table I brought from home and a two-sided layout table. Later, I think we actually went out and *bought* a light table.

Everybody pitched in for Vol. 1, No. 1. Coincidentally Ron's wife, Jan-ice, and my wife, Maggie, were both pregnant and were so big they had to type at full arm's length.

What about circulation? A stroke of pure brilliance on somebody's part,

Bill? Ron? I don't remember which—the idea was to make the nationally renowned East High School marching band the sole seller of subscriptions and give them a cut. It was a huge success. This was due largely to the intense loyalty the blue-ribbon band members felt for their band director, their music and precision marching. In addition they were supported by a large cadre of dedicated band parents and a huge following of fans all over town. How could anyone say no to the Marching Cavaliers? They sold hundreds of subscriptions before we even printed the first paper.

Our first edition hit the streets on March 17, 1969.

And then, it's not a hyperbole to say, the subscriptions just poured in like rain. The town was so thirsty for a good paper that they literally embraced us. Those were heady times.

Ron named it *THIS WEEK* and subtitled it "Rutherford County's *Modern* Newsweekly." As if to say, we're OFFSET, and the competition wasn't. And as if to say, "*THIS WEEK* is an odd name for a paper, but well, that's modern, for you."

Bill handled everything on the business side: sold the ads, pasted them up, did the billing, did the books, paid the bills and basically kept us afloat.

Ron and I called ourselves co-editors, but that term was misleading. Ron, the older and more experienced and locally better known, was the de facto managing editor. I was sort of a glorified feature editor with a big title and a roving camera. But as co-editors, we did have one working rule: He didn't tell me what to do and I didn't tell him what to do. Mostly, it just worked. Here's how we split up the coverage.

First of all, in our county with three municipalities and three high schools, there was no way we could cover the whole county with what we had. In effect we drew a vertical line through the middle of the county and said we'd cover everything to the right of this line: the eastern half of Rutherford County, Forest City and two high schools. Then someday, maybe later if and when we grew, we'd start covering Spindale and the county seat of Rutherfordton with another high school there. County commissioners met at the county courthouse in Rutherfordton, and Ron covered that. But for years we felt like we were in enemy territory when we'd go cover something in Rutherfordton.

Editorial Page

We completely filled the editorial page each week without a shred of canned copy. We even used local cartoons when we could find them. Not an easy task. Each co-editor did a column, usually humorous, and shared the

The "Newsroom" at *THIS WEEK* in 1969. We're all one happy family, and we'd better be, because there's nowhere else to go. Co-editors Paris (seated), Lauterer (foreground) and Business Manager Blair wade through another all-nighter during the paper's infancy.

editorial space with initialed edits so we could have differing opinions on the same question. Also, there was no shortage of letters to the editor.

Sports Coverage

We knew we couldn't afford the luxury of a sports editor at first. So each of the co-editors took a high school. I took East and Ron took Chase. We decided to go whole hog for high school football, and gave each school a whole page each week for each game. Ron and I each wrote (and photographed) an exhaustive game story, post-game coach interview, and an advance story on the upcoming week's game. When East played Chase, we combined our efforts for a mammoth two-page spread.

In addition, to whip up public interest, I'd rush back to the darkroom, develop and print the pictures late Friday after the game, and put them in the window of Smith's Drug Store on Main Street by 10 a.m. Saturday morning. Once the word got out, the entire ball team started showing up in front of the drug store every Saturday morning to see the 20 or so pre-publication 8×10s. It may not have been CNN, but for that little town in 1969, next-day photos from the big game was a big deal. Plus, it was a subtle way for a weekly to partly scoop the semiweekly *Courier*, which otherwise scooped us on football coverage with their Monday edition.

School Coverage

That arrangement spilled over into our school coverage. We each took "our" respective high schools. We quickly found that the East and Chase journalism classes wanted to produce their own copy, so we let them, and took photos to bolster their stories. Each school had its own page about once a month. It was another of *THIS WEEK*'s unheard-of practices that paid off.

Community Correspondents

Through Ron and Virginia's contacts from the *Courier,* we were able to put together a corps of community correspondents who basically reported on visits, church news and the so-called "chicken-dinner circuit." Most all wrote for the paper for eons, and some, such as Mrs. N.C. Melton, are still at it. One of the most beloved community correspondents, Mrs. Charles Self of Sunshine-Golden Valley wrote such colorful stuff that we quickly realized the only way to handle her copy—and everyone else's—was to turn it in unedited. For to edit it would have been to destroy that very thing that made the copy wonderfully individual. In time, she became the most popular feature of the paper. People read Mrs. Self even if they'd never been to Sunshine-Golden Valley. And they'd tell us to our faces that the first thing they read was Mrs. Self. The following example recounts a birthday party with a very special surprise guest:

> Rev. Billy Rich preached real good sermon on Sunday, at Mountain View.
> After services the Church went to Sunshine Club House for dinner. It was Appreciation Day for the Pastor, Rev. Rich, it was his birthday. A beautiful Birthday Cake was made for him. I don't believe the Pastor knew about the birthday dinner, until He got there.

Production

Ron did the front page, hard news, local news and governmental coverage, and took photos if needed. I took the second front, B-1, and each week filled it with whatever I wanted from a feature angle. No ads were allowed on that page. I was also in charge of coordinating the photography, and doing darkroom work.

In no small way, the success of *THIS WEEK* was due to Virginia Rucker, a former women's editor of the old *Courier*, who joined us, working part-time in that area. Because of her long-standing solid reputation around town as a fine lady and respected writer, *THIS WEEK* gained credibility because of her work.

When it came to production on Tuesdays, after Bill pasted up ads, Ron took over his pages, and I took mine. If I finished my areas sooner than Ron, then I'd take other inside pages. Meanwhile I shot PMTs (screened prints, short for Photo-Mechanical Transfers, or Veloxes) for ads, and half-tones (to be stripped into knock-out blocks for the sake of photographic reproduction quality), and finally page negatives, which I hand-developed by tray in the same tiny darkroom, which on Tuesdays was converted into an offset darkroom. (All my photos had to be out and printed from the same darkroom by Monday.)

The newspaper was an instant success. No one complained then or later about staying up all night on Tuesdays to get the thing out, reminding me of the old Arab maxim: "On the day of victory, no one is tired."

We'd drive the negatives down to the Gaffney *Ledger* where the paper was run off on a King offset press for $130 an issue. At our first edition, I remember Ron standing there cussing as the first papers came off the press. If I remember correctly, I think he was upset by the goofy hyphenation our typesetting machine produced. Instead of leaping for joy as I was, his response was to be openly and vocally critical. Not *at* anybody in particular, it was just his own inner critic with its high standards giving vent. "DAMN!" he snarled at the first paper as I danced around happy as a spotted pup.

But that example served as a metaphor for how opposites could combine to work toward a common end. Ron was the practical, rational, unemotional quality-control manager. I was the wild intuitive impulsive one. Together, through this yin-yang process, somehow we complemented one another. The synergy may have been a happy accident. Regardless, we put out some great papers.

That first year in the state press association competition, *THIS WEEK* won an unprecedented 10 awards, many of them firsts, too. From then on, "those boys from Forest City" were on the map. Not only were we the best weekly in the state, but quite possibly the best non-daily, the best community newspaper in the state. People started watching what we did. Heady times, indeed.

GROWING LIKE TOPSY

The paper grew like Topsy. Within two years, we rented the place next door, knocked a door through the brick wall, re-did the front to look like a real newspaper office instead of a bunch of fly-by-nighters in a former beauty shop/cab stand. We got air conditioning. We paneled the new side and hung our awards on the walls. We made the backshop distinctly separate from our office, though the three of us still shared the same space. Because we had doubled our space, we felt like kings. The paper continued to prosper and grow, while the competition across the street went through a raft of short-time editors. In the words of Andy Griffith: "They'd tote one in—and tote another 'n' out."

The Monday and Thursday *Courier* scooped us on Monday, but then we scooped them on Wednesday. But the real difference was in how the two papers *looked*. They were either hot-type or stereotype printed in Morganton. In short, their photo reproduction was terrible. And it was made worse by comparison because not only were we offset, but we were the best offset you could be. We took the extra time and effort to shoot half-tone negatives individually and strip each one in on knock-out blocks on the page negs for the maximum repro quality. People noticed. Pictures looked better, ads looked better, type looked better.

By 1974 and the Arab oil embargo, when all printing and printing products doubled in price, we were strong enough to survive and absorb the financial shock. The web size got smaller, the news hole shrank, and we tightened our belts and slid right on through. The competition suffered though,

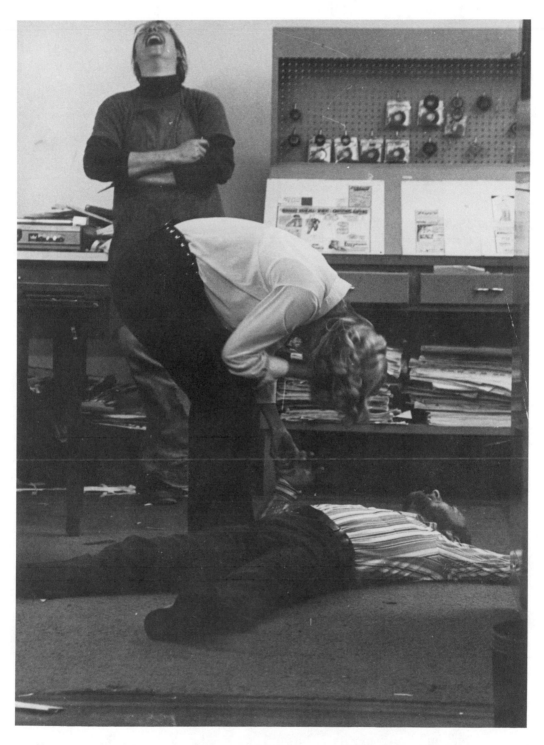

There's nothing like "a happy shop." *THIS WEEK* and the *Daily Courier* were that and more. Here, on yet another production night, the author cracks up as typesetter Billie Faulkner doubles over in laughter after Co-Editor Paris lands on the backshop floor during a not-so-successful demonstration of cartwheeling. (*Photo by Joy Franklin*)

With a little help from our friends: One corner of the "newsroom" is dominated by the clattering typesetting equipment, manned by visiting itinerant journalist Steve Knowlton, here sharing a laugh with Co-Editor Paris. The sign on the wall is an honest typo from the nearby commercial print shop. Paris is now executive editor of the *Daily Courier*. Knowlton is now an author and assistant professor of journalism at Penn State.

and was forced to consolidate with the smaller weekly Spindale *Sun* into the "*Courier-Sun*." They finally went offset, but we'd already had the jump on them for six years.

The next year, we turned the corner. In April of 1975, we bought a big building up on main street that let each of us have our own offices. The building's real strength was its full concrete basement—perfect for a press. We began looking for a used Goss Community. We found three units and a folder in Metarie, La., got a whopping big loan, and took the biggest leap a community publishing outfit can make.

Maybe the news got out, and maybe that was the proverbial straw that broke the camel's back. In early summer we began to get overtures from the competition through their lawyer. Back to the bank we went again. And on Aug. 27, 1975, we announced the purchase of the *Courier-Sun.*

The following week, after we'd figured out the details of combining the two staffs—who to keep and who to let go and how to tell them—the new (used) press arrived.

Ron wrote in an editorial, "The events of this week have been monumental ones for us."

By fall of '75, we were up and running smoothly with our own press thrumming away in the basement. For the next three years, *THIS WEEK,* with its own press, with an enlarged staff and almost no competition in sight, entered its glory days.

By now we had hired a sports editor. We made Virginia Rucker associ-

THIS WEEK grows. The paper gets a new logo for our flag and a new shiny black front for the office, which after two years has expanded to include the adjacent beauty shop.

Inside the backshop well after midnight on another sleepless Tuesday. Co-editors put the final product together, amid drying half-tone negatives and a confetti of headline clippings on the floor. (*Photo by Joy Franklin*)

ate editor and kept the women's editor from the *Courier* to do engagements and weddings. We added two production women in typesetting and ad paste-up, two men on the press and—glory be—a receptionist. Up until then, we were answering our own phones and meeting walk-ins.

This was in lock step with the fortuitous development of the entire county. The community college built back in the mid-60s was growing and gaining community support. Our paper put its back to the wheel and did everything we could to help. The result: another symbiotic relationship that was mutually beneficial for the college, the community and *THIS WEEK*.

Also, a vigorous community Arts Council got cranked up the same year we started *THIS WEEK*, and the paper got on that bandwagon too. Full-scale community theater productions of *Camelot; Jesus Christ, Superstar; Oklahoma; South Pacific* and the *Wizard of Oz* received reams of coverage. We sold papers like hotcakes. And the community found itself in something of a backwoods cultural renaissance.

Meanwhile, a new four-lane bypass from Shelby up to Rutherfordton finally was completed. "Progress is going to march right up that road to you," a Chamber of Commerce gathering had been told prior to the road's

New press.

opening. The speaker was so correct. The business community now had somewhere to expand. It may have been strip-growth, but it was growth, and that meant increased ad revenues. We tried a semiweekly experiment briefly, but quickly reverted.

By the summer of 1978 a mall had been built, and we were putting out 60- and 72-page weekly editions, printing sections and inserting our lives away. Something had to give.

That fall, the merchants at the new mall put out the word to us and the *County News*: Whoever has the most toys wins. *The Rutherford County News*, owned by a South Carolina chain, began publishing the *Enterprise*, a free, total-market coverage shopper with canned Copley News Service stories so it looked like a newspaper. What were we going to do? "Progress" had marched up that road, all right, and now was in our face. If we didn't keep pace with the economic development of the business community, no matter what a great newspaper we were, the new mall merchants were going to run off and leave us standing there with our awards.

Unless we went freebie too, we'd never have the numbers of the *Enterprise*. The only other thing we could do to meet the competition was to fight back with frequency. That meant going daily.

Bill was for it. Ron saw the practical necessity. And I was dead set against it. But eventually even I realized the old weekly had to pass. We'd outgrown it. Or perhaps the county's economic growth had made the weekly obsolete. In the face of this challenge, if we didn't go daily, we might not survive. Reluctantly, I threw my vote in for the conversion. In November of 1978, we began publishing five days a week.

I think it was the right thing to do, financially and journalistically. But my heart just never got on board. I did my best for two more years to get excited about the new daily, which we named the *"Daily Courier,"* but my passion for the new daily was muted compared to what I'd felt for *THIS WEEK*.

THE GAZETTE: A TOWERING HIT—BUT A SACRIFICE FLY

(Author's note: For reasons of privacy and fairness, the following segment uses fictitious names. As with any newspaper failure, there are still some hard feelings. But one learns infinitely more—not from success, but from failure.)

By late 1979 I had become easy prey for a new dream, no matter how implausible. At all costs I wanted another weekly. Looking around, I immediately was taken with the possibilities of the nearby town of Bosco. The

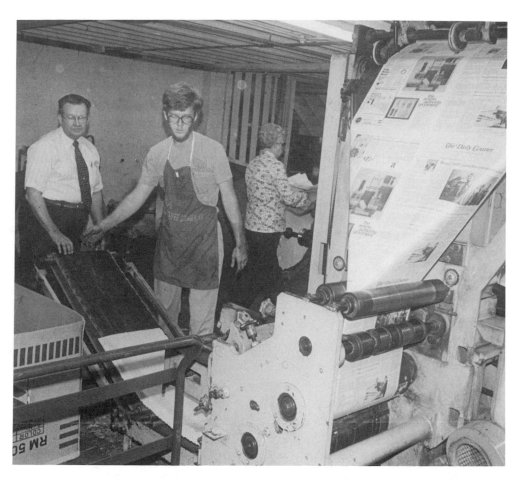

Nine years after start-up, *THIS WEEK* evolves into the *Daily Courier*.
Here we print the first edition of the daily.

county seat of a neighboring county had an entrenched, but truly bad semi-weekly, the *Times*, owned by a relatively small chain which seemed to care about nothing but the bottom line. The long-time editor of the *Times* was feared and openly disliked by many Bosco people with whom I spoke—merchants, governmental, educational, civic and church leaders. Great. The idea looked better and better. We would have an immediate base of support.

Optimistically projecting my desires on the new community, I decided the Bosco *Times* was vulnerable. Why not? If *THIS WEEK* could take the entrenched *Courier*, why couldn't I repeat the miracle with the *Gazette*? All I had to do was duplicate the *THIS WEEK* formula for success—with one twist: This time *we* would be the TMC weekly.

The idea was fairly novel for the times. To our knowledge, no other paper in the state had tried it: to be distributed free, going to every household in the county (total market coverage) through the mail (third-class pre-sort to enhance delivery time). We would take advantage of the shopper concept, but in all actuality be a true community newspaper with a generous news hole and generating all our own copy and pictures.

Since nobody I'd known had done it, my partners at Forest City quite rightly thought me a little daft to step so boldly out off that ledge, and kindly bought me out at a quickly agreed upon fair price; I left the *Daily Courier* with no hard feelings.

Now all I had to do was to find clones of Ron and Bill. I went through all my files and names of people wild enough to take such a risk. I settled on Jim, an older man in his late 30s with little journalism experience but with a great deal of raw talent, drive and sense of humor. With 11 years behind the helm as a founding co-publisher and co-editor, I became uneasy with sharing the reigns equally with such a relatively untested man, in spite of his age. Since I owned 60 percent of the paper, I summarily promoted myself to editor-in-chief and named Jim news editor. His wife, a younger woman, would work part-time keeping the books and serving as receptionist. He seemed to accept the arrangement.

To find my business manager/ad salesman, I called a nearby university school of journalism and asked the business professor for any recommendations. He had a bright prospect who was currently an ad salesman on a nearby big-city daily. Within two days, I'd arranged an interview with Bob. The young man, several years out of college, impressed me with his drive and his apparent grasp of the business side. In addition, he wanted to have his own paper, too. In spite of the fact that he was from urban California, I hoped that the rural, Southern mountain town of Bosco would learn to like and accept Bob. Besides, Bob's wife wanted to sell ads, and she was from the region. It seemed like a perfect fit.

In addition, with my wife doing the women's page and Jim's wife handling the front office, we had a real extended family team thing going on. If the three couples could stay together and get along, I felt sure the *Gazette* would be an instant success.

And in many ways it was.

But first, I had to put together the shop. I found a vacant former law office on main street at the right price. I bought a used Justowriter from the *Courier*, bought a reconditioned used Compugraphic 7200 for headlines, a new vertical copy camera, new light table, new waxer, an ancient Addressograph machine and even older plate maker, a slew of used typewriters, used desks and chairs—and with some help from Bob and Jim, partitioned offices and layout desks and a darkroom.

When it came to circulation, all three of us shared the job of circulation manager. From public records in the county tax office, we got names and addresses and began constructing a mailing list and making Addressograph plates of approximately 10,000 households in the county. Making the labels alone was a huge undertaking. It seems that the three men and three wives were typing labels for weeks prior to the premier issue of the *Gazette*. Then, with the advice of the local postmaster, we sorted them by zips and postal routes. We realized we would have to make a profit early, since the monthly mailing bill was huge. We were the PO's largest customer in town.

Part of my payoff at the *Daily Courier* had been six months of "free printing," so from March until September we had no printing bills. We went to Forest City with pages already shot and on negatives with half-tones stripped in, or "plate-ready."

On Wednesday, March 19, 1980, we published Vol. 1, No. 1 of the *Gazette*, a 24-page broadsheet full of nothing but local news, columns, editorials and photos. Our ad percentage started at a scant 17 percent. No grocery stores. To win, we knew we'd have to get all four of the biggies with their full-page ads.

Within three months, we had three of the four.

Heady times in Bosco. The community hungrily embraced the *Gazette*. We were constantly told things like: "You're the best thing that's happened to Bosco in 50 years." On the business side, we were winning. Our ad percentage had gone from that 17 percent beginning to a healthy 48 percent.

Not until then, did the competition start to take us seriously.

Just as in Forest City, the competition had sat back, fat and smug when we started up, waiting for us to fall on our faces. In both cases, the competition did nothing in response at first, when we were the most vulnerable. And in both cases, we lapped the competition before they knew what had hit them.

When they did respond, it was out of desperation. They did the thing we couldn't do: They lowered ad rates to get advertisers back. And in some critical cases, gave away ads and "gifts." We refused to play that game. We started losing ads. We were further hampered by our ad-rate structure. Because of our huge circulation and mailing costs, we had to construct our ad rates higher than the competition. That's always a dangerous thing for a new paper to try. And now that the *Times* was playing hardball all over town with its ad rates, making deals left and right, different rates for different people, we became increasingly positioned as the expensive and at times the out-of-reach alternative.

And nine months after start-up, we were forced to change printers. Our response was to shake things up: go semiweekly and convert from free to paid circulation. It seemed to work, but gone were the big expansive news-hole 24-pagers of the first six months.

Then, after a year, Bob informed Jim and me that he didn't like selling ads. Stunned by the suddenness of it all, we agreed Bob should sell out quickly. Luckily, we found a new business partner in Ted, a well-liked and respected business and community leader who'd been laid off by a large local factory. But even Ted's wise handling of the books and selling ads could not stop the recession of 1981-82. We felt as if we were caught in the jaws of something huge and malevolent.

I remember one night sitting there at my typewriter, trying to write something creative but so worried because we had just lost the third and final grocery store ad to the *Times*, that all my creative juices had frozen solid. Writer's block? Terminal burnout? Publisher's night-terror? Whatever, I couldn't write anymore. I just went through the motions.

In desperation, we tried buying the competition. And at times, it seemed as if the out-of-state chain managers were willing to sell. But in the end, they were just stalling, while we lost more and more money. At last we realized, while the *Times* could be bought, they were too proud to sell to us—just as we were too proud to sell out to them. We were like two bloodied fighters standing on Main Street slugging it out, each refusing to fall or admit defeat.

At last, Jim wisely engineered a third-party deal in which another out-of-state chain accepted our invitation and came to town and soon bought both papers. We were saved. Jim was hired by the new outfit as a midrange editor. Ted landed on his feet and was quickly snapped up as an executive for a local industry. The *Times* was converted to a five-day-a-week daily and our dear old *Gazette* relegated to a shopper.

Bitter and emotionally devastated, I left town—*evacuated* would be a better term. I never wanted to see the place again. I felt as if two-and-a-half years of hard work had been for nothing. I knocked around the region for a year in a series of jobs until, eureka, in 1983 a teaching position was offered me at the university.

WHAT WENT WRONG?

Wrong people in the wrong place at the wrong time.

Three outsiders in a town not ready for a great paper, with a recession looming on the economic horizon.

From the very start, we weren't "dug in" at all. We were three complete unknowns, outsiders in a community that distrusted outsiders. Even though Jim and I were from the region, to the folks from Bosco, we might as well have been from Mars. While we definitely caused a newspaper revolution and a creative renaissance in Bosco and won some hearts, we didn't win enough of the ones that counted, the big advertisers who caved in to the *Times* under pressure. What I didn't know about Bosco: that most of the population was fiercely xenophobic and unwilling to welcome newcomers.

The town and county had such a bad self-image that if someone actually chose to move there, the residents' first reaction was: "What or who are you running from? Why would anyone *want* to live here? There must be something dark and sinister behind your reasons." We wasted a lot of energy just trying to justify our existence in Bosco.

In picking partners for a start-up, always go with as much experience as you can find and afford.

Part of my buyout at the *Courier* had been six months of printing for the new *Gazette*. While this sounded like a good idea at first, when it came to tax time, I got soaked for capital gains. This occurred initially because of poor financial counseling, but I still should have been canny enough to have figured this out for myself.

Finally and most importantly, we were undercapitalized. We started the *Gazette* for about $35,000 (and my part of that was $21,000 in "free printing") and the remainder wasn't enough to float us very long—especially after those first six months of artificially optimistic and inflated P&L (profit-and-loss) sheets. This was especially hurtful in a situation where our overhead was so steep due to high mailing costs for TMC and high printing costs because of the number of papers we were doing.

Also, we were undercapitalized in the face of the type of competition we went up against. We misjudged their emotional resolve and financial ability to hang on. A larger chain than the one that owned the old *Courier*, the *Times* chain had more resources to draw on.

If we'd had more financial reserves, the *Gazette* might have been able to ride out the recession, and then to have either survived, strengthened and/or bought them out.

COMPARISONS AND CONTRASTS

Start-up Funds: Both newspapers were undercapitalized at start-up. The difference was not just paid circulation vs. free, but the times. In the early '70s you could still make a little go a long way. When prices for film, paper, ink, chemicals skyrocketed after the oil embargo, it became a different ballgame. For a start-up today, depending on the size of the paper, you'd be wise to have a generous financial safety net. Say, at least six months of padding.

Circulation: While both papers were weeklies, their methods of distribution were different. Forest City was paid circulation, mailed out second class and sold in racks around town. Bosco was free—and most importantly, through the mails to every household in the county via "controlled circulation," a third-class presort classification that was relatively fast and very, very expensive.

Both methods have their risks. Starting out with paid circulation means you start literally with zero circulation and build; you have no "numbers" to show potential advertisers. But on the other hand, it's the most economical way to start. You're basically Mom 'n' Poping it. Starting small and growing. In some cases, that's the right way to do it. With TMC, you have huge overhead with the post office or your delivery system, but in return you have instant numbers with which to sell to advertisers. It's hard for an advertiser to say no to a paper that goes to every household in the county. The gamble is that ad revenues will recoup your delivery expenses because of your impressive numbers. That's the shopper concept. It's the hit-the-ground-running approach. If you're up against stiff competition and you've got a big bankroll, that might be the way to go. But be forewarned: You're at the mercy of the U.S. Post Office, which can and will raise rates, change classifications and delivery times without regard to your paper's survival.

Researching and Backgrounding the Community: Starting or buying a paper is like buying a house. According to the old saying, when buying a house there are three important factors: Location, Location and Location. In Forest City, Bill and Ron had done their homework. They had been dug in, taking samples, gathering information, taking the community pulse, getting the feel for the business community's response to the idea of a new paper—all very quietly and thoroughly. You just can't beat that. In Bosco, I projected what I wanted to see: another Forest City. But that was not to be the case.

Timing: Both papers started in the spring. That's when one of the cyclical advertising surges occurs. That's good. But the other factor in timing is this: How long have you been planning and plotting and researching? In Forest City, the team took its time and waited until they were really ready. In Bosco, the team rushed onto the playing field, bright and eager and naive. Perhaps a closer examination of the competition, the market, and prevailing economic trends would have warned us away from Bosco.

The Competition: No matter where you are, whether it's a start-up or a buyout, you are going to run into competition somewhere. You need an honest appraisal of that competition. Is it a family-owned operation? Then they may be more vulnerable. Is it owned by a chain? Which one? How big are they? Where are they headquartered? What is the chain's typical response to competition? Do they just sit there passively or do they respond proactively? For instance, a small, family-owned chain run by a single elderly CEO might be more vulnerable than a fairly large, aggressive chain run by a younger management team. Also, before you take on a paper, scope out the competition and do a worst-case scenario. What would you do if the competition started a total market coverage shopper in response?

Partners: In Forest City, Bill and Ron knew the community and the community knew them. The most important familiar face must be your ad person. In spite of all the weight some of us newsies tend to give the editorial side, it's the success of the business side that drives a start-up. In Forest City, our ad man was a known factor. Not only was he a native, but he'd worked there all his life. I can't over-emphasize the importance of this factor. On the other hand, in Bosco, our ad man was from another region of the country, which only compounded the fact that every single person on the staff was an out-of-towner—strangers, if you will. One friend who bailed out of his paper after only six months cited "a lousy partner" as his reason. "It's like marriage," he said. "Once you've said *I Do*, you're stuck with the sucker. You've got to live or die by your choice." Had I realized early how suspicious Boscoites were going to be of the *Gazette*'s personnel and purposes, I might have scuttled the whole project.

What gives your community its distinct flavor? One of the functions of a good community newspaper is to reflect what poet Elizabeth Sewell calls "a sense of place." Area festivals are especially rich with such essence.

20

Speedbumps and Trouble-shooting

WHEN'S THE LAST TIME YOU CHANGED YOUR OIL?

Your car needs gas, maintenance and periodic oil changes. You know all too well what happens if you don't put gas in the car: You find yourself on the side of the road when you least need to be stranded. If you defer maintenance, you really can get into trouble. And not changing your oil means Old Betsy won't be long for this world.

The irony is that people tend to be better to their cars than they are to themselves.

In community journalism, we're running flat out all the time. We're red-lining it. Our tachometers are pushing the limits every time a paper comes out. So, when's the last time you changed *your* oil?

People at community papers face a different set of problems than folks at big-city dailies and people in the electronic media. Therefore our response must be different too. Here is a sampling of questions most often asked by community newspaper people I encounter.

WHERE DO I DRAW THE LINE ON COMMUNITY INVOLVEMENT?

As has been said, community newspaper people have to be involved with and in their communities at a level far more "dug in" than our brothers and sisters at the big papers. However, we can't enjoy the relative obscurity

275

and anonymity of the big-city reporter. When we go to Bi-Lo, everybody knows us. When we go get gas, we are recognized. Wherever we go all over the county, anywhere in town we play, shop, worship or socialize, we are known and recognized. People are likely to treat us more for what we do than who we are as individuals. Our professional identity is our personal identity.

For instance, what church you join will be noted by the community. Some will accuse you of giving your church more coverage. Some in your church will expect you to give that church special preferential treatment.

If you join the Rotary Club and give too much coverage to their activities according to the Woodmen of the World, you are going to hear about it. Will you be able to defend your coverage? You'd better be ready.

How to deal with that?

The solution is prioritization. Your first allegiance is to journalistic fairness and balance. Just be aware of your special responsibility to keep your news judgment fair and equal. Remember, the word is Balance.

The higher up the editorial or publishing ladder you go, the more prudently you should be making these choices. This is not a job you can take off and hang on a peg each night. Your involvement with civic clubs, schools and your kids' involvement with Little League, scouts, band—everything—should be thought out carefully. No need to get overly paranoid, but editors and publishers must be aware that people are watching the paper's coverage.

And an inviolate rule of community newspaper involvement: Absolutely no politics. The quickest way to wreck your paper's credibility is for you to get involved in politics.

HOW DO I DEVELOP MY TALENT WHEN THERE'S NO ONE TO HELP ME?

If you're at a paper where you're not getting edited, or where you're the top dog but want to improve and are committed to not turning into mush …

• Never be satisfied with your work. That means: Take some joy and satisfaction in what you do, but don't get smug about it.

If you're not putting your full heart, talents and effort into your work because you figure, "Well, it's just a little weekly … just wait until I get to the *Observer*." What makes you think you'll ever *get* to the *Observer*? And if you *do*, that you'll be able to turn on the talent juice like a faucet? Instead, you should do like James Carville, Clinton's gifted '92 campaign adviser, who said, "When you hire me, you pay for my head; I throw in the heart for free."

• Take compliments graciously but with a grain of salt. Just the way you take criticism: Do you really respect the source?

• Read and look at everything you can get your hands on outside of your own area—other papers, larger papers, magazines, books, and especially trade magazines such as *Editor & Publisher*, *Columbia Journalism Review* and *Publishers' Auxiliary.*

• Strike up friendships with outside journalists your own age who may be having the same challenge. Peer counsel each other. Exchange clips and comments.

• Contests can be useful to get you psyched up for your work and to give you feedback, although it's not the gospel. However, every so often it's good to go out there and risk it.

• Workshops, short courses, National Public Radio, Public Television, books—seek out inspiration.

• Finding a role model, and certainly a mentor who is willing to critique your work, is probably the scariest yet most useful way of staying sharp or getting back your edge.

HOW CAN I ESTABLISH CREDIBILITY?

Credibility is a function of accretion. It takes lots of accuracy, trust and time to build up. It will come to you. You can't chase it and catch it. Lots of good works over a period of time will establish your credibility. Newcomers, and recent journalism school grads: There are no shortcuts here.

HOW DO I DEVELOP MY SENSE OF CURIOSITY AND PRECISION?

Without precision, without accuracy, there is no reason to continue working in the news business. What we're about is accuracy. Otherwise, people could get their news from reading tea leaves or by listening to gossip. It is a goal worth striving for. And you can never let down your guard, no matter how experienced you are.

Without curiosity, we might as well be mollusks. To the extent we are good as journalists is a function of our curiosity. We're only as good as our questions. If you're not born inquisitive, then it may be something you have to nurture. Usually journalists self-select; newspaper people tend to get into this crazed business because we *are* curious—about life, about what makes things tick, about how government works, about who pays for what, about where our money goes, about what old men think when they sit on porches, about what went through the quarterback's mind in the last five seconds of the game, what was it like to live in your town in 1900, what is it going to be like to live in your town in 2020 … ?

HOW DO I SPOT NEWS AND TAKE ADVANTAGE OF OPPORTUNITIES?

News for community newspaper is anything that affects your world (defined as your coverage area—your county, for instance).

News is like a hurricane, the closer it gets, the more important it becomes to you. Hugo wasn't important as long as it was knocking around the Lesser Antilles—but then, guess what? The Bosnian civil war may not be riveting news in Whiteville until the local guard unit is called up—and then it's in-your-face news.

Developing the nose for news means you must stay alert, pay attention all through the day, and most importantly, stay current on state, national and international happenings. You've got to track those hurricanes.

On a more personal level, try this news perspective at your paper—that *every person is a story,* and every person has a story to tell. For us, it's just a matter of finding the right time and place and circumstance. It may develop into a news story, a personality profile or a news feature—even a column someday—depending on how it spins out.

If we recognize the power and significance of the human interest story, we go into each story armed with a special insight. We know readers eat these things up because people have an insatiable appetite for learning about each other.

OK, I'VE READ THE BOOK—NOW WHAT?

If you're a student completing a college course in community journalism and you feel like this line of work appeals to you, perhaps you're asking yourself where and when do I start. The answers are immediate and accessible as our business: Now and close to home.

Start by introducing yourself to your own hometown community newspaper editor. Tell him/her about this class and your interest in community journalism. Show the editor your clips and inquire about an internship, either now or during the summer. Perhaps they will have a stringer position open. You could even go so far as to volunteer. Many community papers are short-handed and would welcome such an offer. If you hang in there, it might get parlayed into a paying position.

I'VE HAD IT WITH THIS RAG—I'M OUTTA HERE

If you're a working pro at a community paper and feel like you're ready to move on or up, the guidelines are common sense. Before leaving your own newsroom, make sure there's no room higher up. Start by going to your editor or publisher and expressing your interest in advancement or change within the structure of your paper. Speak forthrightly. After all, what do you have to lose? You might be surprised by his/her response. Unbeknownst to younger employees, many bosses yearn for and welcome such honest, constructive discussions.

But if you get a negative response and do choose to make the jump, ask yourself these questions honestly (and try to write down answers). Remember though, just leaving doesn't guarantee that a new job will be better than your present situation. Sheer change for the sake of change can be counterproductive. Changing jobs is not something to be entered into lightly; moving is stressful and life-boggling (especially if there's a relt involved). So now ...

- Why do you *really* want to leave?
- How does money figure into your decision?
- What do you want/need from a new position?
- Why can't you get all of the above where you are?
- What will you be giving up (what will you miss) if you leave this job?
- What kind of paper do you want to work on (size, publication frequency)?
- What kind of community or city do you want to work in?
- Does it matter where it is geographically?
- How would you describe your ideal job or dream job?
- Who in your personal life will be affected by your leaving? How do they fit in?

Finally, keep your resume current, get your clips in order, make sure your presentation is professional, put the word out to your media friends, watch the want ads in trade magazines and network-network-network. Your new job will most likely come as a result of one-on-one contacts you've made over the years in community journalism.

You can live in a town your whole life and still find new ways of looking at the same place. But it takes energy, enterprise and the realization
that you, too, occasionally need to recharge your creative batteries.
Workshops, seminars and short courses offer inspiration, support and
technical expertise.

21

Addendum

COMMUNITY JOURNALISM AND HIGHER EDUCATION

*Today's journalism training needs revamping
to match tomorrow's journalism.*

There's the bottom line, right out of a recent Poynter Institute for Media Studies seminar on the future of journalism: J-schools need to reinvent themselves to "match tomorrow's journalism."

But how do we do that when we don't know where the leading edge, cutting edge or trailing edge *is*. Indeed, the technology is flying so low and fast, just below radar, that it's more akin to a stealth edge.

We can't see it, but we certainly are aware that it's moving at a frightening velocity, leaving us all a little confused about what it all means. However, one thing is clear: J-schools had better start heeding the words of Lee Iacocca: "Either lead, follow, or get out of the way."

So, what are the needs of industry? How is the industry changing? And how can higher education respond? We don't know what newspapers are going to look like in 20 years, but it's a cinch they'll be more visual, they'll take every advantage of emerging technology, and they'll be heavily community oriented.

281

1. Newspapers are becoming more visual. We don't laugh at *USA Today* anymore; we copy it. Emerging journalists must be familiar with graphics, visual communication and the language of photojournalism. These should be core courses in our journalism curriculum.

2. Emerging Technology, the trend that's really got us all in a future-shock dither: the Digital Newspaper, New Media, Multimedia, Star Wars Journalism, Newsrooms that look like Mission Control.

The next generation of journalists emerging from J-schools needs to be computer-literate in accessing computer databases; editing digital filmless photography and video; creating computer-generated pages, informational graphics and ads, to name a few of the new required skills.

3. There is a renewed interest and emphasis on in-depth community coverage. The one thing that TV can't do well and we can: great community journalism, reporting that is "relentlessly local."

And yet, how many university journalism schools emphasize or even offer separate courses in community journalism? The number is small but growing as increasing numbers of educators become aware of and sensitized to the needs of the newspaper industry. Newspaper leaders know it. From a marketing as well as philosophical standpoint, communities are "in" and local news is hot. American universities, typically slow to change, are only starting to hear the grass-roots call to arms.

Few have responded as courageously, as comprehensively or as quickly as Kansas State University's A.Q. Miller School of Journalism and Mass Communication. KSU's Huck Boyd National Center for Community Media appears to be light years ahead of the pack and the curve. According to John Neibergall, executive director of the Center, KSU "is pointing the way back to the future, back to journalism's roots, and into the future in which communities and their media reconnect. Kansas State has recognized the inseparable link between communities and communications. It has launched an enterprise that seeks to strengthen local media, thus equipping them to help build better communities."

The Huck Boyd Center for Community Media is a pioneering journalism enterprise in higher education. How do they fold community journalism into their curriculum? And what is the response of students, the faculty, the state's press and the constituency they serve? The story is told by Carol Oukrop, director of the A.Q. Miller School of Journalism and Mass Communication at K-State.

John Neibergall, executive director of the Huck Boyd National Center for Community Media, offers advice on pasting up the front page of a weekly newspaper to Kansas State University journalism student Bill Spiegel, while Alianna (Laney) Bowers, a part time employee of the *Westmoreland* (Kan.) *Recorder,* checks an inside page. Keli Huddleston works behind the Media Temps team at another light table to help produce the week's issue. Neibergall and the students were part of a Huck Boyd National Center Media Temps team that kept the newspaper running for a few weeks after the death of its 39-year-old editor and co-publisher. (Photo by Dan Donnert, Kansas State University Photographic Services)

John Neibergall observes as Bill Spiegel, a Temps team student volunteer, pastes up Page One of the *Westmoreland* (Kan.) *Recorder.* (Photo by Dan Donnent, Kansas State University Photographic Services)

Here Bill Spiegel pastes up Page One of the *Westmoreland* (Kan.) *Recorder.* (Photo by Dan Donnert, Kansas State University Photographic Services)

Keli Huddleston (*left*) and Bill Spiegel (*right*), students at Kansas State University who had done computer pagination for their campus publications, working at the light tables of the *Westmoreland* (Kan.) *Recorder,* learning to paste up pages of the newspaper. (Photo by Dan Donnert, Kansas State University Photographic Services)

OTHER VOICES; OTHER NEWSROOMS

From the Heartland: A Case for Grass-roots Community Media

Community and communication come from the same linguistic root. You cannot have community without communications.

By Carol Oukrop

That is the deep-seated belief that led to the formation in 1991 of the Huck Boyd National Center for Community Media, which is a part of the A.Q. Miller School of Journalism and Mass Communications at Kansas State University.

The Center is appropriately named for McDill "Huck" Boyd, a noted Kansas publisher and state leader who was a firm believer in the values, lifestyles and resources of rural America. He believed, as we do, that media are the glue that holds a community together. They sustain a community's identity. They allow community members to communicate with one another, and they furnish information that citizens need to plan for their futures.

By 1989, several of us in the School of Journalism and Mass Communications at K-

State had long felt the need to be doing more than we were with community journalism. Harry Marsh had submitted several community media proposals, Nancy Hause was a regular contributor to a nearby community newspaper, and a member of the School's development committee had prepared a community media proposal.

In early 1990, I included in my weekly faculty memo the following invitation:

"Faculty members interested in participating in a brainstorming session about a community journalism center proposal are invited to a 7-9 p.m. meeting ..."

That initial brainstorming session was attended by only three persons, but we stayed for hours and got truly excited about the possibilities. After distributing a summary of our brainstorming session, I scheduled another meeting and our Huck Boyd Task Force was born.

Nine faculty members, most but not all of them in journalism/mass comm, began meeting regularly to discuss the future of community media and how we at K-State could help. The fact that we somehow managed to wrench from two to five hours a week out of our already tight schedules for nearly a year for these planning sessions is one indication of our belief in the importance of community media. Another such indication was the hiring of a community journalist, John D. Neibergall, who had owned and published four community newspapers in Iowa before beginning his graduate work at Iowa State University. He joined the K-State faculty in the fall of 1990.

One member of our task force completed a detailed literature search for information on community journalism activities carried on at other colleges and universities. Leads from her search were followed up by letter, phone or personal interview. We learned that few journalism programs in 1990 were giving special attention to community journalism, and we found no school with a center such as we hoped to establish, with the specific goal of nurturing and strengthening all community media. We did not at the outset envision a national center, but the more we gathered information the more we realized that our concerns were national in scope. We came to believe that a major way in which the Center will be national will be through activities other journalism programs at other schools will want to adopt and adapt.

Early in our brainstorming we realized that a bunch of professors—even those of us who had spent years working in community media—were not the best-qualified sources of information regarding today's community media needs and how a journalism/mass comm education unit could help. We turned to the Kansas State Press Association and the Kansas Association of Broadcasters. With their advice and encouragement, we brought in three advisory groups—12 community newspaper people, nine community broadcasters, and 12 community leaders. We came to think of them as our "fuzzy groups."

We started out talking about doing focus groups. Part way into our planning, we realized we would not be doing true focus groups. One task force member referred to our "unfocused" groups, and soon they became fuzzy groups.

Each of our fuzzy groups spent an entire day with us, talking about their needs and ways in which the Center might help them. With their help and our other fact-finding, we formulated the following mission statement for the Center:

- Interact with communities to determine their communication needs.
- Develop services and hands-on help for community media to meet those needs.
- Examine existing knowledge of the role that media play in the life of communities.
- Carry out research to add knowledge about that role.
- Contribute to the discovery, testing and implementation of appropriate processes, methods, technologies and structures.
- Expand and upgrade the community media dimension in higher education.
- Disseminate the Center's findings.
- Develop the resources needed to carry out its mission.

Late in 1990, the Kansas Board of Regents endorsed the establishment of the Huck Boyd National Center for Community Media at Kansas State University. John Neibergall became director for the Center, and we developed seven strategic tasks to translate the Center's mission into an active agenda:

1. Serving media and community.
2. Teaching.
3. Doing research.
4. Providing training.
5. Putting technology to use.
6. Linking people with information.
7. Nurturing the Center's leadership.

We are pleased with what we have been able to accomplish so far. In carrying out activities, both in our state and nationally, we believe we have created some models other schools might want to adapt to their own areas.

SERVING MEDIA AND COMMUNITY

We think two of the Center's activities here—our Circuit Rider concept and the Media Temps—should become models for other schools of journalism.

The Circuit Ride is one way that Center scholars stay attuned to the concerns of community media in our area. We carve out a section of the state that we can visit in two or three days, and a couple of us hit the road. We visit the media in as many of the communities along our route as possible, both learning and teaching during those visits—but primarily learning. We try to pinpoint concerns that the Center could address in a regional workshop. It's hard to carve out the time for these trips, but we find them well worth our while.

The Media Temp program stems from a very clear message we received from our fuzzy group discussions—community media are very demanding, and sometimes owners and managers need an escape. One weekly newspaper publisher recalled having taken a vacation once during 40 years of ownership. Other owners expressed a fear that an emergency might bring their operations to a complete halt.

Our Media Temp program is a temporary relief service, made up of students and faculty, to help out in such cases. The Media Temp program went into action, for example, when one of the two publishers of the Westmoreland *Recorder* died and the other publisher found himself overwhelmed. Media Temps made it possible for the publisher of the Wamego *Times* to take his first vacation in 12 years, and the Media Temps helped the Council Grove *Republican* with a special edition.

A Minnesota publisher who read about our Media Temp program in a professional journal summed the program up as follows:

"The best part is that it's such a natural meeting of different needs. The weekly editor needs a vacation and can't find the relief help he needs to take one. Even if he can find it, he may not be able to afford both the help and the vacation.

"The students ... need nothing more than hands-on experience and there's no better place to get it than in the arena of community journalism.

"It's a logical blending of needs and resources, and I wish someone in Minnesota would have thought of it 30 years ago."

TEACHING

A primary goal of the Huck Boyd Center for Community Media is to assure that community media have a place in journalism/mass communication education. We do this at K-

State by acquainting our students with the opportunities for creativity, leadership and self-expression, ownership and entrepreneurship available to them in community media.

We do it in our courses. We try not to depend entirely on textbook examples from mega markets. A News and Feature Writing professor shows a tape of a news story from WIBW TV, Topeka, in which citizens of a small town in our area are interviewed after the death of their 100-year-old paper. The citizens are truly upset at the loss of their paper, and, therefore, the loss of the town's identity. The professor discusses the founding and function of the Huck Boyd National Center, and talks about her own reasons for feeling that "community journalism is the heartbeat of America."

Advanced News and Feature Writing students also have opportunities for acquaintance with community journalism. Each spring, for example, up to a dozen members of the K-State chapter of the Society of Professional Journalists and Advanced News and Feature Writing students spend a day in Marysville, about 60 miles from our campus at Manhattan, producing stories for the annual progress edition of the Marysville *Advocate*, the largest weekly newspaper in Kansas, with a circulation of 6,100.

Harry Marsh, SPJ adviser and professor of the class, explains:

"Before the students arrive, publisher Howard Kessinger has selected a theme (education, manufacturing, computer technology, health care) for the edition, has created about three dozen story assignments and has scheduled most of the key interviews. Students are briefed on their assignments by Kessinger and his staff, do their research and write their stories. Perhaps the most valuable part of the field trip is the one-on-one attention the students get from the *Advocate* staff. In particular, Kessinger and his staff edit each story with the student sitting at the computer and explain every change the editor makes and why it is made."

For a number of students, this day in Marysville is their first taste of community journalism. Some like it, and begin thinking of community journalism as a career possibility. A project on this order might be appropriate for other schools.

Another taste of community journalism is available to students who are members of the staff of the college daily, *The Kansas State Collegian. Collegian* staff members work with staffs of four area community newspapers to publish a special tourism section, "Discover Kansas Trails," which is inserted in all the participating papers in early April and is distributed to tourism centers across the state. *The Collegian* is responsible for organizing the entire project. The faculty member who coordinates this project, Gloria Freeland, calls the project "an excellent cooperative venture that ties K-State to community newspapers in a very positive way." This project should also be adaptable to other parts of the country.

Community media issues are also an important part of media management classes at K-State. Roughly half of the guest speakers in Newspaper Management are from larger papers such as the Kansas City *Star* or the Wichita *Eagle*; the others are from the community newspapers. Among the community media guests in 1994 were two from Atwood (population 1,665) who were unhappy with the results of chain ownership of the local paper and started a competing paper; publishers of the Baldwin *Ledger*, who spoke on "Diversification as a survival strategy"; and the editorial page editor of the Salina *Journal* (circulation 30,000) who spoke on "Ethical dilemmas and community connectedness."

Also, strong efforts are made at Kansas State to introduce students to opportunities in community media by involving them as interns and/or members of community service teams.

One of our favorite community service projects has been helping with the birth of a volunteer newspaper, the *Prairie Dog Press,* in Almena, Kansas, in the summer of 1994. Almena, population 550, had been without a newspaper since December of 1990, when the last issue of the 102-year-old *Plaindealer* was printed. John Neibergall and I went to Almena a few months after the death of the *Plaindealer*, and interviewed former *Plaindealer* subscribers and high school students about the impact of the loss of their paper. Needless to say, the community was hard hit by the death of the paper. We began seeking ways to restore Almena's voice, and the K-State Community Service Project program merged well with the Huck Boyd Center to furnish an opportunity.

A team of five visiting university students assisted in publishing four issues of the *Prairie Dog Press* before turning the twice-a-month paper over to volunteer editor Becky Madden and her local, totally volunteer, staff. John Neibergall was the faculty supervisor for the project.

In late October of 1994, after the volunteer newspaper had been on its own for three months, three members of the student team, Neibergall, and a graduate student who plans to do her thesis on the volunteer newspaper visited Almena. They found the *Prairie Dog Press* alive and well, readers appreciative and volunteer staff members eager to continue to produce the paper.

Don Covington, whose family was the host family for one of the students, said, "It's a surprise each week to see who's submitting stories. So many people are so willing to write, and they do such a good job. Every issue gets better."

Another student host, veterinarian Steve Gaf, said, "We have a base of really good people. I worry that they may get burned out." Volunteers say that's not going to happen, but one added, "God forbid there be two people gone at the same time."

What motivates volunteer staff members? One said, "I just missed the Almena *Plaindealer* something terrible." Another said, "It's the camaraderie, the respect, and the fact that each volunteer brings skills they're really good at. That makes the whole thing work."

"In the years since we lost the *Plaindealer*," Editor Becky Madden said, "the community lost its sense of identity." Madden, the other volunteer staff members, the students who were involved, and the Huck Boyd Center Task Force members feel good about what Madden calls "our 'feel good' newspaper."

The volunteer newspaper project was a great learning experience for students and faculty members.

DOING RESEARCH AND LINKING PEOPLE AND INFORMATION

The Center's most ambitious project so far in this area was a joint project with the National Newspaper Association—a symposium on Newspapers and Community-Building, held in connection with the 1994 NNA convention in Orlando, Fla.

It was our belief that there was newspaper and community-building activity going on out there, and that such a symposium might be a workable way to share information about that activity., The Center and the NNA sent out a call for proposals, seeking "research, ideas and case studies that offer relevance to local newspapers." Frankly, we were a little concerned about filling the 12 time slots available for presentation, and also about whether the pre-convention sessions would be attended (they were, after all, going to be competing with Disney World).

We received 75 proposals. The tough part was weeding the stack down to 12. And about 150 journalists and educators attended the symposium, which, according to Diana Kramer in the Oct. 10, 1994, issue of *Publishers' Auxiliary,* was described as "riveting and fascinating."

Frank Garred, publisher of the Port Townsend, Wash., Jefferson County *Leader* and chairman of the National Newspaper Foundation, told Kramer, "We in the business knew academics were doing research in areas that affect us. We also knew that some journalism schools were becoming so research-driven that they were losing touch with what we need as practitioners. It only made sense to get us together."

Michael Stricklin, a University of Nebraska professor who presented a paper at the symposium, said, "Publishing a paper in an academic journal is fine, but the opportunity to present information to working editors and publishers is rare."

We feel that the Center filled a need with the symposium, which according to Tonda Rush, president and CEO of the National Newspaper Association, "was a hit all around." And this is one of the ways, we think, in which the Center functions as a *national* center by involving other schools of journalism.

Another major national project in 1993-94 was producing, again with the NNA, a *Community Newspaper Showcase of Excellence,* a 54-page tabloid that gives a close-up look at the General Excellence award winning newspapers in NNA's annual Better Newspaper Contest. The tabloid was handed out at the NNA convention in late September 1994, and will be distributed through Publishers' Auxiliary as well.

As the foreword to the publication points out, "We hope the message that excellence is thriving in community newspapers reaches journalism educators and students, too." A copy was mailed to each of the 2,700 members of the Association for Education in Journalism and Mass Communication. No journalism educator should be limited to textbook examples from metropolitan markets.

The Center staff began working on the following year's *Showcase of Excellence* right after the 1994 convention of NNA.

Linking people and information on the state level, the Center, in 1992, provided copies of a 30-page publication on *Libel Law in Kansas.* The publication was sent to members of the Kansas Press Association, the Kansas Association of Broadcasters and the Kansas Scholastic Press Association. *Libel Law in Kansas* was written by Paul Parsons, Kansas State faculty member and a faculty associate of the Huck Boyd National Center, as one chapter of a larger book, *Mass Communication Law in Kansas,* part of a 50-state media law series.

PROVIDING TRAINING, PUTTING TECHNOLOGY TO USE, NURTURING THE CENTER'S LEADERSHIP

The Huck Boyd Center has offered workshops, for example, in professional improvement, learning to use new computer software, and working together to strengthen communities and community journalism. We have co-sponsored activities with Stauffer Communications and with the Kansas Press Association.

With Stauffer Communication, for example, we offered a professional improvement workshop intended to combat burnout. The program was aimed at journalists in their first five years in the profession. We feel that this is a rather vulnerable time, especially for those at small papers who have few, if any, colleagues with whom to interact. This program allowed them to share their concerns with others, and learn that "You don't have to work for the *New York Times* for your work to be significant." Our keynote speaker was Ashley Futrell, Jr., of the Pulitzer-winning Washington, N.C., *Daily News.*

Several times we have made our computer lab available for Kansas Press Association workshops to acquaint KPA members with new software. Some of these workshops have been taught by our faculty; some by KPA members.

One of the many things we learned from our fuzzy groups was that workshops and seminars at our school are all well and good, but there is a real need for us to sponsor activities in other locations of the state as well (Manhattan is simply too far away for many of the Kansas media), and we try to do that.

For example, we did a Better Newspaper Workshop in Hill City, 196 miles northwest of Manhattan, We offered a smorgasbord of activities—design, production, advertising, newswriting, postal concerns—hoping to draw a broad spectrum of staff members from northwest Kansas. We succeeded beyond our wildest dreams. Seventy-five newspaper people attended—not just editors and publishers, but copy editors and advertising and production people as well. Comments indicated that the workshop was an emotional boost for many attendees, as well as learning experience. Some valuable networking took place as well.

As we review the Center's work to date we feel both frustration and satisfaction. We wish we could have done more. There's never enough time or money, and none of us can concentrate fully on community media. Our activities so far have been primarily newspaper, and we know that the newspaper is not the only community medium. We wish even more students would come to care as much about community media as we do.

On the satisfaction side, however, we believe the Huck Boyd National Center for Community Media is filling real needs, both in Kansas and nationally.

It is quietly but persistently nudging community media onto the agendas of journalism educators and students.

It is enthusiastically and ably serving the local media.

It is showcasing excellence in community media, inspiring practitioners and reminding educators and students of grass-roots journalism's significance.

It is creating innovative models for serving community media that other academic programs might adopt and improve upon.

Above all, having the Center here at Kansas State University has enriched our program, for faculty members as well as for our students.

INDEX

3187

PN
4784
.C73
L28
1995

DATE DUE

APR 3 0 1996

JAN 02 1997

RET'D DEC 04 1996

MAR 2 8 2000

REC'D APR 0 1 2000

APR 2 1 2003

REC'D MAR 2 9 2003

Demco, Inc. 38-293